OPTIMAL ECONOMIC GROWTH

Shifting Finite Versus Infinite Time Horizon

CONTRIBUTIONS
TO
ECONOMIC ANALYSIS

63

Edited by

J. JOHNSTON

J. SANDEE

R. H. STROTZ

J. TINBERGEN

P. J. VERDOORN

1970

NORTH-HOLLAND PUBLISHING COMPANY
AMSTERDAM-LONDON

OPTIMAL ECONOMIC GROWTH

Shifting Finite Versus Infinite Time Horizon

M. INAGAKI

Professor of Economics
Sir George Williams University, Montreal, Canada

1970

NORTH-HOLLAND PUBLISHING COMPANY
AMSTERDAM · LONDON

Library of Congress Catalog Card Number: 69-18388
Standard Book Number: 7204 3161 1

Publishers:

NORTH-HOLLAND PUBLISHING COMPANY – AMSTERDAM
NORTH-HOLLAND PUBLISHING COMPANY, LTD. – LONDON

PRINTED IN THE NETHERLANDS

INTRODUCTION TO THE SERIES

This series consists of a number of hitherto unpublished studies, which are introduced by the editors in the belief that they represent fresh contributions to economic science.

The term *economic analysis* as used in the title of the series has been adopted because it covers both the activities of the theoretical economist and the research worker.

Although the analytical methods used by the various contributors are not the same, they are nevertheless conditioned by the common origin of their studies, namely theoretical problems encountered in practical research. Since for this reason, business cycle research and national accounting, research work on behalf of economic policy, and problems of planning are the main sources of the subjects dealt with, they necessarily determine the manner of approach adopted by the authors. Their methods tend to be "practical" in the sense of not being too far remote from application to actual economic conditions. In addition they are quantitative rather than qualitative.

It is the hope of the editors that the publication of these studies will help to stimulate the exchange of scientific information and to reinforce international cooperation in the field of economics.

THE EDITORS

PREFACE

The economics of development has again been pushed into the foreground after some decades of slumbering existence. This is largely the result of the interest of low-income countries in economic development. New and interesting contributions to our knowledge have been made in the last decade and the literature on the subject has been continually growing.

One of the most fundamental problems of development policy, however, has remained in an unsatisfactory state; namely, what portion of national income should be saved in order to obtain optimal development over time? This is known as the problem of optimal savings or, more recently, of optimal growth. It is in this area of inquiry that Professor Inagaki has made a significant contribution.

Professor Inagaki's book presents a completely new approach to optimal growth. It is based on the explicit recognition that a nation cannot be identified with an "immortal" government that posseses an infinite time horizon. A nation should, however, be considered as a succession of "mortal" governments, each possessing a finite time horizon and a still shorter political mandate. Professor Inagaki, accordingly, formulates the problem of optimal growth as a group decision problem of successive governments.

A virtue of this book is that its approach establishes, for the first time, a conceptual framework that permits comparison between different definitions of optimal growth. In particular, Professor Inagaki proposes a new optimal growth criterion. His analysis of the new criterion as well as of the classical criterion of utility maximization over time, throws new light on the optimal development (and savings) process. This new approach will not fail to attract the attention of a wider circle of experts, enhance their understanding of the development process, and provide more adequate assumptions on which to base a development policy.

J. Tinbergen

ACKNOWLEDGEMENT

"... we note the fact that in each consecutive time unit a different group of people or generation is living and that postponing consumption also means allocating it to another generation. The missing element (in the traditional theory) is some sort of balance between the consumption levels of consecutive generations ... If, in a practical programme, a compromise between maximum utility and equity were sought, the optimum would depend on the relative weights given to both principles".

JAN TINBERGEN

This analysis owes more to Prof. J. Tinbergen than could ever be expressed in words. During my four year's stay at the Netherlands Economic Institute, he constantly enlightened my work by his extraordinary theoretical intuition, vast practical experience and keen sense of social justice. In fact, the basic philosophy of this book is his; an "optimal" growth program must be fair to all generations, both present and future.

This book also owes much to the discussions I am privileged to have had with Prof. T. C. Koopmans. They contributed greatly to clarifying my thoughts and deepened my understanding of both the time discount rate and the instantaneous utility function.

I would further like to express my warmest thanks to Prof. F. Loonstra for the interest he has shown in my work, to Ir. J. van IJzeren for checking the mathematics of Paper 1, and to Mr Boaz for computing the numerical results of Paper 3. My gratitude is also due to Mrs H. Matejka and Miss J. Lermer for improving my English, to Miss G. Desmarais and Mr. K. Hudson for completing the bibliography and for establishing the subject index, and to Mrs. C. Kleinpeter and Mrs. E. Whittaker for typing the manuscript.

Finally, I wish to acknowledge my Debt to the Netherlands School of Economics, the Netherlands Economic Institute, and Sir George Williams University, for the material support they have given to this project.

CONTENTS

Introduction to the Series v
Preface vi
Acknowledgement vii
Introduction xiii

PART I
AN APPRAISAL OF THE CLASSICAL THEORY, OUTLINE OF A NEW THEORY

Chapter 1
The growth model 3
1.1 Purpose of the growth model 3
1.2 The choice of the growth model 3
1.3 The exponential growth or EG model 4
1.3.1 The variables 4
1.3.2 The equations 5
1.3.3 Economic interpretation 6
1.4 The quasi-exponential growth or Q-EG model 8
1.4.1 Formal definitions 8
1.4.2 Economic interpretation 10
1.4.3 Realism 11
1.5 Exponential growth properties of the EG and Q-EG models 15
1.5.1 The EG model 15
1.5.2 The Q-EG model 16
1.6 Feasible growth 18
1.6.1 Paths, programs and strategies 18
1.6.2 Feasible paths 19
1.6.3 Feasible programs 19
1.6.4 Feasible strategies 20

Chapter 2
The concept of an optimal growth strategy 23
2.1 Organization of the chapter 23

2.2 The concept of the instantaneous government 24
2.2.1 General definition 24
2.2.2 Formal definition 26
2.2.3 The Bernoulli functions 27
2.3 The concept of national allegiance 28
2.4 The concept of unanimous preference 28
2.5 Two particular definitions of the optimal strategy 30
2.5.1 The classical definition: a case of extreme national allegiance 30
2.5.2 A more realistic definition 32

Chapter 3
Utility maximization over infinite time (UMIT) 34
3.1 Purpose of the chapter 34
3.1.1 Consistency and existence 34
3.1.2 The three basic questions 35
3.2 The existence problem 36
3.2.1 Non-technical introduction 36
3.2.2 Euler's equation 37
3.2.3 The efficiency condition 40
3.2.4 Necessary and sufficient conditions for UMIT-optimality 41
3.2.5 The condition of minimum convergence 43
3.3 Properties of the UMIT-optimal program 45
3.3.1 The UMIT capital, production and consumption programs 45
3.3.2 The UMIT savings program 46
3.4 Difficulties with the economic interpretation 48
3.4.1 Necessity of a constant time discount rate 48
3.4.2 The principle of minimum impatience 49
3.4.3 The Bliss alternative 51

Chapter 4
Marginal utility equilibrium over finite time (MUEFT) 53
4.1 Introduction 53
4.2 Marginal utility equilibrium over infinite time 54
4.2.1 Generalized MUEFT 54
4.2.2 The MUEFT condition 55
4.3 Properties of the MUEFT program 56
4.3.1 The golden utility MUEFT program 56
4.3.2 MUEFT under a constant capital-output ratio 58
4.4 A comparison of MUEFT and UMIT 60
4.4.1 The choice of the time discount rate 60

4.4.2 The critical time horizon 61
4.4.3 The fundamental conjecture 63
4.4.4 How much "better" is MUEFT than UMIT? 64
4.4.5 Generalized MUEFT 67
4.5 Confrontation of the MUEFT strategy with real world data 68
4.5.1 An econometric definition of the time horizon ω 68
4.5.2 A numerical experiment 69

Chapter 5
Conclusion 71

PART II
FIVE PAPERS ON UTILITY MAXIMIZATION OVER INFINITE TIME 73

Paper 1
A general existence theorem 75
Objective 75
Plan 75
1. Definition of Theorem X1 76
2. Proof of Theorem X1 92
3. Appendix 98

Paper 2
Case of a constant technology 100
Introduction 100
Objective 100
Plan 100
1. The growth model 101
2. The utility index 102
3. No time discounting 103
4. Positive time discounting 111
5. Conclusion 117

Paper 3
Particular case of a progressing technology 119
Introduction 119
Objectives 119
Plan 119
1. The growth assumptions 120
2. The preference assumptions 121
3. No technological progress and no time discounting 122
4. Technological progress and minimum time discounting under no Bliss 123
5. No technological progress and no time discounting under Bliss 125
6. Technological progress and arbitrarily large time discounting 126

7. Discussion of the results 128
8. A numerical illustration 133
9. Post-scriptum on the UMIT savings path 135

Paper 4
An explicit solution 138
Introduction 138
Objectives 138
Plan 139
1. The growth assumptions 139
2. The preference assumptions 141
3. An explicit UMIT-optimal solution 142
4. Sharpness of the UMIT-optimum 145
5. Interpretation of the results 148

Paper 5
Absolute versus relative utility maximization 153
Introduction 153
Objectives 154
Plan 154
1. The growth model 154
2. The RUMIT index 156
3. The RUMIT solution 161

Mathematical Appendix 165
A. Proof of Theorems in Part I 165
B. Dictionary of notations 177

Bibliography 181

Subject Index 194

INTRODUCTION

SUBJECT MATTER AND OBJECTIVES

Present-day research in optimal economic growth proceeds essentially along two main lines: models that try to maximize welfare over time and models that have as their sole objective the attainment of the best possible state at the end of a given planning period. This book deals only with the former type of models. In other words, it is concerned with the line of research initiated some 40 years ago by F.P. Ramsey's brilliant and by now classical paper "A Mathematical Theory of Saving" [R]. It is remarkable that no satisfactory alternative to the basic principle of this paper has hitherto been suggested.

Ramsey's principle is nowadays known as "Utility Maximization over Infinite Time" or UMIT. *Grosso modo,* it says that:

(1) a well defined utility can be ascribed to every instantaneous state of the economy;

(2) it is optional to maximize, over *infinite* time the sum of these instantaneous utilities (possibly discounted over time).

This book is primarily an attempt to make a systematic appraisal of the UMIT principle. Our conclusion is that UMIT does not provide a satisfactory answer to the problem of optimal economic growth. Three reasons support this negative judgment.

The first refers to the existence of a UMIT-optimal program. Under technological progress, this existence generally requires either a positive and constant time discount rate or a finite upper limit ("Bliss" level) to the instantaneous utility which can be derived from consumption.

Now the first of these conditions raises serious difficulties in relation to the economic meaning of the time discount rate. It will be seen that the so-called "social" interpretation of the time discount rate cannot be defended. The value of the latter can only be determined on the basis of some "ethical" principal. We argue that the only principle which is meaningful in this context is the "Principle of Minimum Impatience". This principle prescribes the smallest non-negative time discount rate for which a UMIT program can be established. (No UMIT solution exists if the time discount rate is smaller than a certain value i_0; see Section 3.2.3.) Unfortunately, it is not certain whether such a smallest value does generally exist. (It may happen that a UMIT solution exists only if the time discount rate is greater than, but not equal to, a certain value i_0.)

The second of the above-mentioned conditions, namely that of a finite Bliss level of utility, avoids this last problem. Whenever this second condition is satisfied, the prime discount rate may be chosen as equal to zero. It should be pointed out, however, that the principle of minimum impatience is still needed in order to justify this particular choice. Moreover, it seems unlikely that the Bliss condition will be fulfilled by any "actual" social utility function.

Our second objection to the UMIT principle concerns the properties of its optimal program. If one does not assume a Bliss level of utility, the optimal value of the savings ratio may easily exceed what is thought to be enforceable in practice. What is worse, the UMIT principle does not necessarily ensure a "fair" distribution of welfare among the successive generations. It may very well require the highest relative sacrifices from the poorest generations.

Our third and main reason for rejecting the UMIT principle is of a more fundamental nature. We contend that this principle oversimplifies the problem of optimal growth to the point where it becomes almost meaningless. Assuming a "Society of Immortals", the classical theory completely overlooks the fact that Society is made up of an infinite sequence of overlapping generations with a limited life span and, consequently, with conflicting material interests of the problem of optimal economic growth. Any realistic theory of optimal economic growth should take this conflict explicitly into account.

In support of this view, we set forth the framework of a theory which provides a rational solution to the above conflict. For this purpose, we introduce four new concepts: "Instantaneous Government", "National Allegiance", "Unanimous Preference" and "Feasible Growth Strategy". All four have a precise mathematical definition.

These four concepts enable us to conceive of the problem of optimal economic growth as being a particular type of group decision problem. The members of the group are the successive *instantaneous governments* or IGs. An IG is a being characterized as follows:

(1) it can only act at the point in time t of its instantaneous existence; it can co-decide upon the value of the savings ratio at time t;

(2) it has a finite time horizon ω: it is only interested in what happens between t and $t + \omega$;

(3) it has a well defined preference pattern with regard to all growth programs which are feasible over this time horizon ω.

By virtue of their *national allegiance,* all IGs are willing to choose their respective savings ratio according to one out of a given set of *indefinitely feasible growth strategies.* If one of these strategies is *unanimously preferred* by all IGs, it will be considered as optimal.

We then define the strategy of "Marginal Utility Equilibrium over Finite Time" or MUEFT. Contrary to UMIT, MUEFT does not prescribe that the marginal utility of per capita consumption at time t to be equal to the marginal utility of the per capita returns derived over infinite time from investments made at time t, but only to the marginal utility of the per capita returns derived over the finite period extending from t to $t + \omega$. We argue that MUEFT is always unanimously preferred to UMIT. Our conclusion is, therefore, that UMIT cannot be considered as an optimal strategy in the sense of unanimous preference without arbitrarily excluding all competing strategies as, for instance, MUEFT.

To sum up, the general objective of this book is to make a constructive critique of the optimal growth strategy known as Utility Maximization over Infinite Time or UMIT. In order to attain this general objective, we also pursue a very important side objective, namely the development of a more realistic theory of optimal economic growth. Our overall conclusion is that the UMIT strategy does not provide a satisfactory definition of optimal growth. Incidentally, a "better" growth strategy is suggested, namely "Marginal Utility Eqilibrium over Finite Time" or MUEFT.

Our entire analysis is conducted in terms of a certain class of neoclassical one-sector models of growth. We argue that the main conclusions derived on the basis of this class are generally valid.

ORGANIZATION OF THE BOOK

The book consists of two parts, followed by a mathematical appendix, a rather extensive bibliography and a subject index. Part I works out the arguments outlined in the preceding section. The main emphasis is put on the logical structure of the problem of optimal economic growth. The analysis is based on the results of a number of theorems which are proved either in Part II or in the Mathematical Appendix.

Part II is made up of a selection of five papers on optimal economic growth which have hitherto only appeared in mimeographed form as publications of the Netherlands Economic Institute, Division of Balanced International Growth. They are written in a slightly more technical style than the text of Part I. The papers are all self-contained and can be read independently. This advantage has called for some repitition in the definitions.

The Mathematical Appendix contains those proofs of the theorems stated in Part I which are not established in one of the five papers of Part II. It also provides a "dictionary" of the most frequently used symbolic notations.

Part I consists of five chapters. Chapter 1 defines the growth model to be used in the analysis. Great care has been taken to explain and justify the model in terms of the general purpose of this book. Chapter 1 also introduces the important distinction between a *feasible growth program* and a *feasible growth strategy*. In short, Chapter 1 specifies, in technical terms, the growth alternatives that are open to the economy.

Chapter 2 establishes the basis of the new theory referred to in the preceding section. It explains and defines the basic concepts of "Instantaneous Government", "National Allegiance" and "Unanimous Preference". It also introduces the UMIT and MUEFT strategies.

Chapter 3 is entirely devoted to a technical analysis of the UMIT strategy. It considers seperately the respective problems of the existence of the UMIT strategy, of the general properties of a UMIT program, and of the economic interpretation and numerical determination of the time discount rate. Chapter 3 draws extensively on the results of Part II.

Chapter 4 constitutes an attempt to get some insight into the existence conditions and properties of the MUEFT strategy. It turns out that this is even more difficult than it is in the case of the UMIT strategy. We succeed, nevertheless, in showing that MUEFT is likely to be unanimously preferred to UMIT in all cases where both strategies can be applied. We also show that the MUEFT time horizon can be given a perfectly reasonable econometric interpretation. On the basis of the latter, we argue that the United States economy would have to increase somewhat its savings ratio if the United States wanted to apply the MUEFT strategy.

Chapter 5 draws the conclusion that UMIT does not provide an acceptable definition of optimal economic growth. This negative conclusion should not come as a surprise to most students of optimal economic growth. There has been, indeed, a growing feeling of discontent about the UMIT principle. The contribution of this book is that it provides a rational justification for rejecting the UMIT principle by proposing:

(i) a criterion for composing certain types of growth strategies;
(ii) a growth strategy, called MUEFT which is believed to be "better" than UMIT in the sense of the proposed criterion.

PART I

AN APPRAISAL OF THE CLASSICAL THEORY

OUTLINE OF A NEW THEORY

Chapter 1

THE GROWTH MODEL

1.1 PURPOSE OF THE GROWTH MODEL

The purpose of the growth model is to provide a mathematical description of the growth process. Such a description is necessary to define unambiguously the set of growth alternatives from which an optimal one will be selected.

More precisely, we want to define the set of growth strategies which are to be considered as admissible for a given economy in a given initial situation. By a growth strategy, we mean a rule which relates well defined values of the control variables to every given historical situation of the economy. By a growth strategy which is admissible in a given initial situation, we mean a growth strategy which can be applied throughout the period under consideration without violating the assumed technological and social constraints.

It is thus clear that we require a model which states explicitly both the relevant growth variables and the relations or constraints they must satisfy. The definition of this model is the first prerequisite for a rigorous statement of the problem of optimal economic growth and it is with this definition that we begin.

1.2 THE CHOICE OF THE GROWTH MODEL

One would naturally like the growth model to be as realistic as possible. Unfortunately, greater economic realism can only be achieved through greater mathematical complexity. A compromise must therefore be accepted. The problem is to find one which is appropriate for our purpose. Since we want the growth model to be mathematically simple, we cannot expect it to be very realistic. We can only demand that it enables us to draw certain generally valid conclusions which are essential to our purpose.

As has been said, this purpose is to make a constructive critique of the classical theory of optimal economic growth. Now the latter has essentially been devised for growth models which are capable of exponential growth, at least in the infinitely long run. We therefore only consider models which have this property. An economically important class of such models will be defined in Section 1.4. They will be called "Quasi-Exponential Growth" or Q-EG models. It is to these models that our conclusions are believed to apply.

Most of our analysis is conducted in terms of a particular Q-EG model. It is the one (and only one) which is instantaneously capable of exponential growth. For this reason we call it "Exponential Growth" or EG model. It is defined in Section 1.3 and uses a Cobb-Douglas production function.

The question is to what extent the results derived on the basis of the EG model do also apply to the other Q-EG models. Fortunately, as our analysis indicates, the results which are relevant to our purpose depend essentially on the infinitely long term properties of the growth model. Now, *grosso modo,* these properties are the same for all Q-EG models. The Hard core of our results can therefore be expected to hold true for all Q-EG models.

1.3 THE EXPONENTIAL GROWTH OR EG MODEL

1.3.1 The variables

The growth model is stated in terms of seven "primitive" variables (in terms of which all other variables and parameters can be defined). Five of these are economic variables:

x – capital-labor ratio or capital intensity;

y – net production per worker ("worker" is used as a synonym of "labor unit");

c – consumption per worker;

L – employed labor force, i.e. number of workers;

Q – level of technology.

One is a demographic variable:

P – total population.

One is a physical variable:

τ – time.

In addition, we introduce one derived variable which plays an important rôle in our analysis. As a matter of fact, it is our only control or instrument variable. It is:

$$s = 1 - \frac{c}{y} \quad \text{(the savings ratio).}$$

It is assumed that x, y, L, Q and P, on the one hand, and c and s, on the other hand, are respectively continuous and piece-wise continuous functions of time. Moreover, x, y, c, L, Q and P must be positive.

1.3.2 The equations

There are five equations. It is assumed that they obtain for all non-negative values of x, y, c, L, Q, P and τ. They are as follows.

The *production* equation:

$$y = Qx^a, \qquad 0 < \alpha = \text{const.} < 1$$

The *consumption* equation:

$$c = y - \frac{1}{L}\frac{\mathrm{d}}{\mathrm{d}\tau}(xL)$$

$$= y - \left(\frac{\dot{L}}{L}\,x + \dot{x}\right)$$

The *labor* equation:

$$L = mP, \qquad 0 < m = \text{const.} < 1$$

The *technological* equation:

$$Q = \exp[\rho\tau], \qquad \rho = \text{const.} \geqslant 0$$

The *demographic* equation:

$$P = \frac{1}{m}\exp[\lambda\tau], \qquad \lambda = \text{const.} > 0$$

The constant parameters α, m, ρ and λ are given by the model. The origin of the time axis may be arbitrarily chosen. Once this origin has been fixed, the units are chosen such that $Q(0) = L(0) = 1$, $P(0) = 1/m$. This is always possible. Thus, our formulation of the model assumes a convention in the choice of the units. This convention not only greatly simplifies our notations, but it also reduces the statement of the historically given initial condition at $\tau = 0$ to the statement of the value x_0 of $x(0)$. This value will not be considered to be given by the model.

1.3.3 Economic interpretation

The model assumes that the numbers of hours per year during which the production process actually takes place is fixed once and for all. A *worker* is then defined as a member of the population who works this number of hours per year. Notice that two people each working half this number of hours per year make up one worker. The concept of a worker is not associated with a named individual.

The important thing is that the existing capital stock is always fully employed, in the sense that it is always exactly employed during the above defined number of hours per year. The model does not account for variations in this number. We now consider separately the five equations of the model.

The *production* equation says:

(a) technology Q is unembodied;
(b) returns to scale are constant;
(c) the marginal products of capital and labor are positive;
(d) the law of diminishing returns applies to both factors;
(e) no production can take place without some amount of both factors;
(f) the elasticities of production with respect to capital and labor are, respectively, α and $1 - \alpha$.

In short, returns to scale are constant and a Cobb-Douglas production function applies at every given level of (unembodied) technology.

The properties (a), (b) and (e) can be read off at once from the production equation. The others are easily derived.

(c) *Marginal products* of:

$$\text{Capital} \quad \left[\frac{\partial(yL)}{\partial(xL)}\right]_{L,\,\tau} = \left[\frac{\partial y}{\partial x}\right]_{\tau}$$

$$= \alpha\frac{y}{x} > 0$$

$$\text{Labor} \quad \left[\frac{\partial yL}{\partial L}\right]_{xL,\,\tau} = Q(xL)^{a}\,\frac{\mathrm{d}L^{1-a}}{\mathrm{d}L}$$

$$= (1-\alpha)\,y > 0.$$

(d) *Law of diminishing returns* with respect to:

$$\text{Capital}\quad \left[\frac{\partial^2(yL)}{(\partial xL)^2}\right]_{L,\tau} = \left[\frac{\partial^2 y}{\partial x^2}\right]_{\tau} \frac{1}{L}$$

$$= -\alpha\frac{(1-\alpha)}{L}\frac{y}{x^2} < 0$$

$$\text{Labor}\quad \left[\frac{\partial^2(yL)}{\partial L^2}\right]_{xL,\tau} = Q(xL)^{a}\left(\frac{\mathrm{d}^2L}{\mathrm{d}L^2}\right)^{1-a}$$

$$= -\alpha(1-\alpha)\frac{y}{L} < 0.$$

(f) *Elasticities of production* with respect to:

$$\text{Capital}\quad \frac{xL}{yL}\left[\frac{\partial(yL)}{\partial(xL)}\right]_{L,\tau} = \alpha$$

$$\text{Labor}\quad \frac{L}{yL}\left[\frac{\partial(yL)}{\partial L}\right]_{xL,\tau} = 1-\alpha.$$

The *consumption* equation tells us that consumption cL is the difference between production yL and investments $\mathrm{d}(xL)/\mathrm{d}\tau = \dot{x}L + x\dot{L}$. This means that the capital stock is always fully employed (see above) and the economy closed, in the sense that there is no net capital transfer to the rest of the world.

The *labor* equation implies that the demand and supply mechanism works in such a way as to maintain the employed labor-population ratio L/P forever constant. This is the case, *for instance,* if, on the one hand, the labor market is competitive on the demand side [wage rate w = marginal product of labor = $(1-\alpha)y$] and, on the other hand, the labor supply, i.e. the labor-population ratio L/P, depends only on the ratio of the wage rate w to income per capita yL/P. Then, for some function H.

$$\frac{L}{P} = H\left(\frac{w}{y}\cdot\frac{P}{L}\right) = H\left[(1-\alpha)\frac{P}{L}\right]$$

This determines L/P, provided $H(z)$ is continuous and increases monotonically over $0 < z < +\infty$.

The *technological* equation assumes that the rate of technological progress is an autonomously determined non-negative constant ρ. This assumption is further discussed in Section 1.4.2.

The *demographic* equation asserts that the rate of population growth is also an autonomously determined non-negative constant. This condition is relaxed in the definition of the Q-EG models (Section 1.4.1).

1.4 THE QUASI-EXPONENTIAL GROWTH OR Q-EG MODEL

1.4.1 Formal definitions

The EG model contains four constant parameters: α, λ, ρ and m.

α a constant elasticity of production with respect to capital and labor;

λ a constant rate of demographic growth;

ρ a constant rate of technological progress;

m a constant working time per capita.

The general Q-EG model relaxes the first two of these conditions. (It will be convenient to denote by Q-EG λ_0 the Q-EG models where only the first of these conditions is relaxed, i.e. where $\lambda(\tau) = \lambda_0 > 0$, $0 \leqslant \tau < +\infty$.) In other words, it generalizes the production and the demographic equations of the EG model. It maintains, however, the two other conditions, i.e. the labor and technological equations. The reasons for keeping the two latter conditions are explained in Section 1.4.3. As in the case of the EG model, the economy is assumed to be closed. In short, the Q-EG model constitutes a generalization of the EG model.

All the variables and three equations are the same, namely the *consumption*, the *labor* and the *technological* equations. The more general equations are as follows.

The *production* equation.

$$y = Qf(x) \tag{1.4.1}$$

where $f(x)$ is twice continuously differentiable over $0 < x < +\infty$ and satisfies

$$f'(x) > 0,\ f''(x) < 0,\ 0 < x < +\infty \tag{1.4.2}$$

$$f(0) = 0 \tag{1.4.3}$$

$$\lim_{x \to 0} f'(x) = +\infty \tag{1.4.4}$$

$$\lim_{x \to +\infty} f'(x) = 0 \tag{1.4.5}$$

$$\bar{\alpha} < 1 \tag{1.4.6}$$

and either

$$\alpha'(x) \geqslant 0, \quad 0 < x < +\infty \tag{1.4.7}$$

or

$$\alpha'(x) \leqslant 0, \quad 0 < x < +\infty \tag{1.4.8}$$

where

$$\alpha(x) \equiv xf'(x)/f(x) \tag{1.4.9}$$

is the elasticity of production with respect to capital and

$$\bar{\alpha} \equiv \lim_{x \to +\infty} \alpha(x). \tag{1.4.10}$$

The *demographic* equation,

$$P = \frac{1}{m} \exp[\lambda\tau]$$

where $\lambda = \lambda(\tau)$ is positive, continuously differentiable and, from some point of time onwards, decreases monotonically to $\bar{\lambda} \geqslant 0$. Moreover, we require

$$\rho + \bar{\lambda} > 0$$

(otherwise, the classical theory of optimal economic growth does not apply). As before, m, ρ and $\lambda(\tau)$, but not x_0, are given by the model. The units are chosen as in the EG model.

1.4.2 Economic interpretation

As in the case of the EG model, the economic year is assumed to be constant. In words, the *production* equation says that:

(a) technology Q is unembodied;
(b) returns to scale are constant;
(c) the marginal products of capital and labor are positive;
(d) the law of diminishing returns applies to both factors;
(e) no production can take place without some amount of both factors.

The production function is, however, only partly specified. Besides (a) to (e) above, it need only have the two following properties:

(f) that the elasticities with respect to capital and labor tend respectively to the constant values $\bar{\alpha}$ and $1-\bar{\alpha}$, $0 \leqslant \bar{\alpha} < 1$, as the capital-labor ratio x tends itself to $+\infty$;
(g) that the marginal product of a factor tends, respectively, to $+\infty$ or 0 as the factor itself tends to 0 or $+\infty$.

In short, the production equation says essentially that returns to scale are constant and that a strictly concave production function applies at every given level of (unembodied) technology.

The properties (a), (b) and (f) are true by explicit definition. The others are easily derived.

(c) *Marginal products* of:

$$\text{Capital} \quad \left[\frac{\partial(yL)}{\partial(xL)}\right]_{L,\tau} = \left[\frac{\partial y}{\partial x}\right]_{\tau} = Qf'(x) > 0$$

$$\text{Labor} \quad \left[\frac{\partial(yL)}{\partial L}\right]_{xL,\tau} = Q[f(x) - xf'(x)] < 0$$

by using (1.4.2) and (1.4.3).

(d) *Law of diminishing returns* with respect to:

$$\text{Capital} \quad \left[\frac{\partial^2(yL)}{(\partial xL)^2}\right]_{L,\tau} = \frac{1}{L}\frac{\partial^2 y}{\partial x^2} = \frac{Q}{L}f''(x) < 0$$

$$\text{Labor} \quad \left[\frac{\partial^2(yL)}{\partial L^2}\right]_{xL,\tau} = \frac{Q}{L}f''(x)x^2 < 0.$$

(e) No production can take place without some amount of:

Capital $$QLf(0) = 0$$

Labor $$\lim_{\substack{L \to 0 \\ xL = \text{const.}}} QLf\left(\frac{xL}{L}\right) = \lim_{\substack{x \to +\infty \\ xL = \text{const.}}} Qf'(x)xL \quad \text{(using L'Hôpital's rule)}$$
$$= 0.$$

(g) The proof follows at once from (c), (1.4.4), (1.4.5) and (1.4.6).

Granted the assumptions of full aggregation and unembodied technology, none of the conditions (c) to (g) is economically restrictive. The assumption of constant returns to scale is usually interpreted to mean that all enterprises have their optimal size. It seems natural to make this assumption in the context of a theory of long-term growth. The other conditions, except perhaps (f), are also classical. Notice that there is no good reason to assume that $\alpha(x) = xf'(x)/f(x)$ has an extremum for some particular value or values of x. It is therefore reasonable to assume the monotonicity of $\alpha(x)$. This implies the existence of $\bar{\alpha}$, which can easily be seen to lie in $0 \leqslant \bar{\alpha} \leqslant 1$. Economically speaking, it follows that the condition (f) excludes only the case $\bar{\alpha} = 1$.

By Theorem 1.5.2, this condition eliminates all models which are capable of superexponential growth, in the sense that the growth rates of x, y and c will tend to increase at an exponential rate when the savings ratio is maintained above some positive value over a sufficiently long period of time. Now, the classical conception of optimal growth does not apply to such superexponential models, except possibly in a very particular case where the utility function tends to become logarithmic for great values of c.

The *demographic* equation allows the size of the population to become practically constant after some initial period of growth. This assumption seems to be more realistic than an ever exponentially growing population. It is clear, indeed, that there must be some finite upper bound to the size of world population.

The *consumption, labor* and *technological* equations, as well as their respective interpretations, are the same as in the EG model. The previously given particular justification of the labor equation does however not apply to the case where α varies with x, i.e. to the general Q-EG model.

1.4.3 Realism

One may argue about what constitutes a realistic growth model. The purpose of this book is not, however, to make a critical appraisal of the contemporary theory of economic growth, but only of the classical conception of optimal economic growth. In the context of this book, "realistic" will thus be understood to mean "realistic within the limits of present-day theory of growth".

Now, present-day models of growth, which are generally deterministic, differ mainly with respect to:

(i) the number of sectors;
(ii) the number of scarce factors;
(iii) the production functions;
(iv) technological change;
(v) the demand for and supply of the factors;
(vi) the relations with the rest of the world.

Consequently, we shall only discuss the realism of the Q-EG models with regard to the above six points.

(i) The number of sectors From the point of view of realism, the one-sector assumption is undoubtedly rather restrictive. There are, nevertheless, three different reasons for making this assumption:

(a) it is mathematically convenient;
(b) it is, in fact, made in most studies of optimal growth;
(c) it does not affect the general validity of our fundamental argument against the classical theory of optimal growth (Section 2.5.2).

The first reason needs no explanation. The second ensures that our analysis applies to a great part of the literature. There naturally remains the question of the extent to which some of the undesirable properties of the classical solution would be attenuated by the use of a multi-sector model. Because of the third reason, however, we are not greatly interested in this question. We believe that the time necessary to answer it can be put to better use.

(ii) Number of scarce factors This is a typical instance of a case where the simplest possible specification, namely one scarce factor, is not appropriate. Discarding the exceptional and unrepresentative case of abundant capital, a one-factor model can either mean that the labor supply is either abundant or fully employed and constant.

The former cannot be assumed to last forever under optimal planning. Normally, there must come a time when the labor surplus is completely absorbed, i.e. when the assumptions of the model can no longer be considered as valid. This excludes the labor-surplus model for our purpose.

The second of the above-mentioned possibilities constitutes a very particular case of an autonomously determined labor input. It is thus best dealt with within the general framework of a two-factor model.

Finally, given one type of capital only, there is no compelling reason to consider more than one type of labor, i.e. in total more than two factors.

(iii) The production functions Granted our specification of (i) and (ii), the definition of the production function is very general (see Section 1.4.2 and below).

(iv) Technological change Technology has been assumed to be unembodied and to progress at a non-negative ever-constant rate. The assumption of unembodiment is unlikely to be very restrictive for our analysis. It can be shown [1] that embodiment in the Solow sense does not affect the basic exponential growth properties of a model. Only in transition periods does embodiment make investments more rewarding and, consequently, lead to a higher optimal investment ratio. Now we shall see that this can only reinforce our conclusion that the classical definition of optimal growth generally implied a savings ratio which is unrealistically high.

The assumption of an ever-constant rate of technological progress, on the other hand, undoubtedly constitutes one of the weaker points of our analysis. As a matter of fact, it is generally believed that high investments in education and research are beneficial to economic growth because they increase the general level of technology. In a one-sector model, this logically implies that a sustained increase in the investment ratio influences positively the rate of technological progress. Unfortunately, this "productivity effect" has not yet been successfully integrated into the mathematical theory of economic growth. As already pointed out, no theory of optimal growth can be more realistic than its contemporary theory of growth. For the time being, we must therefore content ourselves with the assumption of an automatically progressing technology.

(v) Demand for and supply of the factors As is customary in present-day growth theory, it is assumed that the existing capital stock is always fully employed and that the formation of new capital is completely under the command of, say, the planning authorities. The investment ratio or the savings ratio, which is the same thing in a closed economy, is therefore considered to be a control variable ("instrument variable" in J. Tinbergen's terminology).

The savings ratio is indeed our only control variable. Working time per capita L/P is not considered as an independent control variable. In itself, this is not such an unrealistic assumption, at least if the labor market is competitive on the demand side or, more precisely, if the wage rate w is equal to the marginal product of labor $(1-\alpha)y$. One may expect that the working time per capita L/P increases and decreases, respectively, with the wage rate w and income per capita yL/P.

$$
\begin{aligned}
\frac{L}{P} &= H(w, yL/P) \\
&= H(y(1-\alpha), yL/P) \qquad (1.4.11) \\
&= H^*(x, \tau)
\end{aligned}
$$

where H is some well-behaved function which satisfies

$$\frac{\partial H}{\partial w} > 0, \qquad \frac{\partial H}{\partial (yL/P)} < 0.$$

Now x and, consequently, the working time per capita $H^* = L/P$ can be controlled by the savings ratio s, provided, of course, that H^* is not independent of x (and τ) as in (1.3.1).

The unrealistic aspect of the labor equation (1.3.1) therefore resides much less in the fact that the working time per capita $m = L/P$ is not considered as an independent control variable, than in the assumption that m is constant over time, i.e. independent of both x and τ. It would have been preferable to introduce explicitly the function H. As a matter of fact, it is our conjecture that the main results of this book which hold true for the Q-EG models as defined in Section 1.4.1 remain valid for a more general class of Q-EG models where the labor equation (1.3.1) is replaced by (1.4.11).

It must be admitted, nevertheless, that the assumption of an autonomously determined level of employment is an important simplification of the problem of optimal growth. It is noteworthy that this simplification was not made by Ramsey in his path-breaking paper [R]. Most of his followers, however, have made it, and we follow this tradition. In spite of this simplification, we feel that our model is appropriate for our purpose.

As to the demographic expansion, we have made the usual assumption that it is autonomously determined. However, contrary to most writers on optimal growth who assume an ever-expanding population, we explicitly consider the eventuality that the size of the population will ultimately reach a finite "saturation" level.

(vi) Relations with the rest of the world Our assumption of a closed economy excludes the possibility of foreign aid. The model, as such, applies only to economies which cannot or need not receive foreign aid.

1.5 EXPONENTIAL GROWTH PROPERTIES OF THE EG AND Q-EG MODELS

1.5.1 The EG model

Although the properties of this model are well-known, we state some of them for reference.

An important consequence of the EG assumptions is that the whole development of the economy can be described by the time path of the capital-output ratio $\kappa = x/y$

$$x = \kappa^{1/(1-a)} \exp[\gamma\tau]$$

$$y = \kappa^{a/(1-a)} \exp[\gamma\tau]$$

$$c = (1-s)\, \kappa^{a/(1-a)} \exp[\gamma\tau]$$

$$s = (\gamma+\lambda)\, \kappa + \frac{\kappa}{1-\alpha}, \qquad \gamma \equiv \frac{\rho}{1-\alpha}.$$

The fundamental property of the EG model can be read off at once from the expressions for x, y, c and s: an EG economy is always capable of immediate exponential growth. For every initial positive capital stock, there is a constant and positive savings ratio which ensures an exponential development of the economy over the whole of the future. More precisely, it is seen that x, y and c will grow exponentially from time t onwards if and only if:

(i) the capital-output ratio remains indefinitely constant and positive, i.e.

$$\kappa(\tau) = \kappa_t > 0, \qquad t \leqslant \tau < +\infty$$

(ii) the savings ratio s remains indefinitely constant and equal to $(\gamma + \lambda)\kappa_t$.

It is seen, moreover, that exponential growth can only take place at the so-called equilibrium per capita growth rate $\gamma = \rho/(1-\alpha)$.

If the savings ratio s is indefinitely maintained constant, but at a positive value $\bar{s}$ different from the value $(\gamma + \lambda)\kappa_t$ which ensures immediate exponential growth, the development of the economy nevertheless tends to become ultimately exponential.

THEOREM 1.5.1 Let an EG model, the initial capital-output ratio "κ_t", and an indefinitely constant and positive savings program

$$s(\tau) = \bar{s}, \qquad 0 < \bar{s} \leqslant 1, \qquad t \leqslant \tau < +\infty$$

be given. Then,

$$\kappa = \bar{\kappa} + (\kappa_t - \bar{\kappa}) \exp\left[-\left\{(1-\alpha)\lambda + \rho\right\}\tau\right], \qquad \bar{\kappa} \equiv \frac{\bar{s}}{\gamma + \lambda}.$$

(Proof left to the reader)

In other words, the capital-output ratio remains forever constant whenever it is initially equal to $\bar{\kappa}$. This agrees with observations (i) and (ii). If κ is initially different from $\bar{\kappa}$, then $\kappa(\tau)$ approaches strictly monotonically the asymptotic value $\bar{\kappa}$ from below or from above, depending on whether the initial value of κ lies below or above $\bar{\kappa}$. Writing

$$\bar{x} = \bar{\kappa}^{1/(1-a)}$$

$$\bar{y} = \bar{\kappa}^{a/(1-a)}$$

$$\bar{c} = (1 - \bar{s})\bar{\kappa}^{a/(1-a)}, \qquad \bar{s} = (\gamma + \lambda)\bar{\kappa}$$

this means that $x(\tau)$, $y(\tau)$ and $c(\tau)$ coincide with their respective exponential paths $\bar{x}\exp[\gamma\tau]$, $\bar{y}\exp[\gamma\tau]$ and $\bar{c}\exp[\gamma\tau]$ over $t \leqslant \tau < +\infty$, whenever $\kappa_\tau = \bar{\kappa}$. Otherwise, the former tend, *in the relative sense of* (1.5.1) (see below), strictly monotonically to the latter from below or from above, depending on whether κ_t is smaller or greater than $\bar{\kappa}$.

1.5.2 The Q-EG model

Under the general Q-EG assumptions, immediate exponential growth is no longer possible. As a matter of fact, straightforward time differentiation of the production equation gives

$$\frac{\dot{y}}{y} = \alpha(x)\frac{\dot{x}}{x} + \rho, \qquad \alpha = \frac{xf'}{f}.$$

It follows that the growth rate of x and y can only be constant, i.e. the time paths of x and y can only be exponential, if $\alpha(x)$ is itself constant. Now, this is only the case under the EG assumptions.

In view of Theorem 1.5.1 and the Q-EG assumption that $\alpha(x)$ tends to a constant value smaller than 1 as t tends to infinity, a Q-EG economy is, however, capable of exponential growth in the infinitely long run.

THEOREM 1.5.2 Let a Q-EG model, the initial capital-output ratio κ_t, and a savings program which satisfies both

$$0 < s(\tau) < 1, \qquad t \leqslant \tau < +\infty$$

and

$$\lim_{\tau \to +\infty} s(\tau) = \bar{s} > 0$$

be given. Then the time path $\kappa(\tau)$ of the capital-output ratio is completely determined by its initial value κ_t and satisfies both

$$0 < \kappa(\tau) < \max(\kappa_t, \bar{\kappa}), \qquad t \leqslant \tau < +\infty$$

and

$$\lim_{\tau \to +\infty} \kappa(\tau) = \bar{\kappa}$$

where

$$\bar{\kappa} \equiv \bar{s}(1-\bar{\alpha})/[\rho + \lambda(1-\bar{\alpha})].$$

(Proof in Mathematical Appendix)

In other words, the time paths of x, y and c tend ultimately to the exponential paths $\bar{x}\exp[+\bar{\gamma}\tau]$, $\bar{y}\exp[+\bar{\gamma}\tau]$ and $\bar{c}\exp[+\bar{\gamma}\tau]$ in the relative sense. More precisely,

$$\lim_{\tau \to +\infty} \frac{x(\tau)}{\bar{x}\exp[+\bar{\gamma}\tau]} = \lim_{\tau \to +\infty} \frac{y(\tau)}{\bar{y}\exp[+\bar{\gamma}\tau]}$$

$$= \lim_{\tau \to +\infty} \frac{c(\tau)}{\bar{c}\exp[+\bar{\gamma}\tau]} = 1, \qquad \bar{\gamma} \equiv \rho/(1-\bar{\alpha}), \tag{1.5.1}$$

provided only that the savings ratio s remains always positive and tends ultimately to a positive value $\bar{s}$.

1.6 FEASIBLE GROWTH

1.6.1 Paths, programs and strategies

The purpose of this section is to define the three concepts of feasible path, feasible program and feasible strategy.

In terms of our six primitive variables x, y, c, Q, L and P, a *growth path* is a six-dimensional time path $[x(\tau), y(\tau), c(\tau), Q(\tau), L(\tau), P(\tau)]$ which has positive and piece-wise continuous components over the time interval under consideration.

The economist is only interested in growth paths which are feasible, i.e. which satisfy both the historically given initial conditions and the technological constraints characterizing the production process. The concept of a feasible growth path is defined in Section 1.6.2. For the time being, let us only stress that all the components of a growth path do not have to be continuous everywhere.

It has been traditionally assumed that an economy which is establishing a program of optimal economic growth is completely free with regard to the initial value of the savings ratio. This means that the savings path may have a jump the instant optimal planning is initiated. Now, if the savings path can have a discontinuity at one point of time, there is no reason why it could not have another discontinuity at some later point of time. On the other hand, it is clear that the savings path cannot have infinitely many jumps over any finite time interval. We shall therefore assume that it is piece-wise continuous.

It seems natural to associate a discontinuity of the savings path with a change of program. The connotation of the expression "optimal economic program" implies the idea of continuity. We shall therefore define a feasible *growth program* over a given period as a feasible growth path which is everywhere continuous over the said period.

Both a feasible growth path and a feasible growth program are descriptions of a time path over some given time interval (which may be infinite). A feasible *growth strategy* is something completely different. It is a rule, more precisely a continuous function, which relates a well-defined savings ratio to every conceivable historical economic situation (Section 1.6.4). In terms of the Q-EG variables, this situation is completely determined by the variables x, y, Q, L and P (the value of the variable c is not historically predetermined, in the sense that s and, consequently, c need only be piece-wise continuous). Now, under the Q-EG assumptions, x, y, Q, L and P are functions of κ and τ only. A growth strategy is consequently a continuous function $S(\kappa, \tau) < 1$ which relates the savings ratio $s = S(\kappa, \tau)$ to every historically conceivable situation (κ, τ).

It is useful to distinguish between different classes of growth strategies. There are, for instance, the positive growth strategies, i.e. those which relate a positive value of s (<1) to all economic situations (κ, τ). These strategies have an important property: given the Q-EG assumptions, a positive strategy determines an indefinitely feasible program for every positive and historically conceivable initial value of the capital stock (Definition 1.6.3). We call *feasible strategy*, any strategy, positive or not, which has this property (Definition 1.6.4). Every feasible growth strategy consequently defines a whole class of indefinitely feasible growth programs. A more precise definition of the concept of a feasible growth strategy is provided in Section 1.6.4.

The concept of a feasible growth strategy plays a very important part in our statement of the problem of optimal economic growth (Sections 2.3 and 2.4). It permits us to state this problem in a new and, we believe, more realistic way than has hitherto been done. This, in turn, enables us to formulate clearly our fundamental objection against the classical definition of optimal growth.

1.6.2 Feasible paths

We now give a formal definition of a feasible growth path.

DEFINITION 1.6.1 A growth path $[x(\tau), y(\tau), c(\tau), Q(\tau), L(\tau), P(\tau)]$ is feasible over $t \leqslant \tau < T$ if it satisfies:

(i) the given Q-EG model over $t \leqslant \tau < T$;

(ii) the given initial condition $x(t) = x_t$, where $x_t < 0$.

A growth path is indefinitely feasible at t if it is feasible over $t < \tau < T$ for every $T > t$.

It will be convenient to denote a growth path by either $x(\tau)$, $y(\tau)$, $\kappa(\tau)$, $c(\tau)$ or $s(\tau)$ only. This is always possible since $Q(\tau)$, $L(\tau)$ and $P(\tau)$ are predetermined and, given the initial condition, either one of $x(\tau)$, $y(\tau)$, $\kappa(\tau)$, $c(\tau)$ and $s(\tau)$ univocally determine the four others (proof left to the reader).

It should be noticed that, by definition of the Q-EG model, x, y, κ, c, Q, L and P are everywhere continuous functions of time, except $c(\tau)$ which is only piece-wise continuous.

1.6.3 Feasible programs

DEFINITION 1.6.2 A feasible growth program is a feasible growth path which is everywhere continuous. The set of all feasible programs over $t \leqslant \tau < T$ will be alternatively denoted by $[x(\tau)_t^T]$, $[y(\tau)_t^T]$, $[\kappa(\tau)_t^T]$, or $[c(\tau)_t^T]$. In the case of the set of all indefinitely feasible programs at t, the letter T is replaced by the sign $+\infty$.

In other words, the concept of a feasible growth program requires that $c(\tau)$ and, consequently, $s(\tau)$ be continuous. As already stated, Section 1.6.1, a discontinuity in the time paths of consumption and investments is identified with a *change of growth* program. Such an identification does not only seem economically reasonable, but it also provides the concept of a change of program with a mathematically simple and unambiguous definition. The possibility of a change of program constitutes an important aspect of the definition, given in Chapter 2, of the problem of optimal economic growth.

To complete this section we state necessary and sufficient conditions for the feasibility of a growth program.

THEOREM 1.6.1 Given a Q-EG model and the initial value $\kappa_t > 0$, $\kappa(\tau)$ is a feasible growth program over $t \leqslant \tau < T$ if and only if:

(i) $\kappa(t) = \kappa_t$;

(ii) $\kappa(\tau)$ is positive and continuously differentiable over $t \leqslant \tau < T$;

(iii) $-\infty < \dot{\kappa} < (1-\alpha)\,[1-(\gamma+\lambda)\kappa]$, $\quad t \leqslant \tau < T$

Notice that production cannot be totally invested, but that some part of it must be reserved for consumption. This is an explicit assumption of the Q-EG model (Section 1.3.1).

(Proof left to the reader)

1.6.4 Feasible strategies

This section formally introduces the important concept of a *growth strategy,* which is a new concept in the literature on optimal economic growth. As already said, we believe that this concept permits us to formulate the problem of optimal economic growth more precisely than it has been done hitherto.

In what follows, the concept of a feasible growth strategy is defined with respect to the Q-EG model. Generally speaking, it should be clear that a strategy can only be defined with respect to the rules of a given game. In the context of optimal growth, this game is a growth model; in the context of this book, it is the Q-EG model.

The definition we adopt is a somewhat particular one. We believe, however, that our purpose is best served by sacrificing some degree of generality for the sake of expository simplicity. We therefore take advantage of the fact that the capital-output ratio of a Q-EG economy remains forever below some well-defined value, provided only that it had already been initially smaller than this value.

THEOREM 1.6.2 Given a Q-EG model and the initial condition $\kappa(\tau) = \kappa_t > 0$, there is a $\kappa_+ > 0$ such that every indefinitely feasible growth program at t satisfies

$$0 < \kappa(\tau) < \kappa_+, \qquad t \leqslant \tau < +\infty \tag{1.6.1}$$

provided only that $0 < \kappa_t < \kappa_+$. Writing $g = \gamma + \lambda$ and g_{lb} for the greatest lower bound of g over $0 < x < +\infty$, one has

$$\kappa_+ = 1/g_{lb} \tag{1.6.2}$$

(Proof in Mathematical Appendix)

When λ is constant and positive, it follows that the value of κ remains smaller than κ_+ along any indefinitely feasible growth program starting from an initial value $0 < \kappa(0) < \kappa_+$. We therefore introduce the following definition.

DEFINITION 1.6.3 Under the Q-EG λ_0 and IG assumptions, we call *historically conceivable* any initial capital stock which satisfies

$$0 < \kappa(0) < \kappa_+ \tag{1.6.3}$$

where κ_+ is defined by (1.6.2).

Theorem 1.6.2 explains the following definition of a feasible growth strategy.

DEFINITION 1.6.4 Given a Q-EG model, we say that a function

$$S(\kappa, Q, L, P) = S(\kappa, \tau)$$

defines a feasible growth strategy in $\kappa_1 < \kappa < \kappa_2$, where $0 \leqslant \kappa_1 < \kappa_2 \leqslant \kappa_+$ at time $\tau = t$ if:

(i) it is continuous in the region $\kappa_1 < \kappa < \kappa_2$, when $t \leqslant \tau < +\infty$;
(ii) and if the equation

$$S(\kappa, \tau) = (\gamma + \lambda)\,\kappa + \frac{\dot{\kappa}}{1-\alpha}$$

defines an indefinitely feasible program [hence $S(\kappa, \tau) < 1$, $\kappa_1 < \kappa < \kappa_2$, $t \leqslant \tau < +\infty$ (see Theorem 1.6.1 iii)] at t which satisfies

$$\kappa_1 < \kappa(\tau) < \kappa_2, \qquad t \leqslant \tau < +\infty,$$

provided only that $\kappa_1 < \kappa_t < \kappa_2$. A growth strategy is feasible in $\kappa_1 < \kappa < \kappa_2$ if it is feasible at every $t \geqslant 0$. A growth strategy is simply called feasible if it is feasible in $0 < \kappa < \kappa_+$.

Condition (i) has been imposed for the same reason that a savings program is required to be continuous: a discontinuity of the savings path is interpreted as a change in growth strategy. Condition (ii) says that, starting from any initial capital-output ratio $\kappa_1 < \kappa_t < \kappa_2$, a feasible growth strategy in $\kappa_1 < \kappa < \kappa_2$ should generate an indefinitely feasible growth program which satisfies $\kappa_1 < \kappa(\tau) < \kappa_2$, $0 \leqslant \tau < +\infty$. Given an EG model, $S(\kappa, \tau) = (\gamma + \lambda)\, \kappa_2$, $0 < \kappa_2 < \kappa_+$, is a simple instance of a feasible strategy in $\kappa_1 < \kappa < \kappa_2$ for every $0 < \kappa_1 < \kappa_2$ (Theorem 1.5.1). This strategy is, however, also feasible in $0 < \kappa < \kappa_+$. An instance of a strategy which is only feasible in

$$\frac{\kappa_+}{4} < \kappa < \kappa_+, \qquad \kappa_+ = \frac{1}{\gamma + \lambda}$$

is, under the EG assumptions,

$$S(\kappa, \tau) = 1 - \frac{3}{16}\frac{\kappa_+}{\kappa}.$$

It implies a capital-output ratio $\kappa(\tau)$ which is, over $t \leqslant \tau < +\infty$:

(i) strictly concave and decreasing if $0 < \kappa_t < \kappa_+/4$;
(ii) constant if $\kappa_t = \kappa_+/4$;
(iii) strictly increasing if $\kappa_+/4 < \kappa_t < 3\kappa_+/4$;
(iv) constant if $\kappa_t = 3\kappa_+/4$;
(v) strictly decreasing if $3\kappa_+/4 < \kappa_t < \kappa_+$.

Chapter 2

THE CONCEPT OF AN OPTIMAL GROWTH STRATEGY

2.1 ORGANIZATION OF THE CHAPTER

As stated in the Introduction, the purpose of this book is to make a constructive critique of the classical theory of optimal economic growth. *A priori,* the most natural way to make this critique appears to be:

(i) to define and explain the classical theory;

(ii) to determine and discuss its respective merits and shortcomings;

(iii) to suggest how it could be improved.

However, this seemingly logical program cannot easily be applied. The difficulty resides in the fact that the economic interpretation of the classical theory has never been satisfactorily stated. The reason for this apparently surprising fact is very simple: the classical theory does not possess an economically meaningful interpretation.

The main conceptual weakness of the classical approach is that it does not refer to any meaningful economic decision maker. It reduces the problem of optimal growth to a one-person decision problem by introducing a virtual and unrealistic being which we shall call the Society of Immortals. This deprives the classical theory of any meaningful economic interpretation. In view of this fact we do not apply the program defined by (i), (ii) and (iii). Instead, we:

(i*) set forth a new conceptual framework for the analysis of the problem of optimal economic growth;

(ii*) discuss the classical definition in the light of this new conceptual framework;

(iii*) propose a better definition of optimal growth.

The three subsequent sections define and explain the three basic concepts of the new theoretical scheme advanced in this chapter. Section 2.5 shows how the classical definition can be integrated into this scheme. At the same time, it clearly brings out the fact that the classical definition corresponds to an extreme case of devotion to all future generations.

Finally, it defines what is believed to be a more realistic criterion of optimal economic growth.

The respective technical properties of the classical criterion and this more realistic criterion of optimal growth are analyzed in Chapters 3 and 4.

2.2 THE CONCEPT OF THE INSTANTANEOUS GOVERNMENT

2.2.1 General definition

The problem of optimal economic growth is unquestionably a decision problem. It can therefore not be rigorously stated unless the decision makers involved in this problem are unambiguously specified. Now, to the best of my knowledge, this has never been done. The present section attempts to fill this lacuna.

The first question to ask is: *who can actually control the growth process?* Given the Q-EG class of models, the question put more precisely is: who can actually decide upon the time path $s(\tau)$ of the savings ratio?

In order to answer this question, we start from the obvious fact that only people alive can act. The people living between t and $t + \delta$ must therefore somehow be able to perform the macro-economic act of choosing $s(\tau)$, $t \leqslant \tau \leqslant t + \delta$. For this purpose they need some institutional mechanism. It seems natural to call this mechanism "government". For the sake of simplicity, we assume that the life span δ of all governments is equal to one year. In this discrete description of the growth process, the answer to our first question then reads: in every given year, the savings path $s(\tau)$ is decided upon by the yearly government in power.

Let us now amend this answer to make it consistent with a continuous description of the growth process. In other words, let us see how the above answer must change if we let δ tend to zero. The yearly governments become then *instantaneous governments* or, shortly, IGs. Now, an IG can only act at a given instant of time, namely at the point of time t of its instantaneous existence. Therefore, the IG at t by itself has no power to enforce the value $s(t)$ of the savings ratio it would like to have at t. Indeed, by definition, this value depends on the time path of $x(\tau)$ throughout some neighbourhood of t, i.e. on decisions which do not only depend on the IG at t. Moreover, at time t, the left value $s(t^-)$ of the savings ratio, if this value exists at all, is already historically determined. The only thing that the IG at t can really do is to plan for a given $s(t^+)$, i.e. for a given right value of the savings ratio at t.

The next question to ask is: *for whom should optimal growth be optimal?* In some sense, of course, for the individual members of the economy. The problem is in which sense. There is, indeed, a conflict of interest between people living at different points of time. Clearly, less investments today mean more consumption today, but less tomorrow. On the other hand, more investments today mean less consumption today, but more tomorrow.

Notice that the choice of the savings ratio $s(t^+)$ also causes a conflict of interest among the individuals of different income classes co-existing at time t. This conflict is, however, traditionally considered as a separate problem. In this context, we assume that it has already been solved. In other words, we assume that the IG at t always expresses the will of the people living at time t. More precisely, we assume that an IG at t has a preference pattern which can be considered as the expression of the economic will of the people living at time t.

This raises the last question we have to ask: *what are the alternatives with respect to which the preference pattern of the instantaneous government at time* t *is defined?* In the context of the Q-EG models, it seems natural that this preference pattern refers to all per capita consumption paths $mc(\tau)$ which are feasible over some finite time interval $t \leqslant \tau < t + \omega$. We thus assume that the instantaneous government at time t has a finite time horizon ω. The latter can be interpreted as some weighted average of the economic time horizons of the individuals living at time t. We shall see later that ω can be given an unambiguous econometric definition (Section 4.5.1).

Finally, we assume that the preference pattern of the IG at time t can be described by a utility functional $I[c(\tau)_t^{t+\omega}]$ defined over the set $\{c(\tau)_t^{t+\omega}\}$ of feasible $c(\tau)$ over $t < \tau < t + \omega$. This functional is defined below.

In short, the *instantaneous government* or IG at time t is a being which:

(i) represents the economic interests of the people living at time t;

(ii) can only act at time t, namely, plan for a given value of $s(t^+)$, i.e. of $c(t^+)$;

(iii) has nevertheless a well-defined preference pattern with respect to all per capita consumption paths which are feasible over $t \leqslant \tau < t + \omega$.

It is important to realize that different IGs have different economic interests, even though they are all characterized by the same time horizon ω and the same functional $I[c(\tau)_t^{t+\omega}]$. The difference between two IGs, say at times t and t^*, is that one IG is interested in the time interval $t \leqslant \tau < t + \omega$ and the other IG in the time interval $t^* \leqslant \tau < t^* + \omega$.

The IG concept turns out to be very fruitful. It permits us to integrate the conflict of interests between the successive IGs into our formulation of the problem of optimal economic growth. We also believe that it does provide a relatively realistic schematization of reality, where economic development plans are prepared and enforced by governments. These governments always have a finite time horizon. Both their plans and their own existence usually cover a still shorter period of time. In a continuous formulation of the problem of optimal growth, it was therefore natural to reduce this period to an instant of time.

2.2.2 Formal definition

(i) The instantaneous utility function. The preference pattern of the IG at t, $0 \leqslant t < +\infty$, with respect to instantaneous consumption, i.e. consumption at t, can be described by a strictly concave and thrice continuously differentiable utility function $U(c)$ defined over $0 < c < +\infty$, which satisfies

$$u(c) > 0, \qquad u'(c) < 0, \qquad u''(c) > 0 \tag{2.2.1}$$

$$\lim_{c \to 0} u(c) = +\infty \tag{2.2.2}$$

$$\lim_{c \to +\infty} u(c) = 0 \tag{2.2.3}$$

and

$$\Phi'(c) \geqslant 0 \tag{2.2.4}$$

where $u(c)$ denotes the marginal utility $U'(c)$ and $\Phi(c)$ the elasticity of marginal utility (Frisch's flexibility):

$$\Phi(c) = \frac{cu'(c)}{u(c)}. \tag{2.2.5}$$

The function $U(c)$ is the same for all IGs.

(ii) The time discount rate. The IG at t, $0 \leqslant t < +\infty$, discounts the utility of future per capita consumption at the constant and non-negative rate i. Writing $U_t(c_{t^*})$ for the utility at t of consumption at t^*, $t \leqslant t^* \leqslant t + \omega$, one has

$$U_t(c_{t^*}) = U(c_{t^*})\exp[-i(t^* - t)]$$

The value of the time discount rate i is the same for all IGs.

(iii) The utility index. Between any two c-paths which are feasible at t, the IG at t, $0 \leqslant t < +\infty$, prefers the one which gives the greater value to the Lebesgues integral:

$$I[c(\tau)_t^{t+\omega}] = \int_t^{t+\omega} U[c(\tau)]\exp[-i(\tau - t)\mathrm{d}\tau]. \qquad (2.2.6)$$

(iv) Terminological convention. The above three sets of assumptions (i), (ii) and (iii) are referred to as the IG assumptions.

2.2.3 The Bernoulli functions

A very simple class of utility functions which satisfy our general utility assumptions 2.2.2(i) are the Bernoulli functions. These are defined by a constant and negative elasticity of marginal utility:

$$\Phi = -\nu, \qquad \nu > 0 \qquad (2.2.7)$$

The integration of equation (2.2.7) yields three different "subclasses" of Bernoulli functions, depending on whether $\nu < 1$, $\nu = 1$ or $\nu > 1$.

If $\nu < 1$, then

$$U(c) = Ac^{1-\nu} + U^* \qquad (2.2.8)$$

where A and U^* are arbitrary constants and $A \neq 0$.

If $\nu = 1$, then

$$U(c) = \ln(c/c^*)^a \qquad (2.2.9)$$

where c^* and a are positive constants.

If $\nu > 1$, then

$$U(c) = U^* - Ac^{-(\nu-1)} \qquad (2.2.10)$$

where A and U^* are arbitrary constants and $A \neq 0$.

Throughout the rest of Part I, we generally assume a Bernoulli utility function. This considerably reduces the mathematical difficulties of our analysis, enabling us to concentrate on the exposition of our main chain of arguments.

2.3 THE CONCEPT OF NATIONAL ALLEGIANCE

Having already mentioned the conflict of interests between successive instantaneous governments or IGs, we now consider it in some more detail.

For the sake of argument, we assume for a moment that not only the initial condition $\kappa(t) = \kappa_t$, but also the terminal condition $\kappa(t + \omega) = \kappa_{t+\omega}$ are given. In this case, the IG at t naturally prefers the feasible κ-path which maximizes its utility index $I[c(\tau)_t^{t+\omega}]$. Granted that it exists, we denote this path by $\bar{\kappa}(\tau; \kappa_t, \kappa_{t+\omega})$ and write $\bar{I}(\kappa_t, \kappa_{t+\omega})$ for the resulting value of $I[c(\tau)_t^{t+\omega}]$. Now, it is known that $\bar{\kappa}$ must satisfy Euler's equation (Theorem 3.2.1). It follows by Lemma 2.4.1 (Paper 1) that $\bar{I}(\kappa_t, \kappa_{t+\omega})$ is a strictly decreasing function of $\kappa_{t+\omega}$ and attains its maximum at $\kappa_{t+\omega} = 0$.

The IG at t prefers therefore $\bar{\kappa}(\tau; \kappa_t, 0)$ to any other κ-path which is feasible over $t \leqslant \tau < t + \omega$. It is, however, clear that the program $\bar{\kappa}(\tau; \kappa_t, 0)$ will never be enforced by the IGs succeeding to the IG at t. As a matter of fact, $\kappa_{t+\omega} = 0$ implies that no capital stock is left over at time $t + \omega$ and, consequently, all people die of starvation after $t + \omega$. The IG at t must therefore content itself with a value of $I[c(\tau)_t^{t+\omega}]$ smaller than $\bar{I}(\kappa_t, 0)$. The question then is how high a value it can actually hope to attain. In order to answer this question we endow the IGs with a further property.

ASSUMPTION 2.3.1 Let the Q-EG and IG assumptions obtain. Every IG has a feeling of *national allegiance* which ensures that it views the choice (in the sense of adopting a plan) of the right-hand value of the savings ratio at its instant of existence as a choice from among some given set of growth strategies which are feasible in some given interval $\kappa_1 < \kappa < \kappa_2$, $0 \leqslant \kappa_1 < \kappa_2 \leqslant \kappa_+$. These strategies, called "admissible", are the same for all successive IGs.

2.4 THE CONCEPT OF UNANIMOUS PREFERENCE

By Assumption 2.3.1, every IG has to make its choice (in the sense of choosing a plan) from among a given set of admissible growth strategies. The problem is to determine what constitutes an optimal decision for a given IG. Unfortunately, this problem does not always possess a satisfactory solution. Nevertheless, there are specifications of the set of admissible growth strategies for which such a solution does exist.

In order to define the solution in question, we introduce the fundamental concept of *unanimous preference.*

DEFINITION 2.4.1 Let S and S^* denote two growth strategies which are both feasible in $\kappa_1 < \kappa < \kappa_2$, $0 \leqslant \kappa_1 < \kappa_2 \leqslant \kappa_+$ at time t (Definition 1.6.4).

We say that S^* is unanimously preferred to S in $\kappa_1 < \kappa < \kappa_2$ over the infinite time interval $t \leqslant \tau < +\infty$ if every IG in this time interval prefers S^* to S in $\kappa_1 < \kappa < \kappa_2$ in the sense of Definition 2.4.2 below. If $t = 0$, the explicit reference to the time interval $t \leqslant \tau < +\infty$ is omitted.

DEFINITION 2.4.2 Let $0 \leqslant \kappa_1 < \kappa_2 \leqslant \kappa_+$, where κ_+ is defined by (1.6.2). Let S^* and S denote two growth strategies which are feasible in $\kappa_1 < \kappa < \kappa_2$ at time t. We shall say that the IG at t prefers S^* to S in $\kappa_1 < \kappa < \kappa_2$ if, for any κ_t satisfying $\kappa_1 < \kappa_t < \kappa_2$, the utility index $I[c(\tau)_t^{t+\omega}]$ takes on a greater value along the indefinitely feasible program defined by S^* than along the one defined by S.

Clearly, if there is an admissible strategy S^* which is unanimously preferred to all other admissible strategies, then it is to the advantage of all IGs that S^* be actually enforced. Their rational choice is thus S^*.

DEFINITION 2.4.3 Let the set of admissible growth strategies be defined in $\kappa_1 < \kappa < \kappa_2$. The admissible growth strategy which is unanimously most preferred in $\kappa_1 < \kappa < \kappa_2$ is optimal.

In order to further clarify the concept of unanimous preference, let us stress the fact that the choice of a strategy by an IG is exclusively based on considerations which refer to the future.

It is a matter of fact that the past cannot be changed. The IG at time t must accept the value of the capital stock (as well as the values of Q, L and P) as historically given at time t. This, of course, does not change the fact that the higher the historically given capital stock at time t, the better off the IG at time t. Given two admissible growth strategies, the IG at time t would naturally have preferred all IGs before t to have applied the strategy which would have accumulated the greater capital stock. In general, however, the strategy in question is not the one it wants to see applied in the future, i.e. from t onwards.

Indeed, every IG naturally likes to inherit as much capital stock as possible from the past IGs and to leave as little as possible to the IGs lying beyond its time horizon. This precisely accounts for the conflict of interests between successive IGs. The point is, however, that the IG at time t cannot do anything about what happened before t. It can only try to act at time t in a way which best serves its purpose with regard to the period extending up to its time horizon, i.e. from t to $t + \omega$. The only preferences of an IG relevant to the framing of an optimal economic policy are, consequently, those which refer to the said period.

2.5 TWO PARTICULAR DEFINITIONS OF THE OPTIMAL STRATEGY

2.5.1 The classical definition: a case of extreme national allegiance

The classical approach to optimal growth considers only one admissible growth strategy. It thus ignores completely the problem of choosing from among different admissible strategies. In our terminology, it puts the whole weight of the definition of optimal growth on a particular specification of national allegiance.

POSTULATE 2.5.1 Every IG should behave as if it had an infinite time horizon. More precisely, every IG should apply the strategy of Utility Maximization over Infinite Time or UMIT as defined by Definition 2.5.1.

DEFINITION 2.5.1 Let the Q-EG and IG assumptions obtain and an initial capital stock be given at time t. Then the indefinitely feasible program $\hat{c}(\tau)$ will be called UMIT-optimal if there is a T^* for every other indefinitely feasible program $c^*(\tau)$ such that

$$I[c^*(\tau)_t^T] - I[\hat{c}(\tau)_t^T] < 0, \qquad T^* \leqslant T < +\infty. \tag{2.5.1}$$

A UMIT-optimal growth program is said to "maximize" the UMIT-index

$$I[c(\tau)_t^{+\infty}] = \int_t^{+\infty} U(c)\exp[-i\tau]\mathrm{d}\tau \tag{2.5.2}$$

in the sense of the Carl von Weisszäcker's *overtaking principle* [W].

A feasible strategy is a UMIT strategy in $\kappa_1 < \kappa < \kappa_2$ if it defines a UMIT-optimal program for every point of time $t \geqslant 0$ and every initial capital stock at time t which satisfies $\kappa_1 < \kappa_t < \kappa_2$. The explicit reference to κ_1 and κ_2 is omitted if $\kappa_1 = 0$ and $\kappa_2 = \kappa_+$, where κ_+ is defined by (1.6.2).

We see in Section 3.2.2 that the existence of a UMIT-optimal program under the Q-EG and IG assumptions requires the satisfaction of Euler's condition

$$-\frac{\dot{u}}{u} = \frac{\partial y}{\partial x} - (i + \lambda), \qquad 0 \leqslant \tau < +\infty. \tag{2.5.3}$$

Furthermore, we see in Section 4.2.1 that (2.5.3) follows from

$$u[c(t)] = \int_t^{+\infty} \frac{\partial y}{\partial x}(\tau)u[c(\tau)]\exp[-i(\tau - t) - \int_t^{\tau} \lambda(\tau')\mathrm{d}\tau']\mathrm{d}\tau, \tag{2.5.4}$$

$$0 \leqslant t < +\infty.$$

The latter condition means more than (2.5.3) to the economist. It states the following.

> *The marginal utility of instantaneous consumption should equal at every point of time* t *the marginal utility of the returns per capita derived over the whole of the future from investments at* t. *In short, the classical definition of optimal growth may be said to require Marginal Utility Equilibrium over Infinite Time or MUEIT.*

The expression

$$\frac{\partial y}{\partial x} u \exp[-i(\tau - t) - \int_t^\tau \lambda(\tau')d\tau']$$

represents the marginal utility of the returns per capita at τ from investments made at t. The term

$$\exp[- \int_t^\tau \lambda(\tau')d\tau']$$

takes into account that a growing population decreases the individual share of income over time. The time discount function $\exp[-i(\tau - t)]$ plays the same rôle here as in $I[c(\tau)_t^{+\infty}]$: it expresses a certain impatience to consume.

It is important to realize that *the MUEIT condition corresponds to an extreme degree of national allegiance.* I do not believe, indeed, that anybody wants the marginal utility of instantaneous consumption to be greater than the marginal utility of the per capita returns derived over infinite time from investments. This means that a given IG should forego, in terms of utility units, more than the sum-total of the resulting benefits which would accrue to all later IGs. We may thus safely postulate that the left-hand side of (2.5.4) should never be greater than its right-hand side; the most which can be asked is that both sides of (2.5.4) be equal. This is precisely what the MUEIT condition requires.

In practice, however, the MUEIT condition seems difficult to fulfill. It is too altruistic to be realistic. No actual IG can reasonably be expected to identify its own interests with those of all later IGs, whatever their distance in time.

2.5.2 A more realistic definition

As already mentioned, we see in Section 4.2.1 that the UMIT strategy is a result of marginal utility equilibrium over infinite time. This means that, in terms of utility, people should always invest much more than the returns which their investments can ever yield during their own lifetime. As a consequence, the UMIT strategy will often prescribe an unrealistically high savings ratio (see Papers 3 and 4, Part II), i.e. one which is inconceivable to enforce in practice. It seems therefore worthwhile to investigate the desirability of replacing the "severe" MUEIT condition by the following "softer" MUEFT condition.

DEFINITION 2.5.2 An indefinitely feasible growth program establishes Marginal Utility Equilibrium over Finite Time (or MUEFT) if it satisfies

$$u[c(t)] = \int_t^{t+\omega} \frac{\partial y}{\partial x}(\tau)u[c(\tau)]\exp[-i(\tau - t) - \int_t^{\tau} \lambda(\tau')d\tau']\,d\tau, \quad (2.5.5)$$

$$0 \leqslant t < +\infty.$$

In other words, MUEFT requires that the marginal utility of per capita consumption at t should be equal to the marginal utility of the per capita returns derived over the finite period ω from investments made at t. If ω is defined as the weighted economic life expectancy of the people alive at the same instant of time (Section 4.5.1), the MUEFT condition can be interpreted to say the following.

> *In terms of utility, people should always invest exactly as much as the returns they can expect to get from their investments over their common economic time horizon ω.*

In order to use the MUEFT condition to define the admissible strategy which is to replace the UMIT strategy, we must naturally ascertain whether it defines a unique and feasible growth strategy. Moreover, this strategy must be efficient in the sense of Definition 2.5.3.

DEFINITION 2.5.3 An indefinitely feasible growth program $c(\tau)$, $t \leqslant \tau < +\infty$, is efficient at t if there is no other such program which satisfies

$$c^*(\tau) \geqslant c(\tau), \qquad t \leqslant \tau < +\infty \quad (2.5.6)$$

and

$$c^*(t^*) > c(t^*) \qquad \text{for some } t^* \geqslant t. \quad (2.5.7)$$

An efficient growth strategy in $\kappa_1 < \kappa < \kappa_2$ at t is a feasible growth strategy in $\kappa_1 < \kappa < \kappa_2$ at t which defines an efficient growth program at t for every κ_t in $\kappa_1 < \kappa_t < \kappa_2$. An efficient growth strategy in $\kappa_1 < \kappa < \kappa_2$ is one which is efficient for every $t \geqslant 0$. If $\kappa_1 = 0$ and $\kappa_2 = \kappa_+$, the reference to $\kappa_1 < \kappa < \kappa_2$ is omitted.

Simply, an indefinitely feasible growth program is efficient if there is no other one which provides never less (2.5.6) and sometimes more (2.5.7) consumption. A feasible growth strategy is efficient if it defines an efficient growth program at every point of time t and for every historically conceivable initial capital stock at t.

We need the condition of efficiency since an inefficient indefinitely feasible and historically conceivable MUEFT program could possibly exist. This could also be the case under the MUEIT condition. We have not mentioned the possibility of inefficiency in connection with the MUEIT condition, because a UMIT-optimal program is obviously efficient. Now, we have defined the classical strategy of optimal growth in terms of UMIT and not MUEIT. It is necessary, however, to require efficiency in the definition of MUEFT as the only admissible and, consequently, optimal strategy.

POSTULATE 2.5.2 If the MUEFT condition defines a unique and efficient growth strategy in an interval $\kappa_1 < \kappa < \kappa_2$, including the initial value κ_t, all IGs should consider it as the only admissible growth strategy.

Granted that one does restrict the set of admissible strategies to a single strategy, this definition of the optimal strategy seems preferable to the classical one. I indeed argue that the MUEFT strategy is unanimously preferred to the UMIT strategy in any interval $\kappa_1 < \kappa < \kappa_2$ over which they both exist (Section 4.4.3). Now, if one of two given admissible growth strategies is unanimously preferred, it is certainly the more realistic one.

Only a convincing ethical argument could therefore rule out MUEFT strategy in favor of the UMIT strategy. I do not believe that such an argument exists. As already pointed out, utility maximization for a "Society of Immortals" does not make much sense. Moreover, within the conceptual framework developed in the first three sections of this chapter, it appears to me that MUEFT, and not UMIT, constitutes the ethically more attractive proposition.

Let me make it clear, however, that I do not propose the MUEFT strategy as *the* solution to the problem of optimal economic growth. I only believe that MUEFT is more realistic than UMIT and that, consequently, UMIT should be rejected as an optimal growth strategy.

Chapter 3

UTILITY MAXIMIZATION OVER INFINITE TIME (UMIT)

3.1 PURPOSE OF THE CHAPTER

3.1.1 Consistency and existence

One of the main problems arising in connexion with the UMIT criterion is the determination of the conditions under which it defines a feasible growth strategy in the sense of Definition 1.6.4. To be precise, there are really two separate questions to be answered.

(i) Is the definition of the UMIT strategy consistent with the definition of a feasible strategy? In other words, is Postulate 2.5.1 consistent with Definition 1.6.4?

(ii) Under what conditions does a UMIT strategy exist?

Another way of formulating the first question is to ask whether a UMIT-optimal program is necessarily self-consistent in the sense of the following definition.

DEFINITION 3.1.1 Let a Q-EG model, a UMIT index and the initial capital stock at time 0 be given. Let $\hat{x}(\tau)$ denote the indefinitely feasible program at time 0 which maximizes the UMIT index $I[c(\tau)_0^{+\infty}]$ in the sense of the overtaking principle. Moreover, let $\hat{x}^*(\tau)$ denote the indefinitely feasible program at time $t > 0$ which satisfies the initial condition $\hat{x}^*(t) = \hat{x}(t)$ and maximizes the UMIT index $I[c(\tau)_t^{+\infty}]$. We say that the UMIT program $\hat{x}(\tau)$ is *self-consistent* if it coincides with $\hat{x}^*(\tau)$ over $t \leqslant \tau < +\infty$ for all $t > 0$.

Put simply, the condition of self-consistency requires that a growth program which is optimal at a given point in time should remain so at any later point in time. The UMIT criterion applied at any later point in time should confirm the initial UMIT-optimal program. If this were not so, UMIT would hardly constitute a criterion of optimality. Fortunately the following theorem holds.

THEOREM 3.1.1 Under the Q-EG and IG assumptions, a UMIT-optimal program is necessarily self-consistent.

(Proof in the Mathematical Appendix)

It follows at once that, under the Q-EG and IG assumptions, UMIT defines a feasible strategy in $\kappa_1 < \kappa < \kappa_2$ if:

(a) a UMIT-optimal program exists over $0 \leqslant \tau < +\infty$ for every initial capital stock which satisfies $\kappa_1 < \kappa_0 < \kappa_2$;

(b) every UMIT-optimal program $\hat{\kappa}(\tau)$ which satisfies the initial condition $\kappa_1 < \kappa_0 < \kappa_2$ also satisfies

$$\kappa_1 < \hat{\kappa}(\tau) < \kappa_2, \qquad 0 \leqslant \tau < +\infty.$$

This brings us to the second of the above questions, namely the problem of the existence of a UMIT strategy. Both questions (i) and (ii) require the determination of the conditions under which a UMIT-optimal program can exist. This last question constitutes the traditional existence problem of UMIT. It is dealt with in Section 3.2.

3.1.2 The three basic questions

We are now in a position to specify the purpose of the present chapter. It is to try to answer the following three basic questions:

(i) Under what conditions does a UMIT-optimal program exist?

(ii) What are its main properties?

(iii) How should the value of the time discount rate be chosen?

The first question is the existence question mentioned in Section 3.1.1. It will be further elaborated in a non-technical form in Section 3.2.1.

The second question can be answered either by a general analysis of the conditions which every UMIT-optimal program must satisfy or by the explicit determination of the *x*-, *y*-, *c*- and *s*-paths of a particular UMIT-optimal program. Both lines of approach are followed and the main results are presented in Section 3.3. The reader is also referred to Papers 3 and 4 in Part II. In short, the UMIT strategy often turns out to be unrealistically severe on all generations, with, moreover, an "unfair" bias in favor of the future and richer ones.

The third question raises the problem of the meaning of the time discount rate i in the case of the UMIT strategy. It is shown that the assumption of a constant i cannot be relaxed and that, consequently, i can hardly be considered to represent a "social" time discount rate. It is argued that the most appropriate way to determine the value of i is to choose it according to what we call the principle of "minimum impatience".

Unfortunately, we are not able to ascertain whether or not this principle can always be applied. In any case, the analysis shows that there are serious difficulties associated with the economic interpretation of the UMIT strategy (Section 3.4).

The discussion of these three basic questions provides a fair insight into the problem of UMIT-optimal growth. It also constitutes an appropriate introduction to our discussion of the MUEFT-strategy.

3.2 THE EXISTENCE PROBLEM

3.2.1 Non-technical introduction

The determination of the conditions which are necessary and sufficient for the existence of a UMIT solution is not a simple matter. Under the general Q-EG and IG assumptions, it raises some delicate and yet unsolved mathematical problems. Fortunately, the solution of these is not essential to our purpose. As a matter of fact, we only want to set forth the basic characteristics of the UMIT strategy. We therefore conduct our analysis of the existence problem mainly under the EG and Bernoulli assumptions. No essential feature of the UMIT strategy is believed to be lost by this simplification which, on the contrary, is beneficial to the clarity of our argumentation.

To begin with, it is appropriate to distinguish between those existence conditions which can be applied without solving any further mathematical problem and those which cannot. These two types of existence conditions are called *explicit* and *implicit*, respectively:

A typical instance of an implicit existence condition is that Euler's equation should have a solution. This is a well-known necessary condition in the calculus of free variations. Now, under our growth and preference assumptions, UMIT constitutes precisely a problem of free variations. If a UMIT-optimal program exists, it must therefore be Eulerian. This condition is, however, implicit and its practical application generally raises serious mathematical difficulties. Another implicit condition is that a UMIT-optimal program must be efficient. Indeed, no other indefinitely feasible program should exist which yields never less and sometimes more consumption.

A UMIT-optimal program must thus be both Eulerian and efficient. It is interesting that these two necessary conditions can also be shown to be sufficient for UMIT optimality under the EG and Bernoulli assumptions (Theorem 3.2.8). It is our conjecture that they remain sufficient under our general Q-EG and IG assumptions: *a growth programme is UMIT-optimal if and only if it is Eulerian and efficient.*

This is a very simple and, conceptually, a very neat existence theorem.

It can be interpreted as saying that marginal utility equilibrium should be indefinitely maintained, provided that it can be done efficiently. The theorem is, however, implicit in the sense that it does not state under what conditions an efficient Eulerian program does actually exist. The real difficulty is to find explicit existence conditions to help answer this last question. As a matter of fact, the derivation of necessary and sufficient explicit existence conditions constitutes a very difficult and as yet unsolved problem under the general Q-EG and IG assumptions.

It is only in two particular, though important, cases that this problem has been solved. The first is the case of a constant technology ($\rho = 0$) and a utility function such that the elasticity of marginal utility does not tend to zero as consumption grows infinite ($\nu > 0$) (Theorem 2 in Paper 2, Part II). The other is the case of the EG and Bernoulli assumptions. In both cases, a UMIT-optimal program does exist for every historically conceivable initial capital stock if and only if the time discount rate i is not smaller than a certain value i_0 which may be positive under technological progress. (In the first case i_0 is always equal to zero and the condition $i \geqslant i_0$ is automatically fulfilled, since, by definition $i \geqslant 0$ [Section 2.2.2(ii)])

Our discussion of the existence problem is completed by relating the efficiency condition to a certain "minimum convergence" condition which the UMIT index must satisfy along the optimal program. We see that, at least under the EG and Bernoulli assumptions, this minimum convergence condition is completely equivalent to the efficiency condition.

The interested reader can find in Part II a more general existence theorem, though under somewhat different growth assumptions (Paper 1). The proof of this theorem indicates the kind of mathematical difficulties one is bound to meet as soon as one tries to relax the EG and Bernoulli simplifications under technological progress.

3.2.2 Euler's equation

As already said, UMIT under the Q-EG and IG assumptions is a problem of the calculus of free variations. It is not, however, a classical one. It can be considered as a generalization of the classical fixed end-points problem where one of the end-points is situated at infinity. Now it is well known that Euler's condition constitutes a necessary condition for the existence of an extremum in the classical fixed end-points problem. We shall see that Euler's condition remains necessary under our UMIT generalization of this problem.

The classical fixed end-points theorem which establishes the necessity of Euler's equation may be stated as follows.

THEOREM 3.2.1 Let (z_1, τ_1) and (z_2, τ_2) be two straight lines in some open and convex region R of the $(\tau, z, \dot{z})$-space. Let, on the other hand, the function $W(\tau, z, \dot{z})$ be twice continuously differentiable in R. The curve, if any, which strictly maximizes

$$\int_{\tau_1}^{\tau_2} W(\tau, z, \dot{z}) d\tau$$

among all continuous curves connecting the lines (z_1, τ_1) and (z_2, τ_2) in R satisfies Euler's equation

$$\frac{\partial}{\partial z} W - \frac{d}{d\tau} \frac{\partial}{\partial \dot{z}} W = 0, \qquad \tau_1 \leqslant \tau \leqslant \tau_2 .$$

(Proof: see any textbook on the calculus of variations)

Our problem differs from the one dealt with by Theorem 3.2.1 in so far as our maximand is an improper integral of the type

$$\int_{\tau_1}^{+\infty} W(\tau, x, \dot{x}) d\tau$$

where

$$W(\tau, x, \dot{x}) = U(c) \exp[-i\tau] = U\left\{\exp[\rho\tau] f(x) - \lambda x - \dot{x}\right\} \exp[-i\tau]$$

is defined in the region

$$R: -\infty < \tau < +\infty, \qquad 0 < x < +\infty, \qquad -\infty < \dot{x} < \exp[\rho\tau] f(x) - \lambda x.$$

The problem is to find a continuous curve in R connecting the initial line (τ_1, x_1) to the "plane at infinity" $\tau = +\infty$ and maximizing the improper integral (Section 3.2.6). In short, ours is a problem of the calculus of free variations over an infinite time interval. It can be shown that Euler's equation remains a necessary condition.

THEOREM 3.2.2 Let the Q-EG and IG assumptions obtain and an initial capital stock be given. The growth path, if any, which strictly maximizes $I[c(\tau)_0^{+\infty}]$ from among all indefinitely feasible growth paths must satisfy Euler's equation

$$\left[\frac{\partial}{\partial x} - \frac{d}{d\tau} \frac{\partial}{\partial \dot{x}}\right] U(c) \exp[-i\tau] = + \Phi \frac{\dot{c}}{c} + \frac{\alpha}{\kappa} - (i + \lambda) = 0$$

(Proof in the Mathematical Appendix)

Since $\Phi\dot{c}/c = u'\dot{c}/u$ and $\partial y/\partial x = \alpha/\kappa$, (3.2.1) is just another way of writing (2.5.3). Still another way is

$$\ddot{\kappa} = (1-s)(1-\alpha)\left\{\gamma + \frac{1}{\Phi}\left(\frac{\alpha}{\kappa} - i - \lambda\right) + \frac{\dot{\kappa}}{\kappa}\left[\frac{\alpha}{1-\alpha} - \frac{(\gamma+\lambda)\kappa}{1-s}\right]\right\}$$
$$-\dot{\alpha}\left(\gamma\kappa + \frac{\dot{\kappa}}{1-\alpha}\right) - \dot{\lambda}(1-\alpha)\kappa \tag{3.2.2}$$

Under the assumptions of an EG model and a Bernoulli utility function, (3.2.2) becomes

$$\ddot{\kappa} = (1-s)(1-\alpha)\left\{\gamma - \frac{1}{\nu}\left(\frac{\alpha}{\kappa} - i - \lambda\right) + \frac{\dot{\kappa}}{\kappa}\left[\frac{\alpha}{1-\alpha} - \frac{(\gamma+\lambda)\kappa}{1-s}\right]\right\} \tag{3.2.3}$$

i.e. an autonomous second order differential equation of the form

$$\ddot{\kappa} = h(\dot{\kappa}, \kappa) \tag{3.2.4}$$

where h is continuously differentiable in the region

$$R: -\infty < \dot{\kappa} < (1-\alpha)(1-g\kappa), \qquad 0 < \kappa < +\infty.$$

This last property is known to ensure the existence of a unique solution in the small

$$\tilde{\kappa}(\tau; \dot{\kappa}_t, \kappa_t)$$

through every point $(\dot{\kappa}_t, \kappa_t)$ in R. This solution can be continued to the border of R. Moreover, if there exists an indefinitely feasible $\tilde{\kappa}(\tau; \dot{\kappa}_t, \kappa_t)$, it must be monotonic over $t \leqslant \tau < +\infty$ by virtue of the autonomy of (3.2.4).

The main question is, however, whether an indefinitely feasible Eulerian program (i.e. one which satisfies Euler's equation) exists at all. This is a very difficult question which can generally not be answered with the aid of elementary mathematical techniques. The two following theorems are an exception to this rule.

THEOREM 3.2.3 Let the Q-EG λ_0 and IG assumptions obtain with the restriction that there is no technological progress ($\lambda = \lambda_0 > 0, \rho = 0$). Let, moreover, the elasticity of marginal utility $\Phi(c)$ tend to a negative value $-\nu$ as c grows infinite. Then, there exists an indefinitely feasible Eulerian program for every historically conceivable initial capital stock.

(Proof: Theorem 4.1 in Paper 2, Part II)

THEOREM 3.2.4 Let the EG and IG assumptions obtain under the restriction of a Bernoulli utility function. Provided only that

$$i \geqslant i_0, \qquad i_0 = (1-\nu)\frac{\rho}{1-\alpha}$$

there exists an indefinitely feasible Eulerian program for every historically conceivable initial capital.

(Proof: Theorem 4.1 in Paper 2, Part II)

3.2.3 The efficiency condition

We have already pointed out that a UMIT-optimal program is necessarily efficient in the sense of Definition 2.5.2. Let us now turn to the problem of replacing the efficiency condition by an equivalent explicit condition. Since we have seen that the UMIT-optimal must be Eulerian, we need only consider the problem of deriving necessary and sufficient conditions for the efficiency of an indefinitely feasible Eulerian program.

We base our technical discussion on the EG and Bernoulli assumptions. Then, on the one hand, we have the following theorem.

THEOREM 3.2.5 Let the EG assumptions and an initial capital stock be given. An indefinitely feasible growth program which satisfies

$$\lim_{\tau \to +\infty} s(\tau) = \bar{s}$$

is efficient if $\bar{s} < \alpha$ and inefficient if $\bar{s} > \alpha$.

(Proof: For $\bar{s} < \alpha$, see Theorem 3 in Paper 1, Part II; for $\bar{s} > \alpha$ see the theorem on p. 59 in [P2]

On the other hand we have the following theorem.

THEOREM 3.2.6 Under the EG and IG assumptions, and given a Bernoulli utility function, an indefinitely feasible Eulerian program satisfies

$$\lim_{\tau \to +\infty} s(\tau) = \alpha \frac{(\gamma + \lambda)}{(\gamma + \lambda) + i - i_0}, \qquad i_0 = (1-\nu)\gamma. \tag{3.2.5}$$

(Proof in the Mathematical Appendix)

It follows at once from these last two theorems that, under the said assumptions, an indefinitely feasible Eulerian program is efficient if $i > i_0$ and inefficient if $i < i_0$. It is my conjecture that these results are generally valid.

CONJECTURE 3.2.1 Let the Q-EG and IG assumptions obtain and an initial capital stock be given. Write

$$i_0 = \left[1 + \lim_{c \to +\infty} \Phi(c)\right] \lim_{x \to +\infty} \gamma .$$

An indefinitely feasible Eulerian program is (a) efficient if

$$i > i_0$$

and (b) inefficient if

$$i < i_0 .$$

The question remains as to whether or not an indefinitely feasible Eulerian program is efficient if $i = i_0$. I am only able to answer this question in a particular case:

THEOREM 3.2.7 Let the EG and IG assumptions obtain under the restriction of a Bernoulli utility function and let an initial capital stock be given. An indefinitely feasible Eulerian program is efficient if and only if

$$i \geqslant i_0 .$$

(Proof in the Mathematical Appendix)

3.2.4 Necessary and sufficient conditions for UMIT-optimality

In the two preceding sub-sections, we have established two necessary conditions for the existence of a UMIT-optimal growth program: it must be Eulerian and efficient. It can be shown that these two conditions are also sufficient for UMIT-optimality under the assumptions of the following theorem.

THEOREM 3.2.8 Let the EG and IG assumptions obtain under the restriction of a Bernoulli utility function. Then, given a historically conceivable initial capital stock, an Eulerian and efficient program is UMIT-optimal.

(Proof in the Mathematical Appendix)

It is my conjecture that Theorem 3.2.8 remains true under our general growth and preference assumptions.

CONJECTURE 3.2.2 Let the Q-EG and IG assumptions obtain and a historically conceivable initial capital stock be given. An indefinitely feasible growth program is UMIT-optimal if and only if it is (i) efficient (Definition 2.5.2) and (ii) Eulerian.

Theorem 3.2.8 and, more generally, Conjecture 3.2.2 are very attractive to the economist. They state two necessary and sufficient conditions for the existence of a UMIT-optimal program which possesses a simple economic meaning. The first speaks for itself and the second implies MUEIT (see Section 2.5.1). The only drawback of these two conditions is that they are both implicit. Fortunately, at least under the assumptions of Theorem 3.2.8, they can be replaced by a very simple explicit condition.

THEOREM 3.2.9 Let the EG and IG assumptions obtain under the restriction of a Bernoulli utility function and let a historically conceivable initial capital stock be given. The condition

$$i \geqslant i_0, \qquad i_0 = (1-\nu)\gamma$$

is necessary and sufficient for the existence of a UMIT-optimal program.

(Proof: Theorems 5.1, 6.1 and 6.2, Paper 3, Part II)

In the general case, we venture to express a somewhat weaker conjecture.

CONJECTURE 3.2.3 Let the Q-EG and IG assumptions obtain under the restriction that $-\Phi$ tends to $\nu > 0$ as $c \to +\infty$ and let a historically conceivable initial capital stock be given. The conditions

$$i \geqslant i_0$$

and

$$i > \max\left\{0, i_0\right\}, \qquad i_0 = (1-\nu) \lim_{x \to +\infty} \gamma$$

are, respectively, necessary and sufficient for the existence of a UMIT-optimal program

3.2.5 The condition of minimum convergence

By Definition 2.5.1, a UMIT-optimal program $\hat{c}(\tau)$ cannot be "worse", *a fortiori* infinitely "worse", than some other indefinitely feasible program $c(\tau)$. It is not possible that

$$\lim_{T\to+\infty} \left\{ I[c(\tau)_0^T] - I[\hat{c}(\tau)_0^T] \right\} = +\infty.$$

THEOREM 3.2.10 Let the Q-EG and IG assumptions obtain and an initial capital stock be given. Only an Eulerian program along which the UMIT index satisfies the condition of minimum convergence (defined below) can be UMIT-optimal.

DEFINITION 3.2.1 Let a Q-EG model, a UMIT index and an initial capital stock be given. We say that the UMIT index satisfies the condition of minimum convergence or MC along the indefinitely feasible program $c^*(\tau)$ if there is no other indefinitely feasible program $c(\tau)$ such that

$$\lim_{T\to+\infty} \left\{ I[c(\tau)_0^T] - I[c^*(\tau)_0^T] \right\} = +\infty.$$

The interesting fact is that the two conditions of minimum convergence along an Eulerian program and of the efficiency of an Eulerian program are completely equivalent under the assumptions of Theorem 3.2.8.

THEOREM 3.2.11 Let the EG and IG assumptions obtain under the restriction of a Bernoulli utility function and let an initial capital stock be given. Then, an indefinitely feasible Eulerian program along which the UMIT index satisfies the MC condition is UMIT-optimal.

(Proof in the Mathematical Appendix)

This theorem is perfectly symmetric to Theorem 3.2.8. It raises the question of whether the MC and efficiency conditions are not also equivalent under the general Q-EG and IG assumptions. This is, however, a difficult question to answer. It is, indeed, not certain that Theorem 3.2.6

remains true under the general Q-EG and IG assumptions. An indefinitely feasible Eulerian program could possibly exist which satisfies

$$\lim_{\tau\to+\infty} s(\tau) = 1. \tag{3.2.6}$$

If $\nu, \bar{\alpha}$ and $\bar{\lambda}$ denote, as usual, the respective limits of $-\Phi$, α and λ as c, x and τ tend to $+\infty$, and if

$$i_0 < i < [\bar{\gamma} - (1-\bar{\alpha})(\bar{\gamma}+\bar{\lambda})] < \nu\bar{\gamma}, \qquad \bar{\gamma} = \rho/(1-\bar{\alpha})$$

then (3.2.6) implies by Theorems 1.5.2 and 3.2.2:

$$\lim_{\tau\to+\infty} \frac{\dot{c}}{c} = [\bar{\gamma} - (1-\bar{\alpha})(\bar{\gamma}+\bar{\lambda}) - i]\frac{1}{\nu} > 0.$$

Now the following theorem holds.

THEOREM 3.2.12 Let a Q-EG model and an initial capital stock be given. An indefinitely feasible program is inefficient if it satisfies

$$\lim_{\tau\to+\infty} s(\tau) = 1 > \bar{\alpha}.$$

(Proof in the Mathematical Appendix)

On the other hand consider the following theorem.

THEOREM 3.2.13 Let the Q-EG and IG assumptions obtain and an initial capital stock be given. Let, moreover, $i > i_0$. Then, the MC condition is satisfied along every indefinitely feasible program which satisfies

$$\lim_{\tau\to+\infty} c(\tau) = +\infty.$$

(Proof in the Mathematical Appendix)

In view of these two theorems and of (3.2.6) and (3.2.7), an indefinitely feasible Eulerian program may possibly satisfy the MC-condition without being UMIT-optimal.

3.3 PROPERTIES OF THE UMIT-OPTIMAL PROGRAM

3.3.1 The UMIT capital, production and consumption programs

The properties of the UMIT-optimal x-, y- and c-programs under either a constant technology and an exponential growing population or the EG and Bernoulli assumptions are discussed in great detail in Papers 3 and 4 of Part II. The main results are as follows.

THEOREM 3.3.1 Let the EG and IG assumptions obtain and a Bernoulli utility function be given. Let, moreover,

$$i \geqslant i_0 \qquad i_0 = (1-\nu)\gamma .$$

Then there exists a UMIT-optimal program for every historically conceivable initial capital stock (Theorem 3.2.9). Its x-, y- and c-components tend, at least in relative terms, strictly monotonically to their respective Golden Utility or GU paths:

$$\begin{aligned} &\bar{x} \exp\,[\gamma\tau] \\ &\bar{x}^{a} \exp\,[\gamma\tau] \\ &[\bar{x}^{a} - (\gamma+\lambda)\bar{x}]\exp\,[\gamma\tau] \end{aligned} \tag{3.3.1}$$

defined by

$$\bar{x} = \left(\frac{\alpha}{\gamma+\lambda+i-i_0}\right)^{1/(1-a)} . \tag{3.3.2}$$

The monotonic approach takes place from below if $x_0 < \bar{x}$ and from above if $x_0 > \bar{x}$. If $x_0 = \bar{x}$, the UMIT-optimal growth program coincides with the GU growth path over $0 \leqslant \tau < +\infty$.

(Proof: Theorems 5.1 and 6.1, Paper 3, Part II)

An immediate corollary of Theorem 3.3.1 is that, under its assumptions, the UMIT-optimal capital-output path $\hat{\kappa}(\tau)$ tends strictly monotonically to its GU value $\bar{\kappa} = \bar{x}^{1-a}$, from below if $x_0 < \bar{x}$ and from above if $x_0 > \bar{x}$. If $x_0 = \bar{x}$, then $\hat{\kappa}(\tau) = \bar{x}^{1-a}$, $0 \leqslant \tau < +\infty$. If the Bernoulli restriction is relaxed, this last result becomes the following theorem

THEOREM 3.3.2 Under the EG and IG assumptions, the UMIT-optimal capital-output program $\hat{\kappa}(\tau)$, if any, can have at the most one extremum. The latter must be a minimum below the Golden Utility value $\bar{\kappa} = \bar{x}^{1-a}$ defined by (3.2.2), where $i_0 = (1 - \nu)\gamma$, $-\nu = \lim \Phi$ as $c \to +\infty$. Thereafter, $\hat{\kappa}(\tau)$ tends strictly monotonically to $\bar{\kappa}$.

(Proof in the Mathematical Appendix)

Under the general Q-EG and IG assumptions, things become still more complicated. If there is no technological progress, Theorem 3.3.1 remains true (paper 2, Part II). If there is a positive rate of technological progress and a constant rate of demographic growth ($\rho > 0$, $\lambda = \lambda_0$), then the following property of the UMIT-optimal x-path can be established.

THEOREM 3.3.3 Under technological progress and the Q-EG λ_0 and IG assumptions, the UMIT-optimal x-program, if any, can have at the most one extremum which must be a minimum. Thereafter, it becomes a strictly increasing function of time.

(Proof: Lemmas 10 and 11, Paper 1, Part II)

I must admit that I am unable to establish a similar theorem for the UMIT-optimal c-program. It however, seems likely that the following holds.

CONJECTURE 3.3.1 Under technological progress and the Q-EG and IG assumptions, the UMIT-optimal x-, y- and c-programs, if any, become strictly increasing functions of time from some finite point of time onwards. Moreover, if $\bar{\alpha} > 0$, they tend in relative terms to their respective GU paths [these paths are only relatively attainable in the sense of (1.5.1)] defined by (3.3.1) and (3.3.2), where α, γ and λ have been replaced by $\bar{\alpha}$, $\bar{\gamma}$ and $\bar{\lambda}$.

3.3.2 The UMIT savings program

The properties of the UMIT-optimal savings program under either a constant technology and an exponentially growing population or the EG and Bernoulli assumptions are also discussed in Papers 3 and 4, Part II. The main result is Theorem 1 in Paper 4. It provides an explicit UMIT-optimal solution if $\alpha = \nu = \frac{1}{2}$ and $i = i_0 = (1 - \nu)\rho/(1 - \alpha) = \rho$. The UMIT-optimal savings program is then

$$\hat{s}(\tau) = \tfrac{1}{2}(1 + m\exp[-(\lambda + 2\rho)\tau])$$

where

$$m = 1 - \frac{\kappa_0}{\overline{\kappa}}$$

and

$$\overline{\kappa} = \frac{1}{2(\lambda + 2\rho)}\,.$$

It can be seen that $\hat{s}(\tau)$ tends strictly monotonically from its initial value

$$\hat{s}(0) = 1 - (\lambda + 2\rho)\kappa_0$$

to its Golden Utility value

$$\overline{s} = \tfrac{1}{2}\,.$$

The important fact is that $\hat{s}(0)$ is greater, equal or smaller than $\overline{s} = \frac{1}{2}$, depending on whether κ_0 is smaller, equal or greater than $\overline{\kappa} = \frac{1}{2}(\lambda + 2\rho)$. Thus, the smaller the initial capital stock, the higher the initial savings ratio. In particular, $\kappa_0/\overline{\kappa} = \frac{1}{2}$ implies $\hat{s}(0) = \frac{3}{4}$, while $\kappa_0/\overline{\kappa} = \frac{3}{2}$ implies $\hat{s}(0) = \frac{1}{4}$!

Now, under the same assumptions, the UMIT-optimal y-program reads

$$\hat{y}(\tau) = \overline{\kappa}(1 - m\exp[-(\lambda + 2\rho)\tau]^2)\exp[2\rho\tau]$$

It follows that $\kappa_0 < \overline{\kappa}$ implies both $\dot{\hat{s}}(\tau) < 0$ and $\dot{\hat{y}}(\tau) > 0$, $0 \leqslant \tau < +\infty$. In other words, at least if $\alpha = \nu = \frac{1}{2}$ and $i = i_0$, the UMIT strategy imposes, in relative terms, the highest sacrifices on the poorest generations. This is a very unsatisfactory result. It shows that the UMIT strategy does not generally agree with what most people accept as a fair distribution of welfare among the successive generations. This is all the more true since, as is shown in Paper 4, Part II, the benefits which later and richer generations may derive from an initially very high savings ratio turn out to be relatively small.

The analysis presented in both Papers 4 and 3, Part II, however, leaves one important question unanswered: will the above results be "corrected" by an elasticity of marginal utility Φ which tends fast enough to $-\infty$ as c tends to zero? Unfortunately, this is a question which I cannot answer in a definite way. Unbounded utility functions might exist which do not associate a decreasing savings ratio with an increasing per capita income. Even if this should be so, however, it would not affect the objection raised in Section 2.5.1 that the MUEIT condition is unrealistically severe on all IGs. In terms of the savings program, it means that the latter can always be expected to be unrealistically high.

3.4 DIFFICULTIES WITH THE ECONOMIC INTERPRETATION

3.4.1 Necessity of a constant time discount rate

It is now time to turn to the problem of the value which should be given to the time discount rate i appearing in the UMIT index. We consider two different solutions to this problem. The first assumes the existence of a "social" time discount rate and identifies the latter with i. The second argues on "ethical" grounds that i should be as small as possible, i.e. chosen according to what may be called the "Principle of Minimum Impatience". For the reasons set forth below, the first of these two solutions is not retained.

As a matter of fact, the "social" interpretation of i raises two major difficulties. One of these is that it requires an objective econometric definition of the concept of a social time discount rate. Now, to the best of my knowledge, no econometric definition of i has ever been proposed which could claim any reasonable degree of scientific consensus.

The second difficulty is of a logical nature. According to the "social" interpretation, the value of i can hardly be conceived of as being independent of the level of per capita consumption c. It seems intuitively clear that "social impatience" to consume cannot be the same when consumption is near its subsistence level or at a much higher level. This idea has already been advanced by Böhm-Bawerk [BB].

A simple way to express the above argument mathematically is to assume that i is a differentiable and strictly decreasing function of c:

$$i = i(c) \geqslant 0 \tag{3.4.1}$$

and

$$i'(c) \leqslant 0, \qquad 0 \leqslant \tau < +\infty. \tag{3.4.2}$$

According to the "social" interpretation of i, one would therefore like to relax the assumption of a constant i and replace it by (3.4.1) and (3.4.2) in the definition of the UMIT index. Unfortunately, however, this is not possible. Indeed, the only way to introduce a time discount rate which depends on c in the UMIT index is to write

$$I^*[c(\tau)_t^{+\infty}] = \int_t^{+\infty} U[c(\tau)]\exp[-i\left\{c(t)\right\}\left\{\tau - t\right\}]\mathrm{d}\tau \tag{3.4.3}$$

Clearly, it does not make much sense to use another time discount rate than the rate which applies at the time t of planning. Now *the index defined by* (3.4.3) *is not self-consistent* in the sense of Definition 3.1.1:

THEOREM 3.4.1 Let a Q-EG model, an index $I^*[c(\tau)_t^{+\infty}]$ and an initial capital-stock x_0 be given. Let there exist an indefinitely feasible program $\hat{x}(\tau)$ which maximizes $I^*[c(\tau)_0^{+\infty}]$ and a program $\hat{\hat{x}}(\tau)$ which maximizes $I^*[c(\tau)_t^{+\infty}]$ in the set of indefinitely feasible programs $\{c(\tau)_t^{+\infty}\}$ defined by the "initial" conditions $x_t = \hat{x}(t)$, $t > 0$. Then $\hat{\hat{x}}(\tau)$ differs from $\hat{x}(\tau)$ over $t < \tau < +\infty$, except if

$$i[\hat{\hat{c}}(0)] = i[\hat{c}(t)]. \tag{3.4.4}$$

(Proof in the Mathematical Appendix)

In other words, except if (3.4.4) obtains, there is no common program which maximizes the index $I^*[c(\tau)_t^{+\infty}]$ for every $t \geqslant 0$. The maximization of this index by all IGs is not possible and, consequently, it does not define a feasible growth strategy in the sense of Definition 1.6.4.

Now, the reader can easily convince himself that the condition (3.4.4) can only be satisfied under the Q-EG and IG assumptions if technological progress is nil and the growth rate of population constant and positive. Moreover, even then, (3.4.4) is only satisfied if

$$\hat{c}(\tau) = f(x_0) - \lambda x_0, \qquad 0 \leqslant \tau < +\infty$$

and

$$\begin{aligned} i[\hat{c}(\tau)] &= i[\hat{c}(0)] \\ &= f'(x_0) - \lambda. \end{aligned}$$

Neglecting this exceptional case, UMIT requires either a constant time discount rate, or, in some cases, none at all. This excludes, in our opinion, the "social" interpretation of the time discount rate in the case of UMIT.

3.4.2 The principle of minimum impatience

We are thus left with the possibility of choosing the value of the time discount rate on the basis of some "ethical" principle. The problem is to find an appropriate principle.

The one suggested is an improved version of the older principle of *infinite patience* or *zero impatience.* The latter states that any positive time discount rate, however small, introduces an unfair bias in the valuation of the welfare of future generations. (This thesis has already been defended by Ramsey [R, page 543]). The implicit assumption is that the only two reasons for time discounting are our imperfect knowledge and our limited control of reality. In other words, the principle of infinite patience states that a Society of Immortals possessing perfect knowledge and complete control of the future has no reason to apply any time discount rate at all. Thus, i should always be set equal to zero in the UMIT index $I[c(\tau)_0^{+\infty}]$.

There is certainly a good deal to be said in favor of the principle of infinite patience. It is undoubtedly true that imperfect knowledge and limited control are usually the two most important reasons for time discounting. In the context of the Q-EG and IG assumptions, however, they cannot be the only ones.

We have seen (Section 3.2.4) indeed, that the existence of a UMIT-optimal program requires a time discount rate which is not smaller than the value $i_0 = (1-\nu)\rho/(1-\overline{\alpha})$. Now i_0 is positive whenever the rate ρ of technological progress is positive and the absolute value of elasticity of marginal utility tends to a limit smaller than 1 as c grows infinite. We see in the next section that this latter condition is almost equivalent to the requirement that the utility function $U(c)$ be not bounded from above. It follows that the principle of zero impatience will be incompatible with UMIT whenever $U(c)$ has no "Bliss" upper-bound.

The logical conclusion in the face of this incompatibility is that, at least under the Q-EG and IG assumptions, *UMIT implies the existence of a cause for time discounting other than imperfect knowledge and limited control of reality.* There is no other solution but to accept the fact that UMIT generally requires some degree of impatience to consume on the part of the planner. Accordingly, we shall call i_0 the *planning time discount rate* and adopt the following postulate.

POSTULATE 3.3.1 Let the Q-EG and IG assumptions obtain. Then UMIT should always satisfy the Principle of Minimum Impatience, i.e.

$$i = \max \left\{ 0, i_0 \right\}$$

This postulate solves the problem of the value of i in all cases where a UMIT-optimal program exists for all values of i equal to or greater than $\max \{0, i_0\}$. It fails, however, if a UMIT-optimal program exists for values of i greater than, but not equal to $\max \{0, i_0\}$. Whether such a situation may occur under the Q-EG and IG assumptions is a question which we have unfortunately not been able to answer (Section 3.2.4). In any case, it would only constitute one more objection against the UMIT strategy.

3.4.3 The Bliss alternative

The Principle of Minimum Impatience prescribes that the UMIT strategy should be applied without any time discounting whenever the planning time discount rate i_0 is equal to or less than zero. It is therefore interesting to determine the conditions under which this is the case.

Since, by definition, $i_0 = (1-\nu)\rho/(1-\bar{\alpha})$, $i_0 \leqslant 0$ implies either $\rho = 0$ or $\nu \geqslant 1$. In the first case, technological progress is nil and i_0 is always equal to zero. (If λ = pos. const., this case is dealt with by Theorem 4.1 of Paper 2, Part II.) It is only under technological progress that the condition $i_0 \leqslant 0$ imposes a restriction on the value of ν and, consequently, on the form of the utility function $U(c)$. It is this latter restriction which we investigate.

Let us first consider the Bernoulli utility function defined by ν = pos. const. We know already from Section 2.2.3 that $U(c)$ is any linear transformation of $c^{1-\nu}$, $\ln c$ or $-c^{-(\nu-1)}$, depending on whether ν is smaller than, equal to or greater than 1. It follows that a Bernoulli utility function is upper-bounded if and only if $\nu > 1$. More generally, one has the following theorem.

THEOREM 3.4.2 Let $U(c)$ satisfy the IG assumptions (Section 2.2.2) and let

$$-\lim_{c\to+\infty} \Phi(c) = \nu.$$

If $\nu > 1$, then

$$\lim_{c\to+\infty} U(c) = \bar{U}, \qquad \bar{U}\text{: finite constant.}$$

If $\nu < 1$, then

$$\lim_{c\to+\infty} U(c) = +\infty.$$

(Proof in the Mathematical Appendix)

It follows that *the existence of a finite upper limit of utility*

$$\bar{U} = \lim_{c\to+\infty} U(c) \tag{3.4.5}$$

implies $\nu \geqslant 1$ and, consequently, $i_0 \leqslant 0$. Since $\bar{U}$ represents complete Bliss, (3.4.5) means that Bliss can nearly be reached, say to 99%, at some finite level of per capita consumption. We shall therefore for short call "Bliss utility function" a utility function which satisfies (3.4.5) for some finite $\bar{U}$. This enables us to state the following concise proposition.

Under the Q-EG and IG assumptions and the restriction of a Bliss utility function, the Principle of Minimum Impatience prescribes that UMIT should be applied without any time discounting.

It can thus be seen that an alternative to the use of a positive time discount rate $i = i_0$ is the use of a Bliss utility function. This is the solution chosen by Ramsey himself [R]. In our opinion, however, the Bliss assumption does not constitute a satisfactory device to avoid the necessity of a positive time discount rate. For one thing, to assume a finite upper limit to the satisfaction derived from consumption, does not seem very realistic. Moreover, the Bliss assumption reintroduces an indetermination to the UMIT solution which had been removed by the principle of minimum impatience. Indeed, granted Conjecture 3.3.1, an immediate consequence of the principle of minimum impatience is under technological progress, that the UMIT-optimal savings ratio $\hat{s}(\tau)$ tends to the same GU value

$$\bar{s} = \bar{\alpha}$$

for all values of $\nu \leqslant 1$. If $\nu > 1$, however, this is no longer true. The GU savings ratio becomes dependent on the value of ν, i.e. on the form of the utility function. As a matter of fact, Conjecture 3.3.1, (3.2.2) and $\nu > 1$ together imply

$$\bar{s} = \bar{\alpha}\frac{\bar{\gamma} + \dot{\bar{\lambda}}}{\bar{\gamma} + \bar{\lambda} - i_0}$$

$$= \bar{\alpha}\frac{\bar{\gamma} + \bar{\lambda}}{\nu\bar{\gamma} + \bar{\lambda}}$$

$$< \quad \bar{\alpha}.$$

If $\rho = 0$, then $\bar{\gamma} = 0$ and $\bar{\alpha}$ must be replaced by $\alpha(\bar{x})$, where $\bar{x}$ satisfies $f'(\bar{x}) = i + \bar{\lambda}$ (see Paper 2, Part II).

Chapter 4

MARGINAL UTILITY EQUILIBRIUM OVER FINITE TIME (MUEFT)

4.1 INTRODUCTION

Chapter 4 discusses some properties of the MUEFT-optimal program and supports the fundamental conjecture that, whenever both are feasible, the MUEFT strategy is unanimously preferred to the UMIT strategy.

This conjecture is by no means trivial, though it is rather obvious that, starting from the same initial conditions, the MUEFT-optimal consumption program $\hat{c}_\omega(\tau)$ lies initially above the UMIT-optimal consumption program $\hat{c}(\tau)$. This means that there must be a critical time horizon Ω such that

$$I\left[\hat{c}_\omega(\tau)_t^{t+\Omega}\right] = I\left[\hat{c}(\tau)_t^{t+\Omega}\right].$$

Indeed, by the definition of UMIT-optimality, $\hat{c}(\tau)$ cannot remain forever below $\hat{c}_\omega(\tau)$. The question remains, however, whether or not the critical time horizon Ω is greater than the true time horizon ω for all initial conditions under consideration. It is to be expected that Ω generally depends on these initial conditions, i.e. on the historical time t and the value of the capital-output ratio κ_t: $\Omega = \Omega(\kappa_t, t)$. Now it is only if

$$\Omega(t, \kappa_t) > \omega, \qquad 0 \leqslant t < +\infty, \kappa_1 < \kappa_t < \kappa_2 \tag{4.1.1}$$

that the MUEFT strategy is unanimously preferred to the UMIT strategy in $\kappa_1 < \kappa < \kappa_2$. Our fundamental conjecture is that (4.1.1) holds true whenever both the MUEFT and the UMIT strategies are feasible in $\kappa_1 < \kappa < \kappa_2$. Theorem 4.4.3 proves the truth of this conjecture in the particular, but important, case where the MUEFT Golden Utility path (4.3.2) is feasible.

Chapter 4 also derives the explicit MUEFT solution in the case of a constant capital-output ratio (Theorem 4.3.2). It turns out that this solution is formally identical to the UMIT solution characterized by the time discount rate

$$i^* = i + i_\omega$$

where i is the MUEFT time discount rate and i_ω is the positive constant defined by (4.3.9).

Finally, Chapter 4 provides an econometric definition of the MUEFT time horizon ω. This enables us to make a numerical exercise with real world data, the results of which are found to be very satisfactory.

4.2 MARGINAL UTILITY EQUILIBRIUM OVER INFINITE TIME

4.2.1 Generalized MUEIT

Our starting point is the following theorem.

THEOREM 4.2.1 Under the Q-EG and IG assumptions, the MUEIT condition (2.5.4) implies Euler's condition (2.5.3).

(Proof left to the reader)

It is worth noting, however, that this implication holds true only under the assumption of a constant time discount rate. We have seen, indeed, that the UMIT condition necessarily requires a constant time discount rate: there is simply no meaningful way of introducing a variable time discount rate in the UMIT index $I[c(\tau)_t^{+\infty}]$ (Section 3.4.1). This is not the case for the MUEIT condition (2.5.4). It seems clear that the time discount rate in (2.5.4) refers to the point of time t. Assuming $i = i(c)$, one may therefore write

$$u[c(t)] = \int_t^{+\infty} \frac{\partial y}{\partial x}(\tau) u\,[c(\tau)] \exp\left[-i\left\{c(t)\right\}(\tau - t) - \int_t^{\tau} \lambda(\tau')\mathrm{d}\tau'\right]\mathrm{d}\tau,$$

$$0 \leqslant t < +\infty \qquad (4.2.1)$$

We call (4.2.1) the *"Generalized MUEIT"* condition. In differential form it may be written

$$\Phi[c(t)]\frac{\dot{c}(t)}{c(t)} + \frac{\partial y}{\partial x}(t) - \left\{i\,[c(t)] + \lambda(t)\right\} =$$

$$-\int_t^{+\infty} \frac{\partial y}{\partial x}(\tau)\frac{u[c(\tau)]}{u[c(t)]}(\tau - t)i'\,[c(t)]\,\dot{c}(t) \exp\left[-i\left\{c(t)\right\}(\tau - t) - \int_t^{\tau} (\tau')\mathrm{d}\tau'\right]\mathrm{d}\tau,$$

$$0 \leqslant t < +\infty\,. \qquad (4.2.2)$$

Granted that $i'(c) < 0$ and c/c tends to $\bar{\gamma}$ along a Generalized MUEFT-optimal program, one has

$$\lim_{\tau \to +\infty} \frac{\partial y}{\partial x} = \text{const.},$$

$$\lim_{\tau \to +\infty} \frac{u[c(\tau)]}{u[c(t)]} = \lim_{\tau \to +\infty} \exp\,[-\nu\bar{\gamma}(\tau - t)]$$

$$= 0,$$

$$\lim_{c \to +\infty} ci' = 0.$$

This means [remember that we assume $\bar{\gamma} + \bar{\lambda} > 0$ (Section 1.4.1)] that the right-hand side of (4.2.2) tends to zero as t grows infinite, provided only that $i(c)$ does not tend to zero as c tends to infinity. In other words, it means that the Generalized MUEFT equation tends to become Eulerian for great values of t. In view of Theorem 3.2.9 and Conjecture 3.2.3, we are therefore tempted to express the following conjecture.

CONJECTURE 4.2.1 Except for the assumption that $i'(c) < 0$, $0 < c < +\infty$, let the Q-EG and IG assumptions obtain and a historically conceivable capital stock be given. A necessary condition for the existence of a Generalized MUEIT-optimal program is that

$$\lim_{c \to +\infty} i(c) \geqslant i_0, \qquad i_0 = (1-\nu)\bar{\gamma}$$

Under the EG and Bernoulli assumptions, this condition is also sufficient.

We shall not pursue the discussion of the Generalized MUEIT condition any further. We do not believe that, in itself, it constitutes a very interesting generalization of the UMIT condition. As a matter of fact, it still has the basic effect of the UMIT condition, namely that it requires all IGs to act as if they had an infinite time horizon (Section 2.5.1).

4.2.2 The MUEFT condition

A much more interesting modification of the MUEIT condition is the MUEFT condition (2.5.5) which has been introduced in Section 2.5.2. For the determination of the properties of the MUEFT-optimal properties, it is convenient to write (2.5.5) in differential form. Straightforward differentiation with respect to time gives:

$$-\Phi_\tau \frac{\dot{c}_\tau}{c_\tau} = \frac{\alpha_\tau}{\kappa_\tau} - (\lambda_\tau + i_\tau) - \frac{\alpha_{\tau+\omega}}{\kappa_{\tau+\omega}} \cdot \frac{u_{\tau+\omega}}{u_\tau} \exp\left[-i\omega - \int_\tau^{\tau+\omega} \lambda_{\tau'}\, d\tau'\right], 0 \leqslant \tau < +\infty. \tag{4.2.3}$$

It can be seen that the MUEFT equation (4.2.3) only differs from Euler's equation (3.2.1) through the adjunction of the term

$$i_\omega = \frac{\alpha_{\tau+\omega}}{\kappa_{\tau+\omega}} \cdot \frac{u_{\tau+\omega}}{u_\tau} \exp\left[-i\omega - \int_\tau^{\tau+\omega} \lambda_{\tau'}\, d\tau'\right]. \tag{4.2.4}$$

Formally, it is as though the time discount rate i had been increased by a variable quantity i_ω. Under the EG and Bernoulli assumptions, (4.2.3) "simplifies" to

$$\nu \frac{\dot{c}_\tau}{c} = \frac{\alpha}{\kappa_\tau} - (\lambda + i) - \frac{\alpha}{\kappa_{\tau+\omega}} \left(\frac{c_\tau}{c_{\tau+\omega}}\right)^\nu \exp\left[-(\lambda + i)\omega\right], \quad 0 \leqslant \tau < +\infty. \tag{4.2.5}$$

Even this last equation is still very difficult to analyze. A qualified programmer to whom I have submitted this equation is of the opinion that its numerical analysis would take him approximately six months. Nevertheless, we try to get some general idea about the existence conditions and properties of a MUEFT-optimal program in the next section.

4.3 PROPERTIES OF THE MUEFT PROGRAM

4.3.1 The Golden Utility MUEFT program

The reader can easily verify that the MUEFT equation (4.2.5) has an exponential growth solution

$$\left.\begin{aligned} \hat{x}_\omega(\tau) &= \bar{x}_\omega \exp[\gamma\tau] \\ \hat{y}_\omega(\tau) &= \bar{x}_\omega^a \exp[\gamma\tau] \\ \hat{c}_\omega(\tau) &= [\bar{x}_\omega^a - (\gamma + \lambda)\,\bar{x}_\omega] \exp[\gamma\tau] \end{aligned}\right\} \tag{4.3.1}$$

defined by

$$\bar{x}_\omega = \left[\frac{\alpha}{\lambda + i + \nu\gamma}(1 - \exp[-(\lambda + i + \nu\gamma)\omega])\right]^{1/(1-a)}. \quad (4.3.2)$$

We call this solution the *"Golden Utility MUEFT-Path"*. Its existence immediately implies the following theorem.

THEOREM 4.3.1 Let the EG and IG assumptions obtain under the restriction of a Bernoulli utility function. Moreover, let $x_0 = \bar{x}_\omega$, where $\bar{x}_\omega$ is defined by (4.3.2). Then the MUEFT-optimal program is identical with the UMIT-optimal program where i has been replaced by

$$i + i_\omega = i + \frac{\alpha}{\bar{x}_\omega^{1-a}} \exp[-(\lambda + i + \nu\gamma)\omega]. \quad (4.3.3)$$

The optimal program is defined by (4.3.1) and (4.3.2).

Now it follows from (4.3.2) and the efficiency condition (Theorem 3.2.5), that the Golden Utility MUEFT-program (4.3.1) can only exist if

$$\begin{aligned} \bar{s}_\omega &= (\lambda + \gamma)\, \bar{x}_\omega^{1-a} \\ &\leqslant \alpha \end{aligned} \quad (4.3.4)$$

that is

$$i + (\lambda + \gamma)\exp[-(\lambda + i + \nu\gamma)\omega] \geqslant i_0, \qquad i_0 = (1-\nu)\gamma. \quad (4.3.5)$$

Under the EG and Bernoulli assumptions, this seems to be the MUEFT condition which corresponds to the UMIT condition $i \geqslant i_0$ (Theorem 3.2.9). It is therefore likely that the following conjecture holds.

CONJECTURE 4.3.1 Under the Q-EG and IG assumptions, a necessary condition for the existence of a MUEFT-optimal program is that

$$i + (\bar{\lambda} + \bar{\gamma})\exp[-(\lambda + i + \nu\bar{\gamma})\omega] \geqslant i_0, \qquad i_0 = (1-\nu)\bar{\gamma}. \quad (4.3.6)$$

where, as usual, ν, $\bar{\gamma}$ and $\bar{\lambda}$ are the respective limits of $-\Phi$, γ and λ as c, κ and τ tend to $+\infty$.

If the initial capital stock is historically conceivable and the EG as well as the Bernoulli (2.2.7) assumptions apply, condition (4.3.6) becomes also a sufficient existence condition. If $\bar{\alpha} > 0$, the MUEFT-optimal x-, y- and c-programs approach strictly monotonically, at least in relative terms, their respective generalized GU paths [these paths are only relatively attainable in the sense of (1.5.1)] defined by (4.3.1) and (4.3.2), where γ and λ are, respectively, replaced by $\bar{\gamma}$ and $\bar{\lambda}$.

4.3.2. MUEFT under a constant capital-output ratio

For the sake of a logical experiment, assume the following Constant Capital-Output or CC-O growth model:

$$\left.\begin{aligned} y &= \frac{1}{\kappa_0} x \\ c &= (1-s)y \\ L &= mP, \qquad 0 < m < 1 \\ P &= P_0 \exp[\gamma\tau] \end{aligned}\right\} \tag{4.3.7}$$

(The four equations are valid over $0 \leqslant \tau < +\infty$.)

Assume as well a Bernoulli utility function ($-\Phi = \nu > 0$). The MUEFT integral condition then reads

$$u_t = \int_t^{t+\omega} \frac{u}{\kappa_0} \exp[-(\lambda + i)(\tau - t)]\mathrm{d}\tau, \qquad 0 \leqslant t < +\infty$$

In differential form, it becomes

$$-\frac{\dot{u}_\tau}{u_\tau} = \frac{1}{\kappa_0} - (\lambda + i) - \frac{1}{\kappa_0} \cdot \frac{u_{\tau+\omega}}{u_\tau} \exp[-(\lambda + i)\omega].$$

It is easy to verify that this last equation is satisfied by the solution

$$u_\tau = u_0 \exp\left[-\left(\frac{1}{\kappa_0} - \lambda - i - i_\omega\right)\tau\right] \tag{4.3.8}$$

where i_ω is defined by

$$i_\omega \kappa_0 = \exp\left[-\left(\frac{1}{\kappa_0} - i_\omega\right)\omega\right]$$

Now (4.3.8) is also the solution of the equation

$$-\frac{\dot{u}_\tau}{u_\tau} = \frac{1}{\kappa_0} - (\lambda + i + i_\omega)$$

which is, under the CC-O and IG assumptions, no other than Euler's equation for the time discount rate $(i + i_\omega)$. More precisely, it can be shown that the following theorem holds.

THEOREM 4.3.2 Let the CC-O (4.3.7) and IG assumptions obtain and an initial capital stock be given. Let i_ω be defined by (4.3.9). If an indefinitely feasible growth program which is UMIT-optimal for the time discount rate $(i + i_\omega)$ exists, it will also be MUEFT-optimal for the time discount rate i and the time horizon.

$$\omega = \frac{\kappa_0}{1 - i_\omega \kappa_0} \ln \frac{1}{i_\omega \kappa_0}$$

A necessary condition for the existence of such a program is that

$$i + i_\omega > (1 - \nu)\left(\frac{1}{\kappa_0} - \lambda\right) \tag{4.3.10}$$

If, moreover, a Bernoulli utility function applies, (4.3.10) becomes necessary and sufficient for the existence of the optimal program in question. The latter reads, in this case, as

$$c(\tau) = \left[(i + i_\omega) - (1 - \nu)\left(\frac{1}{\kappa_0} - \lambda\right)\right] \frac{x_0}{\nu} \exp\left[\left\{\left(\frac{1}{\kappa_0} - \lambda\right) - (i + i_\omega)\right\}\frac{\tau}{\nu}\right]$$

$$x(\tau) = x_0 \exp\left[\left\{\left(\frac{1}{\kappa_0} - \lambda\right) - (i + i_\omega)\right\}\frac{\tau}{\nu}\right]$$

$$s(\tau) = s_0$$

$$= \frac{\kappa_0}{\nu}\left[\frac{1}{\kappa_0} - (i + i_\omega) - (1 - \nu)\lambda\right] \tag{4.3.11}$$

(Proof in the Mathematical Appendix)

It is interesting to compare conditions (4.3.5) and (4.3.10), which are both very similar. Condition (4.3.5) has been derived from the condition that an optimal path must necessarily be efficient. Under the assumptions of Theorem 4.3.1, this implies $s \leqslant \alpha$ (4.3.4). In the case of the assumptions of Theorem 4.3.2, however, every indefinitely positive and constant savings program along which $c > 0$ turns out to be efficient (proof left to the reader). The only condition to be imposed on $s(\tau) = s_0$ in (4.3.11) is, consequently, that $s_0 < 1$. This implies at once (4.3.10).

It is also interesting to notice how ω depends on i_ω. From (4.3.9) we get

$$\frac{\omega}{\kappa_0} = \frac{1}{1 - i_\omega \kappa_0} \ln \frac{1}{i_\omega \kappa_0}$$

$$= 1 + \frac{1 - i_\omega \kappa_0}{2} + \frac{(1 - i_\omega \kappa_0)^2}{3} + \ldots$$

It follows that ω(i) is decreasing if i_ω increases and (ii) has a least upper bound

$$\bar{\omega} = \frac{1}{\dfrac{\nu}{\kappa_0} + (1-\nu)\lambda + i} \ln \frac{1}{(1-\nu)(1-\lambda\kappa_0) - i\kappa_0}$$

whenever

$$i < i_0, \qquad i_0 = (1-\nu)\left(\frac{1}{\kappa_0} - \lambda\right).$$

Similarly, it follows at once from (4.3.6) that ω has a least upper bound if $i < i_0 = (1-\nu)\bar{\gamma}$ under the Q-EG assumptions. This least upper bound is

$$\bar{\omega} = \frac{1}{\nu\bar{\gamma} + \bar{\lambda} + i} \ln\left(\frac{\bar{\gamma} + \lambda}{(1-\nu)\bar{\gamma} - i}\right). \tag{4.3.13}$$

4.4 A COMPARISON OF MUEFT AND UMIT

4.4.1 The choice of the time discount rate

We now try to compare the MUEFT and UMIT strategies on the basis of what we have learned of their respective properties. Our criterion of comparison is naturally the concept of unanimous preference (Definition 2.4.3). In order to apply this criterion, however, we must first specify the value of the time discount rate for which such a comparison can be considered significant.

The question which must be answered is whether or not there exists a time discount rate which makes sense for both the MUEFT and UMIT strategies. Indeed, in view of what has been said in Section 3.4.2, it seems clear that the greater of the two values 0 and i_0 should be used in the case of the UMIT strategy. The problem is whether or not this value can also be applied to the case of the MUEFT strategy.

In this case, we know that the choice of the time discount rate i is closely related to the choice of the time horizon ω. With regard to the asymptotic value of the optimal capital-output ratio, i.e. to the very long-term properties of the optimal program, an increase of i is completely equivalent to a decrease in ω. (The short-term properties of the MUEFT-optimal program depend, however, in a different way on i and on ω. Indeed, i_ω in (4.2.4) is only asymptotically constant.) In other words, the MUEFT-optimal program tends to reach the same Golden Utility path (4.3.1) for different combinations of i and ω (4.3.2). As a matter of fact, i may always be set equal to zero in the case of the MUEFT strategy, provided only that ω has been chosen small enough (4.3.6).

It may therefore be argued that the value of i which agrees best with the MUEFT-strategy is $i = 0$. In a world of complete certainty, there appears to be only one reason which could induce an IG to apply a positive time discount rate within its time horizon: namely the knowledge that the satisfaction which an individual derives from consumption decreases as he grows older. Now there does not seem to be any clear evidence that this is actually so.

Since, however, the UMIT strategy requires that $i \geqslant i_0$, no comparison with the MUEFT strategy is possible unless this condition is satisfied. It therefore follows that we may as well apply the principle of minimum impatience and set i equal to the greater of the two values 0 and i_0. We believe this to be the most appropriate value for a comparison between the MUEFT and UMIT strategies. Moreover, as it follows at once from (4.3.6), this value has the advantage that no upper-bound is imposed on the time horizon ω. We therefore assume that

$$i = \max. \{0, i_0\}$$

for the rest of Section 4.4.

4.4.2 The critical time horizon

We begin with a more detailed definition of the critical time horizon mentioned in Section 4.1.

DEFINITION 4.4.1 Let the Q-EG and IG assumptions obtain, and denote respectively by $\hat{k}_\omega(\kappa_t, t, \tau)$ and $\hat{k}(\kappa_t, t, \tau)$ the MUEFT- and UMIT-optimal programs satisfying the condition $\hat{k}_\omega(t) = \hat{k}(t) = \kappa_t$. Then, the smallest positive number $\Omega(\kappa_t, t)$ such that

$$I\left[\hat{c}_\omega(\kappa_t, t, \tau)\Big|_t^{t+\Omega(\kappa_t, t)}\right] = I\left[\hat{c}(\kappa_t, t, \tau)\Big|_t^{t+\Omega(\kappa_t, t)}\right]$$

is called *critical (MUEFT) time horizon* at t for κ_t. (This formulation of the smallest positive number avoids the necessity of proving that there is only one such number.) Accordingly,

$$\tilde{\omega}_t = \inf_{\kappa_1 < \kappa_t < \kappa_2} \Omega(\kappa_t, t)$$

is called critical time horizon at t in $\kappa_1 < \kappa < \kappa_2$ and

$$\tilde{\omega} = \inf_{0 \leqslant t < +\infty} \tilde{\omega}_t$$

is simply called critical time horizon in $\kappa_1 < \kappa < \kappa_2$.

We now show that a critical time horizon $\Omega(\kappa_t, t)$ must exist, whenever both the MUEFT and UMIT strategies are feasible at t for κ_t. As already pointed out in Section 4.1, the MUEFT-optimal consumption program must initially be above the UMIT-optimal consumption program. Indeed, at least initially, MUEFT requires less investments than UMIT, since, contrary to UMIT, MUEFT equalizes the marginal utility of instantaneous consumption with the marginal utility of the per capita returns from investments derived over a finite period of time only. On the other hand, by definition, the UMIT-optimal consumption program cannot remain forever below the UMIT-optimal one. There must come a time $[t + \delta(\kappa_t, t)]$ such that

$$\hat{c}_\omega(\kappa_t, t, \tau) > \hat{c}(\kappa_t, t, \tau), \qquad t \leqslant \tau \leqslant t + \delta(\kappa_t, t)$$

and

$$\hat{c}_\omega[\kappa_t, t, t + \delta(\kappa_t, t)] = \hat{c}[\kappa_t, t, t + \delta(\kappa_t, t)].$$

Now this implies

$$I\left[\hat{c}_{\omega}(\kappa_t, t, \tau)\Big|_{t}^{t+\delta(\kappa_t, t)}\right] > I\left[\hat{c}(\kappa_t, t, \tau)\Big|_{t}^{t+\delta(\kappa_t, t)}\right]$$

while, by definition

$$I\left[\hat{c}_{\omega}(\kappa_t, t, \tau)\Big|_{0}^{+\infty}\right] < I\left[\hat{c}(\kappa_t, t, \tau)\Big|_{0}^{+\infty}\right]$$

It follows at once that there exists a critical time horizon $\Omega(\kappa_t, t)$ in the sense of Definition 4.4.1. The crucial question is, however, whether or not

$$\tilde{\omega} \geqslant \omega \tag{4.4.1}$$

in the interval $\kappa_1 < \kappa < \kappa_2$, in which both the MUEFT and UMIT strategies are feasible.

4.4.3 The fundamental conjecture

It is our fundamental conjecture that (4.4.1) is always true.

CONJECTURE 4.4.1 Under the Q-EG and IG assumptions, the MUEFT strategy is unanimously preferred to the UMIT strategy in any interval $\kappa_1 < \kappa < \kappa_2$ in which both are feasible.

In support of this conjecture, we first state the following theorem.

THEOREM 4.4.1 Let the Q-EG λ_0 and IG assumptions apply. Denote, respectively, by $\hat{x}_{\omega}(\kappa_t, t, \tau)$ and $\hat{x}(\kappa_t, t, \tau)$ the MUEFT- and UMIT-optimal programs satisfying at $t \geqslant 0$ the condition $\hat{\kappa}_{\omega}(t) = \hat{\kappa}(t) = \kappa_t$. Let, moreover, the MUEFT and UMIT strategies be both feasible in $\kappa_1 < \kappa < \kappa_2$ at any point of time $t \geqslant 0$ and satisfy the condition

$$\dot{\hat{x}}(\kappa_t, t, \tau) > \dot{\hat{x}}_{\omega}(\kappa_t, t, \tau),$$

$$t \leqslant \tau \leqslant t + \infty, \qquad 0 \leqslant t < +\infty, \qquad \kappa_1 < \kappa_t < \kappa_2.$$

Then, the MUEFT strategy is unanimously preferred to the UMIT strategy in $\kappa_1 < \kappa < \kappa_2$.

(Proof in the Mathematical Appendix)

Now we know from Theorem 3.3.1 that, under the EG and Bernoulli assumptions and for $i \geqslant i_0$, $\hat{\kappa}(\tau)$ approaches monotonically the GU value $\bar{\kappa} = \bar{x}^{1-\alpha}$ defined by (3.3.2). We know also that, under the same assumptions and for the same i, there is an initial capital-output ratio $\kappa_0 = \bar{\kappa}_\omega = \bar{x}^{1-\alpha} < \bar{\kappa}$, defined by (4.3.2), such that the GU MUEFT path $\hat{\kappa}_\omega(\tau) = \kappa_0$, $0 \leqslant \tau < +\infty$, is MUEFT-optimal (4.3.1). Hence the following theorem.

THEOREM 4.4.2 Under the EG, IG and Bernoulli assumptions, let $i \geqslant i_0$ and $x_0 = \bar{x}_\omega$ (as defined by (4.3.2)). Then, the MUEFT strategy is unanimously preferred to the UMIT strategy at $x_0 = \bar{x}_\omega$.

(Proof: see preceding text)

At least under the assumptions of Theorem 4.4.2, we are thus certain that no IG wants any later IG to switch from MUEFT to UMIT. It is interesting to consider the symmetric case where $\kappa_0 = \bar{\kappa}$ under the EG, IG and Bernoulli assumptions. Then, $\hat{\kappa}(\tau) = \bar{\kappa}$, $0 \leqslant \tau < +\infty$, while Conjecture 4.3.1 says that $\hat{\kappa}_\omega(\tau)$ tends monotonically to $\bar{\kappa}_\omega < \bar{\kappa}$. Granted Conjecture 4.3.1, the conditions of Theorem 4.4.1 are thus again satisfied and our fundamental conjecture also holds true for $\kappa_0 = \bar{\kappa}$. Finally, it is worth noting that Theorem 4.4.1 remains true under the CC-O assumptions and that, together with Theorem 4.3.2, it implies Theorem 4.4.3.

THEOREM 4.4.3 Under the CC-O assumptions of Theorem 4.3.2, the MUEFT strategy is unanimously preferred to the UMIT strategy provided that $i > (1-\nu)\ (\frac{1}{\kappa} - \lambda)$. (Under the CC-O assumptions, the concept of feasible strategy is not tied to a particular capital-output interval.)

In view of these results it seems likely that Conjecture 4.4.1 holds true, at least under the EG, IG and Bernoulli assumptions.

4.4.4 How much "better" is MUEFT than UMIT?

Granted that $\Omega(\kappa_t, \omega)$ is greater than ω, the question remains how much so? As well, how does $\Omega(\kappa_t, \omega)$ depend on κ_t for a given ω and how far does $\tilde{\omega}$ lie from ω? These questions are, indeed, closely related to the crucial question of how much "better" MUEFT is than UMIT. More precisely, how much greater than 1 is the "gain" coefficient.

$$\delta = \frac{I[\hat{c}_\omega(\tau)_t^{t+\omega}]}{I[c(\tau)_t^{t+\omega}]}$$

and how does δ depend on ω, κ_t and t? We shall now try to get some idea about these two last questions.

We make use of our knowledge of the explicit UMIT-optimal solution in the particular case defined by $\alpha = \nu = \frac{1}{2}$ and $i = i_0 = \rho$ (Paper 3, Part II). This solution tends ultimately to the GU UMIT path defined by the GU UMIT capital-output ratio

$$\bar{\kappa} = 1/2g, \qquad g = 2\rho + \lambda. \tag{4.4.3}$$

With regard to the initial value of the capital-output ratio, we assume that it happens to be equal to the GU MUEFT value (4.3.2)

$$\bar{\kappa}_\omega = (1/2g)\,(1 - \exp[-g\omega]). \tag{4.4.2}$$

Under our present assumptions, this implies that the MUEFT-optimal program coincides with the GU MUEFT path (4.3.1). For the particular initial value (4.4.2) of κ, we are thus in a position to derive an explicit formula for the value of the index $I[c(\tau)_t^{t+\omega}]$ along both the MUEFT-optimal and UMIT-optimal programs.

THEOREM 4.4.4 Let the EG and Bernoulli assumptions obtain under the conditions

$$\alpha = \nu = \tfrac{1}{2}$$

$$i = i_0 = \rho$$

and

$$\kappa_0 = \bar{\kappa}_\omega \,. \qquad \text{[see (4.4.2)]}$$

As before, let us respectively write $\hat{c}(\tau)$ and $\hat{c}_\omega(\tau)$ for the UMIT-optimal and MUEFT-optimal programs. Then,

$$\delta = \frac{I[\hat{c}_\omega(\tau)_t^{t+\omega}]}{I[\hat{c}(\tau)_t^{t+\omega}]} = \frac{(\ln m)\,(1-m^2)^{1/2}}{(\ln m) + m\,(1-m)}$$

where

$$m = 1 - \frac{\overline{K}_\omega}{\overline{K}}$$

$$= \exp\,[-g\omega], \quad g = 2\rho + \lambda.$$

(Proof in the Mathematical Appendix)

By using l'Hospital's Rule, one may verify that

$$\lim_{\omega \to +\infty} \delta = 1$$

and

$$\lim_{\omega \to 0} \delta = +\infty.$$

The first limit must obviously be equal to one, since UMIT is equivalent to MUEIT, the limit case of MUEFT as ω becomes infinite. The second limit gives rise to a more interesting result. It could indicate substantial gain along the MUEFT-optimal program. The question is, of course, how fast this gain decreases as the time horizon increases: is this gain still significant for practically relevant values of ω?

In the following sub-sections, we discuss what constitutes an economically relevant value of the time horizon. For the time being, let us only compute the gain coefficient δ for different values of $g\omega$. We obtain Table 4.1.

TABLE 4.1

$g\omega$	=	0.1	0.5	1	1.5
δ	=	3.0	1.5	1.2	1.1

Thus, if $\lambda = 2\%$ and $\rho = 1.5\%$, i.e. $g = 5\%$, one gets the correspondence given in Table 4.2 between ω and δ. Granted that the time horizon is generally

TABLE 4.2

ω	=	2	10	20	30	years
δ	=	3.0	1.5	1.2	1.1	

smaller than 30 years, as we argue in 4.5.1, these results are definitely in favor of the MUEFT strategy. To be quite impartial, however, I must admit that I do not have any clear idea of the extent to which they depend on the particular assumptions of this sub-section.

To conclude the latter, let us clarify the point in the above exercise which may possibly be the cause of some confusion. We have perhaps not sufficiently stressed the fact that different initial values of the capital-output ratio are associated with the different values of δ in Table 4.1 and Table 4.2. This follows from (4.3.2) and the assumption that $\kappa_0 = \overline{\kappa}_\omega$. It is probably more relevant to keep κ_0 constant and to vary ω alone. This requires, however, an explicit MUEFT solution for $\kappa_0 \neq \overline{\kappa}_\omega$. Lacking such a solution, the above exercise is our only alternative.

4.4.5 Generalized MUEFT

As long as our purpose is to compare MUEFT and UMIT, the appropriate value of the time discount is the one prescribed by the principle of minimum impatience. As already pointed out in Section 4.4.1, however, there is no need to use this value if one considers the MUEFT strategy alone. In the latter case, the most appropriate thing to do is, perhaps, to forego the use of any time discount rate at all.

The only drawback of a zero discount rate is the implication of a finite least upper-bound $\overline{\omega}$ to the values which can be given to the time horizon ω (4.3.12). In the next section we see that this restriction is not very likely to become effective for economically relevant values of ω.

Nevertheless, it may be worth mentioning that, as in the case of MUEIT condition, the MUEFT condition can be generalized by the assumption of a time discount rate which depends on c (4.2.1). This makes it possible to give the time discount rate a "social" interpretation. Moreover, it increases, if need be, the least upper-bound $\overline{\omega}$.

Formulated explicitly, the generalized MUEFT condition reads

$$u_t = \int_t^{t+\omega} \left(\frac{\partial y}{\partial x}\right)_\tau u_\tau \exp\left[-i_t(\tau - t) - \int_t^\tau \lambda_{\tau'}\, d\tau'\right] d\tau, \qquad 0 \leqslant t < +\infty.$$

In differential form it becomes

$$\Phi_t\left(\frac{\dot{c}}{c}\right)_t + \left(\frac{\partial y}{\partial x}\right)_t - (i_t + \lambda_t) - \left(\frac{\partial y}{\partial x}\right)_{t+\omega} \frac{u_{t+\omega}}{u_t} \exp\left[-i_t\,\omega - \int_t^{t+\omega} \lambda_{\tau'}\, d\tau'\right]$$

$$= - \int_t^{t+\omega} \left(\frac{\partial y}{\partial x}\right)_\tau \frac{u_\tau}{u_t} (\tau - t)\, i_t'\, \dot{c}_t \exp\left[-i_t(\tau - t) - \int_t^\tau \lambda_{\tau'}\, d\tau'\right] d\tau,$$

$$0 \leqslant t < +\infty.$$

4.5 CONFRONTATION OF THE MUEFT STRATEGY WITH REAL WORLD DATA

4.5.1 An econometric definition of the time horizon ω

As already mentioned, an important feature of the MUEFT strategy is that the time horizon ω can be given a reasonable econometric interpretation.

The suggested definition rests on the general idea that the time horizon ω should express some economically weighted mean life expectancy of all people living at a given point of time *t*. It has been assumed, indeed, in Section 2.2.1, that the preferences of an IG should somehow express the preferences of the people living at the time *t* of its instantaneous existence.

There are, of course, several ways in which ω can be determined. It seems to us, however, that a simple and reasonable interpretation of ω is the following postulate.

POSTULATE 4.5.1 Let p_n denote the income earning population of age n, e_n the life expectancy of the population p_n and y_n the income per capita of the population p_n. Then, the value of the time horizon introduced by the IG assumptions should be determined according to the formula:

$$\omega = \frac{\sum_{n=1}^{100} y_n e_n p_n}{\sum_{n=1}^{100} y_n p_n}. \tag{4.5.1}$$

To put it simply, Postulate 4.5.1 says that the life expectancy of every age class should be weighted by its total income share.

By way of illustration, let us roughly estimate ω, as defined by (4.5.1), in the case of the US economy. We first notice that ω is certainly significantly smaller than the expression

$$\frac{\sum_n e_n p_n}{\sum_n p_n}. \tag{4.5.2}$$

As a matter of fact, weighting the different age classes by per capita income favors the classes between, say, 40 and 65 years. It is clear that this implies a smaller value for (4.5.1) than for (4.5.2).

The expression (4.5.2) therefore constitutes an upper limit to the value of ω. In order to evaluate (4.5.2), we identify the income earning population p_n with the active population. The value found for the US is 31.7 years. It seems therefore likely that the US value of ω lies somewhere between 20 and 25 years.

4.5.2 A numerical experiment

We now make a logical experiment, the MUEFT counterpart of the logical experiment performed under UMIT in Section 8 of Paper 3, Part II. We use the same numerical values as in Paper 3. These are meant approximately to fit the US economy. They are

$$\left.\begin{aligned} \alpha &= 1/3 \qquad \text{(EG model)} \\ \rho &= 4/300 \\ \lambda &= 1/100 \\ \kappa_0 &= 3.5 \text{ years} \\ y_0 &= 2{,}400 \text{ US \$} \\ s &= 10.5/100 \end{aligned}\right\} . \qquad (4.5.3)$$

These values imply the exponential growth program

$$\left.\begin{aligned} y(\tau) &= y_0 \exp\,[\gamma(2/100)\tau] \\ &= 2{,}400 \exp\,[2\tau/100] \\ c(\tau) &= (1-s)\,y(\tau) \\ &= 2{,}148 \exp\,[2\tau/100] \end{aligned}\right\} . \qquad (4.5.4)$$

The question asked in Paper 3 is then the following: for which value of i does the actual US growth path (4.5.4) become UMIT-optimal? The answer is $i = 6.5\%$. Similarly, we now ask: *Granted that* i = *0, for which value of* ω *does the actual US growth path (4.5.4) become MUEFT-optimal?*

In order to answer this question, we express the GU savings ratio $\bar{s}_\omega$ as a function of the time horizon ω. Remembering our assumption that

$i = i_0$ and substituting the expression (4.3.2) for the GU capital-output ratio $\bar{\kappa} = \bar{x}^{1-\alpha}$ in the exponential growth condition

$$\bar{s}_\omega = g\,\bar{\kappa}_\omega$$

one finds that

$$\bar{s}_\omega = \alpha \frac{g}{g - i_0}(1 - \exp\,[-(g - i_0)\omega]), \qquad i_0 = (1-\nu)\gamma. \qquad (4.5.5)$$

As in Paper 3, we set $\nu = 1$. Now 1 is the greatest value of ν which avoids the assumption of a Bliss utility function. Since $\nu = 1$ implies $i_0 = 0$, this value of ν associates the smallest value of $\bar{s}_\omega$ with a given value of ω under the condition of no Bliss.

Granted that $\nu = 1$, (4.5.5) becomes

$$\bar{s}_\omega = \alpha\,(1 - \exp\,[-g\omega]).$$

Table 4.3 below gives the value $\bar{s}_\omega$ for $\alpha = 1/3$, $g = \lambda + \gamma = 3\%$ and different values of ω. The value $\omega = 12.7$ years corresponds to the actual US savings ratio of 10.5%. In other words, the US economy, as defined by (4.5.1), would not have to follow a significantly different growth program from the one it actually does follow, if it did really apply the MUEFT strategy under a time horizon of about 13 years and an elasticity of marginal utility equal to 1.

If, all things being equal, the US economy applied the MUEFT strategy under a time horizon of 20 to 25 years, as suggested in Section 4.5.1, it would have to increase its savings ratio in the course of time to somewhere between 15 to 18%. Though higher than the actual value of 10.5%, this value is, nevertheless, about 50% lower than the GU value prescribed by the UMIT strategy. Under the principle of minimum impatience, the GU UMIT savings ratio is equal to α, i.e. to 33%.

Table 4.3 also gives the values of the GU MUEFT capital-output ratio corresponding to the different values of ω.

TABLE 4.3

ω	$\bar{\kappa}_\omega$	$\bar{s}_\omega$
12.7	3.5	10.5
15	4	12.1
20	5	15.0
25	5.9	17.6
30	6.6	19.8
$+\infty$	11.1	33.3

Chapter 5

CONCLUSION

The classical theory of optimal economic growth hitherto essentially confines itself to the mathematical investigation of the principle of utility maximization over infinite time. (The few authors who have considered it over finite time have been unable to solve the problem of the capital stock to be left over at the end of the planning period.) It thereby tends to forget its main task: *to propose and compare different optimality criteria.*

The basic problem of the theory of optimal economic growth is, indeed, to discover an appropriate optimality criterion. Optimal economic growth constitutes a decision problem in the sense that one from among all the conceivable optimality criteria must be selected as most appropriate. Once this selection is made, the rest is essentially a problem of mathematics. The classical theory of optimal economic growth "selects" the UMIT criteria without comparing it to any other. In other words, it never states the problem of optimal economic growth as a real decision problem.

It is true, of course, that any given economy at any given point of time has to decide which one of all feasible growth programs it considers as optimal. From the theoretical viewpoint, however, the choice of the optimal program must be formulated in terms of a choice from among a given set of optimality criteria. Indeed, once the latter has been selected, the optimal program is, at least implicitly, completely defined. It is therefore fallacious to speak of the problem of choosing an optimal program once the UMIT criteria has already been adopted.

In other words, the classical theory always by-passes the real problem of optimal economic growth. Accepting the UMIT principle without much discussion, it concentrates mainly on the mathematical analysis of this principle. As we have seen, this analysis reveals a number of unpleasant aspects of the UMIT criteria. It shows that the savings ratio is likely to be unrealistically high, the distribution of welfare over time rather unfair and the choice of the time discount rate subject to certain restrictive conditions.

It is, however, a scientifically unsatisfactory procedure to reject the UMIT principle on the basis of relatively vague objections. Indeed, it is not completely clear what constitutes an excessively high savings ratio or an unfair distribution of welfare over time. As to the difficulty with regard to the value of i, we have seen that it can be solved by the principle of minimum impatience, at least in all cases where we know for sure that UMIT can be applied.

In order to reject the UMIT criterion according to the standards of scientific rigor, it was necessary:

(1) to propose another criterion;

(2) to show that this other criterion was better in a well defined sense.

This book has attempted to fulfil these two conditions. For this purpose, it has introduced the concepts of growth strategy, instantaneous government, national allegiance and unanimous preference. This has enabled us to define both the UMIT-strategy and the new MUEFT-strategy within the same conceptual framework and to compare them according to the well-defined criteria of unanimous preference. As a result, UMIT could be safely rejected as an optimality criterion. This is the theoretical contribution of the present book (Part I).

A necessary prerequisite for the analysis presented in Part I was a sufficient knowledge of the mathematical implications of the UMIT principle. A number of mathematical results are presented in Part II and in the Mathematical Appendix, which together constitute the mathematical contribution of the present book.

PART II

FIVE PAPERS ON UTILITY MAXIMIZATION OVER INFINITE TIME

Paper 1

A GENERAL EXISTENCE THEOREM

OBJECTIVE

To show that Utility Maximization over Infinite Time (UMIT) is feasible under very general economic assumptions.

This objective is realized by the proof of a general existence theorem called "Theorem X1". Contrary to most so-called existence theorems in the field of optimal growth, Theorem X1 is neither restricted to the case of a constant technology, nor stated in terms of mathematical conditions which have no direct economic interpretation and are, moreover, difficult to apply. Finally, it applies to all known one-sector production functions for which UMIT has any meaning.

PLAN

1. Definition of Theorem X1

1.1 The growth assumptions
1.2 The set of feasible growth plans
1.3 The utility index
1.4 Statement and meaning of Theorem X1

2. Proof of Theorem X1

2.1 Outline of the proof
2.2 Tonelli-Cinquini method
2.3 Existence of an absolutely continuous optimal path
2.4 Piece-wise continuity of the optimal investment path

3. Appendix

3.1 Mathematical definitions
3.2 Bibliography

1. DEFINITION OF THEOREM X1

1.1 The growth assumptions

Production per worker y and capital intensity x (capital stock per worker) are assumed to satisfy a neoclassical production relation:

$$y = \exp[\rho\tau]f(x), \qquad 0 \leqslant x, \qquad \tau < +\infty \tag{1.1.1}$$

where

$$\rho = \text{const.} \geqslant 0 \tag{1.1.2}$$

$$f(0) = 0 \tag{1.1.3}$$

$$f''(x) \text{ is continuous,} \qquad 0 < x < +\infty \tag{1.1.4}$$

$$f'(x) > 0, \qquad f''(x) < 0, \qquad 0 < x < +\infty \tag{1.1.5}$$

$$\sigma(x) \leqslant 1, \qquad 0 < x < +\infty. \tag{1.1.6}$$

The primes (″, ′) denote differentiation with respect to x and

$$\sigma(x) \equiv \frac{d(\ln x)}{d(\ln \left\{ [f(x)/f'(x)] - x \right\})} \tag{1.1.7}$$

denotes the elasticity of substitution between capital and labor.

In words, (1.1.1) says that $\exp[\rho\tau]$ is the autonomously growing level of technology and that returns to scale are constant, (1.1.3) that no production can take place without capital, (1.1.5) that production per worker increases with capital intensity, but less than proportionally, and (1.1.6) that the elasticity of substitution between labor and capital does not exceed 1. The purpose of the latter assumption is explained by Theorem 1.1.1 and Theorem 1.1.2.

It is furthermore assumed that the time path of the labor force L is exogeneously determined and satisfies

$$L = L_0 \exp[\lambda\tau], \qquad 0 \leqslant \tau < +\infty \tag{1.1.8}$$

where $L_0 > 0$ and $\lambda > 0$ are historically given constants and $\tau = 0$ denotes the beginning of the planning period. The initial capital stock is also assumed to be historically determined. Thus,

$$x(0) = x_0 \tag{1.1.9}$$

where $x_0 > 0$ is given.

Finally, it is assumed that the economy is either closed or in permanent equilibrium of the balance of payments, i.e. at any point of time, consumption is the difference between production and investments. In other words, it is assumed that

$$c = \exp[\rho\tau]f(x) - \lambda x - \dot{x}, \qquad 0 \leqslant x, c, \tau < +\infty \tag{1.1.10}$$

where c denotes consumption per worker. Assumption 1.1.6 is thus the only "unusual" restriction we are making. Its purpose is to eliminate the possibility of superexponential growth, i.e. of growth paths that satisfy

$$\lim_{\tau \to +\infty} \frac{x(\tau)}{\exp[g\tau]} = +\infty, \tag{1.1.11}$$

for every finite constant $g > 0$. Indeed, the UMIT index is unable to discriminate among such superexponential growth paths. This follows, among other things, from the two following theorems.

THEOREM 1.1.1 Assumptions (1.1.1) to (1.1.6) imply that

$$\alpha'(x) \leqslant 0, \qquad 0 < x < +\infty \tag{1.1.12}$$

where

$$\alpha(x) \equiv \frac{xf'(x)}{f(x)}. \tag{1.1.13}$$

Proof Straightforward computation of the right side of (1.1.7) gives

$$\frac{1}{\sigma} = x \frac{\mathrm{d}}{\mathrm{d}x} \ln \left[\frac{1-\alpha}{\alpha} x \right] \tag{1.1.14}$$

i.e.

$$\frac{\sigma - 1}{\sigma} = \frac{x\,\alpha'}{\alpha(1-\alpha)}. \tag{1.1.15}$$

Now (1.1.3) and (1.1.5) imply

$$0 < \alpha(x) < 1, \qquad 0 < x < +\infty$$

where $\alpha(x)$ is continuously differentiable by virtue of (1.1.4). Hence (1.1.12) must hold true.

q.e.d.

THEOREM 1.1.2 Under Assumptions (1.1.1) to (1.1.6) and (1.1.8) to (1.1.10), an indefinitely constant and positive savings policy

$$s(\tau) = \frac{\lambda x + \dot{x}}{y} = \bar{s}, \qquad 0 < \bar{s} = \text{const} \leqslant 1 \tag{1.1.16}$$

implies

$$\lim_{\tau \to +\infty} \frac{\dot{x}}{x} = \lim_{\tau \to +\infty} \frac{\dot{y}}{y} = \lim_{\tau \to +\infty} \frac{\dot{c}}{c} = \frac{\rho}{1-\bar{\alpha}} \tag{1.1.17}$$

where

$$\bar{\alpha} = \lim_{x \to +\infty} \alpha(x). \tag{1.1.18}$$

Proof Notice first that (1.1.4) and (1.1.16) ensure the continuity of $\dot{x}(\tau)$ over $0 \leqslant \tau < +\infty$. Write $\kappa \equiv x/y$, $\bar{\kappa} \equiv \bar{s}/g_{lb}$, $g - \lambda = \rho/(1-\alpha)$ and $g_{lb} - \lambda = \rho/(1-\bar{\alpha})$. Then $\dot{\kappa}(\tau)$ is also continuous over $0 \leqslant \tau < +\infty$ and

$$\bar{s} = g\kappa + \frac{\dot{\kappa}}{1-\alpha} = g_{lb}\bar{\kappa} \tag{1.1.19}$$

Hence, $\kappa(\tau) > \bar{\kappa}$ requires $\dot{\kappa}(\tau) < 0$, since $\bar{\alpha} \leqslant \alpha < 1$ and, consequently, $g \geqslant g_{lb}$.

On the other hand $\kappa(\tau)$ cannot have a maximum $< \bar{\kappa}$. Indeed, this would require the existence of two points of time ω and $\Omega > \omega$ such that $\kappa(\omega) = \kappa(\Omega)$ and, by the continuity of $\dot{\kappa}(t)$, $\dot{\kappa}(\Omega) < 0 < \dot{\kappa}(\omega)$, $\kappa(\tau) < \bar{\kappa}$, $\omega \leqslant \tau \leqslant \Omega$. Now this is impossible since it implies

$$
\begin{aligned}
\frac{\dot{x}}{x} &= \frac{\overline{s}}{\kappa} - \lambda \\
&> \frac{\overline{s}}{\overline{\kappa}} - \lambda \\
&= g_{lb} - \lambda \\
&\geqslant 0, \qquad \omega \leqslant \tau \leqslant \Omega
\end{aligned}
\tag{1.1.20}
$$

i.e.

$$g(\Omega) \leqslant g(\omega) \tag{1.1.21}$$

and, consequently, by (1.1.19), $\dot{\kappa}(\Omega) > \dot{\kappa}(\omega)$.

It follows that

$$\lim_{\tau \to +\infty} \kappa(\tau) = \text{const.} \tag{1.1.22}$$

where

$$\text{const} = \overline{\kappa} > 0 \tag{1.1.23}$$

by (1.1.19) and $\overline{s} > 0$. (Remember that $\lambda > 0$, i.e. $g_{lb} > 0$.) Hence,

$$\lim_{\tau \to +\infty} \left[(1-\alpha)\frac{\dot{x}}{x} - \rho \right] = \lim_{\tau \to +\infty} \frac{\dot{\kappa}}{\kappa} = 0 \tag{1.1.24}$$

i.e. (1.1.17), since

$$\frac{\dot{c}}{c} = \frac{\dot{y}}{y} = \alpha\frac{\dot{x}}{x} + \rho \tag{1.1.25}$$

and

$$\lim_{\tau \to +\infty} \left[\alpha\frac{\dot{x}}{x} + \rho \right] = \rho \left[\frac{\underline{\overline{\alpha}}}{1-\underline{\overline{\alpha}}} + 1 \right] = \frac{\rho}{1-\underline{\overline{\alpha}}}. \tag{1.1.26}$$

q.e.d.

Since the highest growth rate of x is obtained by investing everything which is produced, i.e. for the indefinitely constant savings policy $s(\tau) = 1, 0 \leqslant \tau < +\infty$, it follows from Theorem 1.1.2 that superexponential growth in the sense of (1.1.11) is not possible under our assumptions. From the proofs of Theorems 1.1.1 and 1.1.2, it is also seen that Assumption (1.1.6) ensures the elimination of superexponential growth. It can be shown, on the other hand, that *ceteris paribus* the condition

$$\lim_{x \to +\infty} \alpha(x) = 1 \tag{1.1.27}$$

is sufficient for (1.1.11).

1.2 The set of feasible growth paths

This section defines the set of growth paths from which the optimal one is to be selected. The importance of a rigorous definition of this set cannot be sufficiently emphasized. Indeed, without a mathematically unambiguous definition of this set, no clear answer can be given to the question of the existence of an optimal UMIT path.

The first question to settle is the minimum degree of "smoothness" we are willing to consider as acceptable for an optimal path. Granted our assumptions, $x(\tau)$ must clearly be required to be continuous. The question is whether $\dot{x}(\tau)$, i.e. $c(\tau)$, should also be continuous. Since UMIT allows an initial discontinuity in the savings path, it seems logical to permit such a discontinuity from time to time. We shall therefore assume that $\dot{x}(\tau)$ is piece-wise continuous.

The next problem to solve is whether or not some positive lower bounds should be imposed on both c and $\dot{x}$. Indeed, it seems clear that, even for a day, $c = 0$ must be excluded as socially unacceptable (over a longer period, it entails the death by starvation of the whole population).

We therefore require c not to fall below a minimum level $c_s > 0$ along any admissible path. On the other hand, it seems economically reasonable to assume that the rate of disinvestment cannot exceed a certain negative value. Moreover, for the sake of generality, we shall introduce a constant lower bound to x which may be chosen as equal to zero.

DEFINITION 1.2.1 Given a growth model satisfying the assumptions of Section 1.1 and given the constants $c_s > 0, \xi \geqslant 0, x_m \geqslant 0, x_0 \geqslant x_m, x_0 > 0$, a path $x(\tau)$, $0 \leqslant \tau < +\infty$, is said to be *indefinitely feasible* if

(i) $\dot{x}(\tau)$ is piece-wise continuous over $0 \leqslant \tau < +\infty$;

(ii) $x(0) = x_0$;

(iii) $x \geqslant x_m$; $0 \leqslant \tau < +\infty$;

(iv) $-\xi \int_{t_1}^{t_2} x \mathrm{d}\tau \leqslant x(t_2) - x(t_1) \leqslant \int_{t_1}^{t_2} (y - \lambda x - c_s) \mathrm{d}\tau$;

for any two points of time $t_2 > t_1 \geqslant 0$. The set of all indefinitely feasible $x(\tau)$ is denoted by $[x(\tau)_0^{+\infty}]^*$.

1.3 The utility index

It is assumed that the instantaneous national preference pattern with respect to the level c of consumption per worker can be described by a strictly concave and time invariant utility function $U(c)$ which satisfies

$$U'''(c) \text{ is continuous,} \qquad c_{lb} < c < +\infty \qquad (1.3.1)$$

$$U'(c) > 0,\ U''(c) < 0,\ U'''(c) > 0 \qquad c_{lb} < c < +\infty \qquad (1.3.2)$$

and

$$\Phi'(c) \geqslant 0, \qquad c_{lb} < c < +\infty \qquad (1.3.3)$$

where

$$\Phi(c) \equiv \frac{\mathrm{d}[\ln U'(c)]}{\mathrm{d}[\ln c]} \qquad (1.3.4)$$

and

$$0 \leqslant \dot{c}_{lb} = \text{const.} \qquad (1.3.5)$$

It is furthermore assumed that the nation discounts the utility of future consumption at the constant rate $i \geqslant 0$: the utility at time 0 of consumption c_t at time t is

$$\exp[-it]U(c_t). \qquad (1.3.6)$$

Finally, the UMIT index is assumed to express the national preference pattern with respect to the set of indefinitely feasible growth paths..

DEFINITION 1.3.1 Maximization of the improper integral

$$I[x(\tau)_0^{+\infty}] \equiv \int_0^{+\infty} U[c(\tau)]\exp[-it]\,\mathrm{d}\tau$$

is called "Utility Maximization over Infinite Time" or shortly UMIT. The integral itself is the UMIT index. If, given a set $[x(\tau)_0^{+\infty}]$ of time paths $x(\tau)$,

$0 \leqslant \tau < +\infty$, there is a $\hat{x}(\tau) \in [x(\tau)_0^{+\infty}]$ which maximizes absolutely $I[x(\tau)_0^{+\infty}]$ in $[x(\tau)_0^{+\infty}]$, $\hat{x}(\tau)$ is called *UMIT-optimal* or, simply, optimal in $[x(\tau)_0^{+\infty}]$. If there is only one such $\hat{x}(\tau)$, optimality is called *strict.*

The above definition of UMIT is thus the usual one, except perhaps for (1.3.3). Notice, however, that the condition (1.3.3) has been satisfied by all specifications of $U(c)$ which have been hitherto used in UMIT.

1.4 Statement and meaning of Theorem X1

THEOREM X1 Given a UMIT index $I[x(\tau)_0^{+\infty}]$, a non-empty set of indefinitely feasible growth paths $[x(\tau)_0^{+\infty}]^*$ contains an optimal path $\hat{x}^*(\tau)$ if

$$\text{(a)} \qquad i > \max \left\{ 0; (1-\nu)\,(g_{lb} - \lambda) \right\}$$

where

$$-\nu = \lim_{c \to +\infty} \Phi(c)$$

$$\text{(b)} \qquad f(x_0) - \lambda x_0 \geqslant c_s > c_{lb}.$$

It is seen that Theorem X1 is extremely simple and general. The condition $i > 0$ is hardly stronger than the economically obvious condition that $i \geqslant 0$. The condition $i > (1-\nu)\,(g - \lambda)$ ensures the convergence of $I[x(\tau)_0^{+\infty}]$ in $[x(\tau)_0^{+\infty}]^*$. Condition (b) ensures that $[x(\tau)_0^{+\infty}]^*$ is not empty.

2. PROOF OF THEOREM X1

2.1 Outline of the proof

Our purpose is to take advantage of the method of proof first developed by L. Tonelli in the case of definite L-integrals and later extended by S. Cinquini to the case of L-integrals with an infinite upper limit.

The logic of the Tonelli-Cinquini method is explained in the next section. At this stage, let us only say that this method requires the set of admissible $x(\tau)$s to be closed. Now the set $[x(\tau)_0^{+\infty}]^*$ is unfortunately not closed. Indeed, the limit path of a sequence of piece-wise continuously differentiable $x(\tau)$s satisfying the conditions of Definition 1.2.1 is not itself necessarily piece-wise continuously differentiable.

We shall therefore proceed as follows. We first extend the set $[x(\tau)_0^{+\infty}]^*$ to a closed set by admitting all absolutely continuous (for definition, see Appendix to this paper) $x(\tau)$s which satisfy Definition 1.2.1 except condition i. It is to this extended set of admissible $x(\tau)$s, say $[x(\tau)_0^{+\infty}]$, that we apply the Tonelli-Cinquini method. Under the conditions of Theorem X1, this enables us to establish the existence of an $\hat{x}(\tau) \in [x(\tau)_0^{+\infty}]$ which is UMIT optimal in $[x(\tau)_0^{+\infty}]$ (Section 2.3).

To prove Theorem X1, it is then sufficient to show that $\hat{x}(\tau)$ is piece-wise continuously differentiable, i.e. that $\hat{x}(\tau) = \hat{x}^*(\tau)$.

2.2 The Tonelli-Cinquini method

The main steps of this method are clearly set forth by the following theorem.

THEOREM 2.2.1 If

(i) $[x(\tau)_0^{+\infty}]$ is a non-empty set of functions $x(\tau)$, $0 \leqslant \tau < +\infty$, which satisfy the initial condition $x(0) = x_0$;

(ii) the members of $[x(\tau)_0^{+\infty}]$ are absolutely equicontinuous over every finite interval;

(iii) $[x(\tau)_0^{+\infty}]$ is closed in the finite;

(iv) $W(\tau, x, \dot{x})$ is an L-integrable function along all $x(\tau) \in [x(\tau)_0^{+\infty}]$ over every finite interval;

(v) $J[x(\tau)_0^{+\infty}] \equiv \int_0^{+\infty} W d\tau$ is upper-bounded on $[x(\tau)_0^{+\infty}]$;

(vi) $J[x(\tau)_0^{+\infty}]$ is uniformly convergent on $[x(\tau)_0^{+\infty}]$;

(vii) $J[x(\tau)_0^T] \equiv \int_0^T W d\tau$ is, for every $T > 0$, upper semi-continuous on the set $[x(\tau)_0^T]$ of all $x(\tau) \in [x(\tau)_0^{+\infty}]$ "truncated" at $\tau = T$;

then there is an $\hat{x}(\tau) \in [x(\tau)_0^{+\infty}]$ which maximizes absolutely $J[x(\tau)_0^{+\infty}]$ with respect to $[x(\tau)_0^{+\infty}]$.

Proof Since $[x(\tau)_0^{+\infty}]$ is not empty (i) and $J[x(\tau)_0^{+\infty}]$ upper-bounded on $[x(\tau)_0^{+\infty}]$ (v),

$$\bar{J} \equiv \sup \left\{ J[x(\tau)_0^{+\infty}];\ x(\tau) \in [x(\tau)_0^{+\infty}] \right\} \tag{2.2.1}$$

exists and is finite. We may therefore extract a so-called "maximizing sequence" $x_1(\tau), x_2(\tau), \ldots$, from $[x(\tau)_0^{+\infty}]$ such that

$$J[x_n(\tau)_0^{+\infty}] + \frac{1}{n} \geqslant \bar{J}, \qquad n = 1, 2, \ldots \tag{2.2.2}$$

The members $x_n(\tau)$ of this sequence being absolutely equicontinuous (ii) and initially bounded (i), the Ascoli-Darbo theorem (Theorem 2.2.2) above does apply and the sequence has at least one limit path in the finite, say $x_l(\tau)$. Moreover, $x_l(\tau) \in [x(\tau)_0^{+\infty}]$, since $[x(\tau)_0^{+\infty}]$ is closed (iii) in the finite.

The uniform convergence of $J[x(\tau)_0^{+\infty}]$ on $[x(\tau)_0^{+\infty}]$ (vi) tells us, on the other hand, that there is an $\Omega > 0$ for every given $\eta > 0$ such that

$$|J[x(\tau)_0^{+\infty}] - J[x(\tau)_0^T]| < \eta \tag{2.2.3}$$

provided only $T \geqslant \Omega$. Finally, we know from the upper semi-continuity of $J[x(\tau)_0^T]$ on $[x(\tau)_0^T]$ for every $T > 0$ (vii), that there is a $\rho > 0$ for every given $\epsilon > 0$ and $T \geqslant \Omega$ such that

$$J[x(\tau)_0^T] < J[x_l(\tau)_0^T] + \epsilon \tag{2.2.4}$$

provided only $x(\tau) \in [x(\tau)_0^T]$ lies in the neighbourhood ρ of $x_l(\tau)$. Now $x_l(\tau)$ being a limit curve of the sequence $x_1(\tau)$, $x_2(\tau)$, ... , there is, in particular, an $x_n(\tau)$, $n \geqslant N$, for every given $N > 0$ which lies in the said neighbourhood ρ of $x_l(\tau)$ over $0 \leqslant \tau \leqslant T$.

It follows from this fact and from the inequalities (2.2.2), (2.2.3) and (2.2.4) that

$$\bar{J} < J[x_l(\tau)_0^{+\infty}] + \frac{1}{n} + \epsilon + 2\eta \tag{2.2.5}$$

where $(\frac{1}{n} + \epsilon + 2\eta)$ can be chosen smaller than any preassigned positive number. Hence,

$$\bar{J} \leqslant J[x_l(\tau)_0^{+\infty}] \tag{2.2.6}$$

i.e. by virtue of the definition (2.2.1) of $\bar{J}$:

$$\bar{J} = J[x_l(\tau)_0^{+\infty}]. \tag{2.2.7}$$

In other words, $x_l(\tau) = \hat{x}(\tau)$.

q.e.d.

THEOREM 2.2.2 (Ascoli-Darbo, simplified version) Let $x_1(\tau), x_2(\tau), \ldots,$ be a sequence of functions which are absolutely equicontinuous over every finite interval $0 \leqslant \tau \leqslant T$ and which satisfy $x_n(0) = x_0$, $n = 1, 2, \ldots,$ where x_0 is a given number. Then the functions of the sequence are uniformly bounded over every finite interval and have at least one absolutely continuous limit function in the finite.

2.3 Existence of an absolutely continuous optimal path

We now define explicitly the extended class of admissible $x(\tau)$s as already indicated in Section 2.1.

DEFINITION 2.3.1 Given a growth model satisfying the assumptions of Section 1.1 and given the constants $c_s > 0, \xi \geqslant 0, x_m \geqslant 0$ and $\leqslant x_0$, a path $x(\tau)$, $0 \leqslant \tau < +\infty$, is said to be *indefinitely admissible if*

(i) $x(\tau)$ is absolutely continuous over $0 \leqslant \tau < +\infty$;

(ii) $x(0) = x_0$;

(iii) $x(\tau) \geqslant x_m$, $0 \leqslant \tau < +\infty$;

and, for any two points, $t_2 > t_1 \geqslant 0$,

$$\text{(iv)} \; -\xi \int_{t_1}^{t_2} x \mathrm{d}\tau \leqslant x(t_2) - x(t_1) \leqslant \int_{t_1}^{t_2} (y - \lambda x - c_s)\, \mathrm{d}\tau$$

(the integrals are L-integrals).

The set of all indefinitely admissible $x(\tau)$s is denoted by $[x(\tau)_0^{+\infty}]$. A path $x(\tau)$ is said to be admissible over a given finite interval $t_1 \leqslant \tau \leqslant t_2$ if it coincides with a member of $[x(\tau)_0^{+\infty}]$ over $t_1 \leqslant \tau \leqslant t_2$.

Having noticed that $[x(\tau)_0^{+\infty}] \supset [x(\tau)_0^{+\infty}]^*$, we carry out the first step of the proof outlined in Section 2.1.

THEOREM X0 Given a UMIT index $I[x(\tau)_0^{+\infty}]$ and a set $[x(\tau)_0^{+\infty}]$ as defined by Definition 2.3.1 there is a UMIT-optimal path $\hat{x}(\tau)$ if

$$i > \max \left\{ 0, (1 - \nu)\, (g_{lb} - \lambda) \right\} \tag{2.3.1}$$

and

$$f(x_0) - \lambda x_0 \geqslant c_s > c_{lb}. \tag{2.3.2}$$

Proof It is sufficient that conditions (i) to (vii) of Theorem 2.2.1 are fulfilled by $[x(\tau)_0^{+\infty}]$ and $I[x(\tau)_0^{+\infty}]$.

(i) $[x(\tau)_0^{+\infty}]$ is not empty since it obviously contains $x(\tau) = x_0, 0 \leqslant \tau < +\infty$.

(ii) The equicontinuity of the $x(\tau)$ over every finite interval $0 \leqslant \tau \leqslant T$ follows from the Lipschitz condition

$$| x(t_2) - x(t_1) | \leqslant \max \left\{ \xi x_s(T), \exp [\rho\tau] f[x_s(T)] \right\} \mathrm{T}, \qquad 0 \leqslant t_1 < t_2 \leqslant T \tag{2.3.3}$$

where $x_s(\tau)$ denotes the solution of

$$\dot{x} = \exp [\rho\tau] f(x) - \lambda x, \qquad 0 \leqslant \tau < +\infty \tag{2.3.4}$$

satisfying $x(0) = x_0$.

(iii) The Lipschitz condition (2.3.3) ensures that every limit curve $x_l(\tau)$ of $[x(\tau)_0^{+\infty}]$ is continuous. It follows that there is an ϵ for every interval $t_1 \leqslant \tau \leqslant t_2$ which satisfies

$$x_l(t_2) - x_l(t_1) + \epsilon = - \xi \int_{t_1}^{t_2} x_l(\tau) \mathrm{d}\tau. \tag{2.3.5}$$

Now if $\epsilon > 0$, this leads, for any $x(\tau)$ which lies in the neighbourhood δ of $x_l(\tau)$, $\epsilon > \delta\ [2 + \xi(t_2 - t_1)]$, to the absurd conclusion that

$$\begin{aligned}\epsilon &\leqslant [x(t_2) - x(t_1)] - [x_l(t_2) - x_l(t_1)] \\ &\quad + \xi \int_{t_1}^{t_2} [x(\tau) - x_l(\tau)]\mathrm{d}\tau \\ &\leqslant [2 + \xi(t_2 - t_1)]\delta \\ &< \epsilon. \end{aligned} \tag{2.3.6}$$

Hence, the first inequality sign in Definition 2.3.1(iv) must hold true. The proof is similar for the second inequality sign.

(iv) The proof that $W(\tau, x, \dot{x}) = U(c)\exp[-i\tau]$ is L-integrable along every $x(\tau) \in [x(\tau)_0^{+\infty}]$ is trivial.

(v) and (vi) We need only consider the case

$$\lim_{c \to +\infty} U(c) = +\infty. \tag{2.3.7}$$

We first notice that (2.3.7) implies

$$\lim_{c \to +\infty} |\Phi| = \nu \leqslant 1. \tag{2.3.8}$$

Indeed, assume that $\nu = 1 + 2\epsilon > 1$. Then

$$(c^{1+\epsilon}\, U')' = c^{\epsilon} U'[\Phi + 1 + \epsilon] \tag{2.3.9}$$

where

$$\lim_{c \to +\infty} [\Phi + 1 + \epsilon] = -\epsilon. \tag{2.3.10}$$

Hence,

$$(c^{1+\epsilon} U')' < 0, \qquad c \geqslant c_\epsilon, \epsilon > 0 \tag{2.3.11}$$

for some $c_\epsilon > 0$. Now this is contrary to (2.3.7) by Weierstrass' test for the convergence of improper integrals.

Now $\nu = 1$, (1.3.1) and (1.3.2) imply

$$\begin{aligned}(cU)' &= U'[\Phi + 1] \\ &\leqslant 0, \qquad c_s \leqslant c < +\infty \end{aligned} \tag{2.3.12}$$

and $\nu < 1$ implies

$$(cU')' = U'[\Phi + 1] > 0, \qquad c^* \leqslant c < +\infty \tag{2.3.13}$$

for some $c^* \geqslant c_S$. Hence,

$$\lim_{c \to +\infty} cU' = \text{const.} \tag{2.3.14}$$

or

$$\lim_{c \to +\infty} cU' = +\infty. \tag{2.3.15}$$

Now, granted (2.3.7), (2.3.14) implies

$$\lim_{c \to +\infty} \frac{cU'}{U} = 0 \tag{2.3.16}$$

and, by l'Hospital's Rule, (2.3.15) implies

$$\lim_{c \to +\infty} \frac{cU'}{U} = 1 - \nu. \tag{2.3.17}$$

It follows that for every $x(\tau) \in [x(\tau)_0^{+\infty}]$,

$$\int_0^{+\infty} U \exp[-i\tau]\,\mathrm{d}\tau < \int_0^{+\infty} U\left\{\exp[\rho\tau] f[x_s(\tau)] + \xi x_s(\tau)\right\} \exp[-i\tau]\,\mathrm{d}\tau \tag{2.3.18}$$

where the second integral converges because

$$\lim_{\tau \to +\infty} \frac{\mathrm{d}}{\mathrm{d}\tau} \ln\left[U\left\{\exp[\rho\tau] f[x_s(\tau)] + \xi x_s(\tau)\right\} \exp[-i\tau]\tau^2\right] = (1\,\nu)\,(g_{lb} - \lambda) - i < 0 \tag{2.3.19}$$

by virtue of Theorem 1.1.2, (2.3.16), (2.3.17) and (2.3.1).

$I[x(\tau)_0^{+\infty}]$ is therefore upper-bounded on $[x(\tau)_0^{+\infty}]$. Moreover, whether (2.3.7) holds true or not, $I[x(\tau)_0^{+\infty}]$ is uniformly convergent on $[x(\tau)_0^{+\infty}]$. Indeed, whatever $x(\tau) \in [x(\tau)_0^{+\infty}]$, one has

$$|I[x(\tau)_T^{+\infty}]|$$

$$<\max\left\{|U(c_s)|\frac{\exp[-iT]}{i},\ \int_T^{+\infty} U[\exp[\rho\tau]f[x_s(\tau)]+\xi\, x_s(\tau)]\exp[-i\tau]\,\mathrm{d}\tau\right\}. \qquad (2.3.20)$$

Now the right side of (2.3.20) can be made smaller than any pre-assigned positive number by choosing T large enough [see (2.3.19)].

(vii) Finally, we prove the upper-semi continuity of $I[x(\tau)_0^T]$ on $[x(\tau)_0^T]$ for every $T>0$ by adapting a proof of Tonelli to our definitions of $I[x(\tau)_0^T]$ and $[x(\tau)_0^T]$.

Let $x^*(\tau)\in[x(\tau)_0^T]$ and $\Pi(\tau)$ be a polygonal curve inscribed in $x^*(\tau)$ (end-points coinciding with $x^*(0)=x_0$ and $x^*(T)$, vertices on $x^*(\tau)$, $0<\tau<T$) the corners of which have been smoothed such that: (a) $\ddot{\Pi}(\tau)$ is continuous over $0\leqslant\tau\leqslant T$ and (b) given an ϵ which satisfies

$$0<\epsilon<c^*(\tau)-c_s, \qquad 0\leqslant\tau\leqslant T \qquad (2.3.21)$$

one has ·

$$|\Pi-x^*|<\epsilon, \qquad 0\leqslant\tau\leqslant T \qquad (2.3.22)$$

and, except at the most over an interval of measure less than ϵ, also

$$|\dot{\Pi}-\dot{x}^*|<\epsilon, \qquad 0\leqslant\tau\leqslant T. \qquad (2.3.23)$$

It follows that, except possibly over an interval of measure less than ϵ, both

$$|\dot{\Pi}|<M, \qquad 0\leqslant\tau\leqslant T \qquad (2.3.24)$$

where

$$M\equiv\max\left\{\dot{x}_s(T),\ -\xi x_s(T)\right\}+\epsilon \qquad (2.3.25)$$

and

$$\begin{aligned} E(\tau,x^*;\dot{\Pi},\dot{x}^*) &\equiv W(\tau,x^*,\dot{x}^*)-W(\tau,x^*,\dot{\Pi}) \\ &\quad -(\dot{x}^*-\dot{\Pi})\,W_{\dot{x}}(\tau,x^*,\dot{\Pi}) \\ &> \left\{W_{\dot{x}}(\tau,x^*,\dot{x}^*)-W_{\dot{x}}(\tau,x^*,\dot{\Pi})\right\}(\dot{x}^*-\dot{\Pi}) \\ &> -2\,\epsilon U'(c_s), \qquad 0\leqslant\tau\leqslant T. \qquad (2.3.26) \end{aligned}$$

Moreover, wherever it exists, the Weierstrass function E is negative since $U(c)$ is strictly concave. Hence,

$$\int_0^T \left\{ E(\tau, x; \dot{\Pi}, \dot{x}) - E(\tau, x^*; \dot{\Pi}, \dot{x}^*) \right\} d\tau$$

$$< 2\epsilon U'(c_s)[T + 2M]. \tag{2.3.27}$$

It follows that

$$I[x(\tau)_0^T] - I[x^*(\tau)_0^T] < 2\epsilon U'(c_s)[T + 2M]$$

$$+ \int_0^T \left\{ W(\tau, x, \dot{\Pi}) + (\dot{x} - \dot{\Pi})\, W_{\dot{x}}(\tau, x, \dot{\Pi}) \right\} d\tau$$

$$- \int_0^T \left\{ W(\tau, x^*, \dot{\Pi}) + (\dot{x}^* - \dot{\Pi})\, W_{\dot{x}}(\tau, x^*, \dot{\Pi}) \right\} d\tau \tag{2.3.28}$$

where

$$\int_0^T \left\{ W(\tau, x, \dot{\Pi}) + (\dot{x} - \dot{\Pi})\, W_{\dot{x}}(\tau, x, \dot{\Pi}) \right\} d\tau \tag{2.3.29}$$

is continuous by Lemma 2.3.1 below.

q.e.d

The following Lemma is an immediate corollary of a theorem established by Tonelli [T].

LEMMA 2.3.1 If $P(\tau, x)$, $Q(\tau, x)$ and $\partial Q(\tau, x)/\partial \tau$ are continuous over $0 < x(\tau) < x_s(\tau)$, $0 \leqslant \tau \leqslant T$, then

$$\int_0^T \left\{ P(\tau, x) + \dot{x} Q(\tau, x) \right\} d\tau \tag{2.3.30}$$

is continuous on $[x(\tau)_0^T]$.

2.4 Piece-wise continuity of the optimal investment path

This section shows that $\hat{x}(\tau) \equiv \hat{x}^*(\tau)$ by proving that $\dot{\hat{x}}(\tau)$ is piece-wise continuous over $0 \leqslant \tau < +\infty$.

THEOREM 2.4.1 Let $\hat{x}(\tau)$ be optimal in a given set $[x(\tau)_0^{+\infty}]$ according to a given UMIT index $I[x(\tau)_0^{+\infty}]$. Then, for every given $\omega \geqslant 0$, there is a $\delta > 0$ such that one of the following conditions holds true over $\omega \leqslant \tau \leqslant \omega + \delta$:

$$\frac{\dot{\hat{c}}}{\hat{c}} \Phi(\hat{c}) + \exp[\rho\tau] f'(\hat{x}) - (i + \lambda) = 0 \tag{2.4.1}$$

$$\hat{c}(\tau) = c_s \tag{2.4.2}$$

$$\dot{\hat{x}}(\tau) = -\xi\hat{x}(\tau) \tag{2.4.3}$$

$$\hat{x}(\tau) = x_m. \tag{2.4.4}$$

Moreover, if $\omega > 0$, there is a $\delta^* > 0$ such that one of these conditions (not necessarily the same one as after ω) holds true over $\omega - \delta^* \leqslant \tau \leqslant \omega$.

(Proof: see below)

It should be noticed that $\dot{\hat{x}}(\tau)$ is continuous over any open interval over which it satisfies one of the four conditions (2.4.1) - (2.4.4). This is obvious for the last three of these conditions and follows from Lemma 2.4.2 for the first. Theorem 2.4.1 excludes the possibility of a limit point of discontinuities of $\dot{\hat{x}}(\tau)$ and implies, consequently, the desired piece-wise continuity of $\dot{\hat{x}}(\tau)$.

We now proceed to the proof of Theorem 2.4.1. For expository convenience, a number of side arguments are stated and proved as Lemmas at the end of the section.

Proof of Theorem 2.4.1 It will be convenient to write $x_s(\tau; \omega, a)$ for the solution of

$$\dot{x} = \exp[\rho\tau] f(x) - \lambda x - c_s, \qquad x(\omega) = a \tag{2.4.5}$$

over $\omega \leqslant \tau < +\infty$ and $x_d(\tau; \omega, a)$ for the solution of

$$\dot{x} = -\xi x, \qquad x(\omega) = a \tag{2.4.6}$$

over its interval of existence beyond ω. Let us further denote by $\tilde{x}(\tau; \omega, a, b)$ the solution of Euler's equation

$$\Phi\frac{\dot{c}}{c} + \exp[\rho\tau]f'(x) - (i+\lambda) = 0, \qquad x(\omega) = a, \dot{x}(\omega) = b \quad (2.4.7)$$

over its interval of existence in the open region

$$R: 0<\tau<+\infty, \quad 0<x<+\infty, \quad -\infty<\dot{x}<\exp[\rho\tau]f(x) - \lambda x - c_{lb}.$$

We prove the theorem over $\omega \leqslant \tau \leqslant \omega + \delta$, $\delta > 0$; we consider separately the cases $\hat{x}(\omega) > x_m$ and $\hat{x}(\omega) = x_m$.

$\hat{x}(\omega) > x$. In this case, there must be a $\delta_1 > 0$ such that $\hat{x}(\tau)$ satisfies either one of the three following conditions over $\omega < \tau \leqslant \omega + \delta_1$:

$$\hat{x}(\tau) = x_s[\tau; \omega, \hat{x}(\omega)] \quad (2.4.8)$$

$$\hat{x}(\tau) = x_d[\tau; \omega, \hat{x}(\omega)] \quad (2.4.9)$$

$$x_d[\tau; \omega, \hat{x}(\omega)] < \hat{x}(\tau) < x_s[\tau; \omega, \hat{x}(\omega)]. \quad (2.4.10)$$

Indeed, by virtue of the Definition 2.3.1 of $[x(\tau)_0^{+\infty}]$, $\hat{x}(\omega_1) > x_d[\omega_1; \omega, \hat{x}(\omega)]$ and $\hat{x}(\omega_1) < x_s[\omega_1; \omega, \hat{x}(\omega)]$, $\omega_1 > \omega$, imply respectively $\hat{x}(\tau) > x_d[\tau; \omega, \hat{x}(\omega)]$ and $\hat{x}(\tau) < x_s[\tau; \omega, \hat{x}(\omega)]$, $\tau \geqslant \omega_1$.

To prove the theorem for $\hat{x}(\omega) > x_m$ over $\omega \leqslant \tau \leqslant \omega + \delta$, it is therefore sufficient to show that (2.4.10) implies (2.4.1) for some $\delta > 0$. For this purpose, we have to consider five different alternatives separately. Alternative 1 is that there is an $\tilde{x}[\tau; \omega, \hat{x}(\omega), b_1]$ and an $\tilde{x}[\tau; \omega, \hat{x}(\omega), b_2]$, $\dot{x}_d[\omega; \omega, \hat{x}(\omega)] \leqslant b_1 \leqslant b_2 < \dot{x}_s[\omega; \omega, \hat{x}(\omega)]$, which are both feasible over some open interval starting at ω and satisfy

$$\tilde{x}[\tau; \omega, \hat{x}(\omega), b_1] \leqslant \hat{x}(\tau) \leqslant \tilde{x}[\tau; \omega, \hat{x}(\omega), b_2], \omega < \tau \leqslant \omega + \delta_2 \quad (2.4.11)$$

for some $\delta_2 > 0$. Now, by virtue of Lemmas 2.4.1 and 2.4.3, this implies (2.4.1) for some $\delta > 0$.

If Alternative 1 does not hold true, then either

$$\hat{x}(\tau) < \tilde{x}[\tau; \omega, \hat{x}(\omega), b], \qquad \omega < \tau \leqslant \omega + \delta_3 \quad (2.4.12)$$

or

$$\hat{x}(\tau) > \tilde{x}[\tau; \omega, \hat{x}(\omega), b], \qquad \omega < \tau \leqslant \omega + \delta_3 \quad (2.4.13)$$

for all values of b which satisfy

$$\dot{x}_d[\omega;\omega,\hat{x}(\omega)] < b < \dot{x}_s[\omega;\omega,\hat{x}(\omega)] \tag{2.4.14}$$

and some δ_3 which may depend on b. Indeed, by Lemmas 2.4.1 and 2.4.2, $\hat{x}(\tau)$ cannot be both optimal and cross $\tilde{x}[\tau;\omega,\hat{x}(\omega),b]$ at some $\omega_2 > \omega$ unless $\hat{x}(\tau) = \tilde{x}[\tau;\omega,\hat{x}(\omega),b]$, $\omega \leqslant \tau \leqslant \omega_2$. Now, each of the two alternatives (2.4.12) and (2.4.13) gives rise to two further alternatives. We are thus left with four alternatives which, together with Alternative 1, constitute the five alternatives we have to consider.

Let us first consider the two alternatives, say Alternative 2 and Alternative 3, which are associated with (2.4.13).

Alternative 2 is that, over some open interval starting at ω,

$$\tilde{x}\{\tau;\omega,\hat{x}(\omega)\ \dot{x}_s[\omega;\omega,\hat{x}(\omega)]\} < \hat{x}(\tau) < x_s[\tau;\omega,\hat{x}(\omega)]. \tag{2.4.15}$$

Now by Lemma 2.4.4, (2.4.15) is contrary to the optimality of $\hat{x}(\tau)$.

Alternative 3 is that

$$\tilde{x}\Big\{\tau;\omega,\hat{x}(\omega),\dot{x}_s[\omega;\omega,\hat{x}(\omega)]\Big\} > x_s[\tau;\omega,\hat{x}(\omega)] \tag{2.4.16}$$

over some interval starting at ω. [Notice that the case $\hat{x}(\tau) < \tilde{x}\{[\tau;\omega,\hat{x}(\omega)], \dot{x}[\omega;\omega,\hat{x}(\omega)]\} < x_s[\tau;\omega,\hat{x}(\omega)]$ over some open interval starting at ω is taken care of by alternative 1.] By (2.4.13) and Lemma 2.4.2, this implies the existence of a $\beta < \dot{x}_s[\omega;\omega,\hat{x}(\omega)]$ and an $\omega_\beta > \omega$ such that

$$\tilde{x}[\tau;\omega,\hat{x}(\omega),\beta] < x_s[\tau;\omega,\hat{x},(\omega)], \qquad \omega < \tau < \omega_\beta \tag{2.4.17}$$

and

$$\tilde{x}[\omega_\beta;\omega,\hat{x}(\omega),\beta] = \dot{x}_s(\omega_\beta;\omega,\hat{x}(\omega)). \tag{2.4.18}$$

This implies, in turn, that there is an ω_b for every b satisfying

$$\dot{x}_s[\omega;\omega,\hat{x}(\omega)]\quad \beta \leqslant b < \dot{x}_s[\omega;\omega,\hat{x}(\omega)] \tag{2.4.19}$$

such that both (2.4.17) and (2.4.18) hold true if β is everywhere replaced by b.

It follows that $\tilde{x}[\tau;\omega,\hat{x}(\omega),b]$, where b satisfies (2.4.19) crosses $\hat{x}(\tau)$ at some point of time ω_b^*, $\omega < \omega_b^* < \omega_b$. Now, if there were an $\tilde{x}[\tau;\omega,\hat{x}(\omega),b]$, admissible over $\omega \leqslant \tau \leqslant \omega_b$, where b satisfied (2.4.19), then $\hat{x}(t)$ could not be optimal unless $\hat{x}(\tau) = \tilde{x}[\tau;\omega,\hat{x}(\omega),b]$, $\omega \leqslant \tau \leqslant \omega_b$. This would, however, be contrary to our assumption that Alternative 1 does not hold true. Hence, no such $\tilde{x}[\tau;\omega,\hat{x}(\omega),b]$ can exist which is feasible over $\omega \leqslant \tau \leqslant \omega_b$. [Notice that it is the feasibility, and not the existence of $\tilde{x}[\tau;\ \omega,\ \hat{x}(\omega),\ b]$, which is here rejected.] By Lemma 2.4.5 this implies that

$$\dot{\hat{x}}(\omega + 0) = \dot{x}_s[\omega + 0;\ \omega, \hat{x}(\omega)]\,. \tag{2.4.20}$$

It follows from Lemma 2.4.1 on the other hand, that, over some interval starting at ω,

$$\left[\frac{\mathrm{d}}{\mathrm{d}x} - \frac{\mathrm{d}}{\mathrm{d}\tau}\frac{\partial}{\partial \dot{x}}\right]\left\{U(\bar{\bar{c}})\exp[-i\tau]\right\} < 0 \tag{2.4.21}$$

where $\bar{\bar{c}}$ is defined by $x_s = x_s[\tau;\ \omega,\ \hat{x}(\omega)]$. This implies, in turn, the existence of an $\epsilon^* > 0$ such that (2.4.21) remains true over some interval $\omega < \tau < \omega_\epsilon$, if x_s is replaced by a path, say $x_{s\epsilon}(\tau)$, which satisfies

$$\dot{x} = \exp[\rho\tau]f(x) - \lambda x - c_s - \epsilon,\quad x_{s\epsilon}(\omega) \geqslant \hat{x}(\omega),\quad 0 < \epsilon \leqslant \epsilon^*,\quad \omega \leqslant \tau < \infty$$

We may thus choose an $\bar{\epsilon}$ in $0 < \bar{\epsilon} \leqslant \epsilon^*$ such that $x_{s\bar{\epsilon}}(\tau)$ crosses $\hat{x}(\tau)$ for the first time after ω at a time $\omega_{\bar{\epsilon}} < \omega_{\epsilon^*}$ and is admissible over $\omega \leqslant \tau \leqslant \omega_{\bar{\epsilon}}$. By Lemma 2.4.1 and (2.4.20), this implies, however, the absurd conclusion that $x_{s\bar{\epsilon}}(\tau)$ is "better" than $\hat{x}(\tau)$ over $\omega \leqslant \tau \leqslant \omega_{\bar{\epsilon}}$.

Next we consider the two alternatives, say Alternative 4 and Alternative 5, which are associated with (2.4.12).

Alternative 4 is the counterpart of Alternative 2 and, as the latter, is excluded by Lemma 2.4.4. It is

$$x_s[\tau;\ \omega,\ \hat{x}(\omega)] < \hat{x}(\tau) \leqslant \tilde{x}\left\{\tau;\ \omega,\ \hat{x}(\omega),\ \dot{x}_d[\omega;\ \omega,\ \hat{x}(\omega)]\right\} \tag{2.4.22}$$

over some open interval starting at ω.

Alternative 5 is the counterpart of Alternative 3. It is

$$\tilde{x}\left\{\tau; \omega, \hat{x}(\omega),\ \dot{x}_d[\omega; \omega, \hat{x}(\omega)]\right\} < x_d[\tau; \omega, \hat{x}(\omega)] \tag{2.4.23}$$

over some open interval starting at ω. This alternative is dealt with in a way perfectly similar to Alternative 3.

$\hat{x}(\omega) = x_m$. In this case, either there is, for every $\delta > 0$ a t_1 and a t_2, $\omega < t_1 < t_2 < \omega + \delta$, such that

$$\hat{x}(t_1) > \hat{x}(t_2) = x_m \tag{2.4.24}$$

or one of the three following conditions holds true over $\omega < \tau \leqslant \omega + \delta_1$ for some $\delta_1 > 0$:

$$\hat{x}(\tau) = x_s[\tau; \omega, \hat{x}(\omega)] \tag{2.4.25}$$

$$\hat{x}(\tau) = x_m \tag{2.4.26}$$

$$x_m < \hat{x}(\tau) < \hat{x}_s[\tau; \omega, x(\omega)]. \tag{2.4.27}$$

In order to prove the theorem (over $\omega \leqslant \tau \leqslant \omega + \delta$), it is sufficient to exclude the alternative associated with (2.4.24). Indeed, the three alternatives (2.4.25), (2.4.26) and (2.4.27) can be formally considered as respectively identical to (2.4.8), (2.4.9) and (2.4.10), where $\xi = 0$ and $\hat{x}(\omega) = x_m$. Hence, the same reasoning applies here as in the case $\hat{x}(\omega) > x_m$, provided the alternative associated with (2.4.24) can be excluded

Now, in this last alternative, there must be a $\delta_0 > 0$ such that

$$\widetilde{x}(\tau; \omega, x_m, 0) > x_m, \qquad \omega < \tau < \delta_0 \tag{2.4.28}$$

$$\widetilde{x}(\omega + \delta_0; \omega, x_m, 0) = x_m. \tag{2.4.29}$$

Indeed, otherwise one would have along $x(\tau) = \overline{x}$, by Lemma 2.4.1,

$$\Phi(c)\frac{\dot{c}}{c} + \exp[\rho\tau]f'(x) - (i + \lambda) < 0, \qquad \omega \leqslant \tau < \delta_4 \tag{2.4.30}$$

for some $\delta_4 > 0$. Again, by Lemma 2.4.1 this would, however, be contrary to the optimality of $\hat{x}(\tau)$. From here on, we proceed formally as in the case of Alternative 5 by setting $\xi = 0$ and $\hat{x}(\omega) = x_m$.

The proof of the theorem over $\omega - \delta^* \leqslant \tau \leqslant \omega$ is perfectly similar and is left to the reader.

q.e.d.

LEMMA 2.4.1 If $x^*(\tau) \in [x(\tau)_0^{+\infty}]$ and if $\dot{x}^*(\tau)$ is absolutely continuous over $\omega \leqslant \tau \leqslant \Omega$, $\Omega > \omega \geqslant 0$, then

$$\exp[-i\omega]\left\{I[x(\tau)_\omega^\Omega] - I[x^*(\tau)_\omega^\Omega]\right\}$$
$$< \int_\omega^\Omega (x - x^*)\left[\frac{\partial}{\partial x} - \frac{\mathrm{d}}{\mathrm{d}\tau}\frac{\partial}{\partial \dot{x}}\right] U'(c^*)\exp[-i\tau]\mathrm{d}\tau \tag{2.4.31}$$
$$-(x - x^*)U'(c^*)\exp[-i\tau]\Big|_\omega^\Omega$$

for all $x(\tau) \in [x(\tau)_0^{+\infty}]$ different from $x^*(\tau)$.

Proof By virtue of the strict concavity of $U(c)$ and $f(x)$, the continuity of $U''(c)$ and $f'(x)$ and the absolute continuity of $x(\tau)$ and $\dot{x}^*(\tau)$ over $\omega \leqslant \tau \leqslant \Omega$,

$$\int_\omega^\Omega [U(c) - U(c^*)]\exp[-i\tau]d\tau$$

$$< \int_\omega^\Omega U'(c^*)(c - c^*)\exp[-i\tau]d\tau$$

$$= \int_\omega^\Omega U'(c^*)\left\{\exp[\rho\tau]\,[f(x) - f(x^*)] - \lambda(x - x^*)\right\}\exp[-i\tau]d\tau$$

$$- \int_\omega^\Omega U'(c^*)(\dot{x} - \dot{x}^*)\exp[-i\tau]d\tau$$

$$< \int_\omega^\Omega U'(c^*)\left[\exp[\rho\tau]f'(x^*) - (i + \lambda) + \Phi(c^*)\frac{\dot{c}^*}{c^*}\right](x - x^*)\exp[-i\tau]d\tau$$

$$- U'(c^*)(x - x^*)\exp[-i\tau]\Big|_\omega^\Omega . \qquad (2.4.32)$$

In applying this lemma, one should be aware that the set $[x(\tau)_0^{+\infty}]$ of the lemma may be defined for any value of $c_s > c_{lb}$ and less than or equal to the value of c_s in the position under consideration.

LEMMA 2.4.2 $\bar{x}(\tau;\,\omega,\,a,\,b)$, as defined in the proof of Theorem 2.4.1, is uniquely determined over its interval of existence. This interval extends on both sides of ω over some finite interval $\omega_1 < \tau < \omega_2$, $\omega_1 < \omega < \omega_2$, if the point (ω, a, b) lies in the region

$$R: 0 \leqslant \omega < +\infty, \qquad 0 < a < +\infty, \qquad -\infty < b < \exp[\rho\omega]f(a) - \lambda a - c_{lb}.$$

Moreover, both $\bar{x}(\tau;\,\omega,\,a,\,b)$ and $\tilde{\dot{x}}(\tau;\,\omega,\,a,\,b)$ are continuous functions of τ, ω, a and b for $(\omega, a, b) \in R$ and τ in $\omega_1 < \tau < \omega_2$.

Proof The lemma follows from the fact that Euler's equation (2.4.1) is of the form

$$\ddot{x} = h(\tau, x, \dot{x}) \qquad (2.4.33)$$

where $h(\tau,\,x,\,\dot{x})$ has partial derivatives of order 1 over $0 < \tau < +\infty$, $0 < x < +\infty$, $-\infty < \dot{x} < \exp[\rho\tau]f(x) - \lambda x - c_{lb}$.

q.e.d.

LEMMA 2.4.3 If $x_l(\tau)$ is continuous over $\omega < \tau \leqslant \omega + \delta$, $\delta > 0$, and

$$\tilde{x}[\tau; \omega, x_l(\omega), b_1] < x_l(\tau) < \tilde{x}[\tau; \omega, x_l(\omega), b_2] \qquad (2.4.34)$$

holds true over $\omega < \tau < \omega + \delta_1$ for some b_1 and b_2, then there is a b^*, $b_1 < b^* < b_2$, and a ω^*, $\omega < \omega^* \leqslant \omega + \delta$, such that

$$\tilde{x}[\omega^*; \omega, x_l(\omega), b^*] = x_l(\omega^*). \qquad (2.4.35)$$

Proof This lemma is a corollary of Lemma 2.4.2. Indeed, $\tilde{x}(\tau; \omega, x_l(\omega), b)$ exists over some finite interval $\omega \leqslant \tau \leqslant \omega_b$ for every b in $b_1 \leqslant b \leqslant b_2$. Let $\omega^{**} = \inf \omega_b$ in $b_1 \leqslant b \leqslant b_2$ and $\omega^* = \min\{\omega + \delta, \omega^{**}\}$. Then $\omega^* > \omega$, and $\tilde{x}[\omega^*; \omega, x_l(\omega), b]$ describes a straight line $\tau = \omega^*$ in the (τ, x)-plane as b varies continuously from b_1 to b_2. Now this line must obviously cross $x_l(\tau)$ at ω^* for some b^* in $b_1 < b < b_2$.

The lemma remains true if, in the definition of $\tilde{x}(\tau; \omega, a, b)$ above, R is replaced by $\bar{R}$: $0 < \tau < +\infty, x_m \leqslant x < +\infty, -x\,\xi \leqslant \dot{x} \leqslant \exp[\rho\tau] f(x) - \lambda x - c_s$.

LEMMA 2.4.4 Let $\hat{x}(\tau)$ be optimal in a given $[x(\tau)_0^{+\infty}]$ according to a given UMIT index $I[x(\tau)_0^{+\infty}]$. Then there is no $\omega \geqslant 0$ and $\delta > 0$ such that

$$\tilde{x}\left\{\tau; \omega, \hat{x}(\omega), \dot{x}_s[\omega; \omega, \hat{x}(\omega)]\right\} < \hat{x}(\tau) < x_s[\tau; \omega, \hat{x}(\omega)], \quad \omega < \tau \leqslant \omega + \delta \qquad (2.4.36)$$

or

$$\tilde{x}\left\{\tau; \omega, \hat{x}(\omega), \dot{x}_d[\omega; \omega, \hat{x}(\omega)]\right\} > \hat{x}_d(\tau) > x_d[\tau; \omega, \hat{x}(\omega)], \quad \omega < \tau \leqslant \omega + \delta. \qquad (2.4.37)$$

Proof We consider first the case (2.4.36). By Lemma 2.4.2 and the fact that $\hat{c}(t) \geqslant c_s > c_{lb}$ obtains, $\tilde{x}\{\tau; \omega, \hat{x}(\omega), \dot{x}_s[\omega; \omega, \hat{x}(\omega)] + \epsilon\}$ exists over $\omega \leqslant \tau \leqslant \omega + \delta$ and is $> x_s[\tau; \omega, \hat{x}(\omega)]$ over $\omega < \tau \leqslant \omega + \delta$ for some $\delta > 0$, provided only that $0 < \epsilon < c_s - c_{lb}$. Hence, by Lemma 2.4.3, (2.4.36) implies that there is an ϵ^*, $0 < \epsilon^* < c_s - c_{lb}$, such that, given any ϵ, $0 < \epsilon \leqslant \epsilon^*$,

$$\hat{x}(\omega + \delta_\epsilon) = \tilde{x}\left\{\omega + \delta_\epsilon; \omega, \hat{x}(\omega), \dot{x}_s[\omega, \omega, \dot{x}(\omega) + \epsilon]\right\} \qquad (2.4.38)$$

and

$$x_s[\omega + \delta'_\epsilon; \omega, \hat{x}(\omega)] = \tilde{x}\left\{\omega + \delta'_\epsilon; \omega, \hat{x}(\omega), \dot{x}_s[\omega; \omega, \hat{x}(\omega) + \epsilon]\right\} \qquad (2.4.39)$$

for some $\delta_\epsilon > \delta'_\epsilon > 0$. Now by Lemma 2.4.1, this implies that $\hat{x}(\tau)$ can only be optimal if

$$\exp[\rho\tau] f'\left\{x_s[\tau; \omega, \hat{x}(\omega)]\right\} - (i + \lambda) > 0, \quad \omega < \tau < \omega^* \qquad (2.4.40)$$

for some $\omega^* < \omega$. It follows that there is an $\bar{\epsilon} > 0$ such that the path

$$\bar{x}(\tau)\begin{cases} x_s[\tau;\omega,\hat{x}(\omega)], & \omega \leqslant \tau \leqslant \omega + \delta'_{\bar{\epsilon}}, \\ \tilde{x}\left\{\tau;\omega,\hat{x}(\omega),\dot{x}_s[\tau;\omega,\hat{x}(\omega)]+\bar{\epsilon}\right\}, & \omega + \delta'_{\bar{\epsilon}} \leqslant \tau \leqslant \omega + \delta_{\bar{\epsilon}} \end{cases} \tag{2.4.41}$$

is feasible and, by Lemma 2.4.1 better than $\hat{x}(\tau)$ over $\omega \leqslant \tau \leqslant \omega + \delta_{\bar{\epsilon}}$.

The proof in the case (2.4.37) is perfectly symmetrical and is left to the reader.

q.e.d.

LEMMA 2.4.5 Let $\hat{x}(\tau)$ be optimal in a given $[x(\tau)_0^{+\infty}]$ according to a given UMIT index $I[x(\tau)_0^{+\infty}]$. If, given $\omega \geqslant 0$ and whatever $\epsilon > 0$,

$$\begin{aligned}&\tilde{x}\left\{\tau;\omega,\hat{x}(\omega),\dot{x}_s[\omega;\omega,\hat{x}(\omega)]\right\} > x_s[\tau;\omega,\hat{x}(\omega)] > \\ &\hat{x}(\tau) > \tilde{x}\left\{\tau;\omega,\hat{x}(\omega),\dot{x}_s[\omega;\omega,\hat{x}(\omega)]-\epsilon\right\}, \qquad \omega < \tau \leqslant \omega + \delta\end{aligned} \tag{2.4.42}$$

for some $\delta > 0$ which may depend on ϵ, then

$$\dot{\hat{x}}(\omega) = \dot{x}_s[\omega;\omega,\hat{x}(\omega)] \tag{2.4.43}$$

if, given $\omega \geqslant 0$ and whatever $\epsilon > 0$,

$$\begin{aligned}&\tilde{x}\left\{\tau;\omega,\hat{x}(\omega),\dot{x}_d[\omega;\omega,\hat{x}(\omega)]\right\} < x_d[\omega;\omega,\hat{x}(\omega)] < \\ &\hat{x}(\tau) < \tilde{x}\left\{\tau;\omega,\hat{x}(\omega),\dot{x}_d[\omega;\omega,\hat{x}(\omega)]+\epsilon\right\}, \qquad \omega < \tau \leqslant \omega + \delta\end{aligned} \tag{2.4.44}$$

for some $\delta > 0$ which may depend on ϵ, then

$$\dot{\hat{x}}(\omega) = \dot{x}_d[\omega;\omega,\hat{x}(\omega)]. \tag{2.4.45}$$

Proof We first consider the case (2.4.42). Given $\epsilon > 0$, denote by $x_l(\tau,\epsilon)$ the straight line in the (τ, x)-plane which goes through the point $[\omega, \hat{x}(\omega)]$ and has the greatest possible slope without lying above $\tilde{x}\{\tau;\omega,\hat{x}(\omega),\dot{x}_s[\omega;\omega,\hat{x}(\omega)]-\epsilon\}$ at any point in $\omega \leqslant \tau \leqslant \omega_\epsilon$, where $\omega_\epsilon > \omega$ denotes the first time at which $\tilde{x}\{\tau;\omega,\hat{x}(\omega),\dot{x}_s[\omega;\omega,\hat{x}(\omega)]-\epsilon\}$ crosses $\hat{x}(\tau)$. Then there is an $\bar{\epsilon} > 0$ such that

$$\dot{x}_l(\tau,\epsilon) < \frac{\hat{x}(\omega_\epsilon)-\hat{x}(\omega)}{\omega_\epsilon-\omega} < \frac{x_s[\omega_\epsilon;\omega,\hat{x}(\omega)]-x_s[\omega;\omega,\hat{x}(\omega)]}{\omega_\epsilon-\omega} \tag{2.4.46}$$

for $0 < \epsilon \leqslant \bar{\epsilon}$. Now as ϵ tends to zero, i.e. as ω_ϵ tends to ω, the first and third members and, consequently, also the second member of the inequality (2.4.46) all tend to $\dot{\bar{x}}_s[\omega; \omega, \mathfrak{X}(\omega)]$.

The proof in the case (2.4.45) is perfectly symmetrical and is left to the reader.

q.e.d.

3. APPENDIX

3.1 Mathematical definitions

DEFINITION 3.1.1 Let $z(\tau)$ and $z^*(\tau)$ be two continuous real functions defined over the real interval $0 \leqslant \tau \leqslant T$. $z(\tau)$ *lies in the interval* $\delta > 0$ of $z^*(\tau)$ (over $0 \leqslant \tau \leqslant T$) if

$$|z(\tau) - z^*(\tau)| < \delta, \qquad 0 \leqslant \tau \leqslant T. \tag{3.1.1}$$

DEFINITION 3.1.2 Let $[z(\tau)_0^T]$ be a set of continuous real functions $z(\tau)$ defined over the real interval $0 \leqslant \tau \leqslant T$. A continuous real function $z^*(\tau)$, $0 \leqslant \tau \leqslant T$, is a *limit curve* of $[z(\tau)_0^T]$ if there is a $z(\tau) \in \{z(\tau)\}$ different from $z^*(\tau)$ in every neighbourhood $\delta > 0$ of $z^*(\tau)$ over $0 \leqslant \tau \leqslant T$.

DEFINITION 3.1.3 Let $[z(\tau)_0^{+\infty}]$ be a set of real continuous functions defined over the real interval $0 \leqslant \tau \leqslant +\infty$. $[z(\tau)_0^{+\infty}]$ is *closed in the finite* if, for every $T > 0$, the "truncated" set $[z(\tau)_0^T]$ contains all its limit curves (over $0 \leqslant \tau \leqslant T$).

DEFINITION 3.1.4 A real function $z(\tau)$ is *absolutely continuous* over the real interval $0 \leqslant \tau \leqslant T$, if there is a δ for every $\epsilon > 0$ such that

$$\sum_{i=1}^{n} (t_i^* - t_i) < \delta \tag{3.1.2}$$

implies

$$\sum_{i=1}^{n} |z(t_i^*) - z(t_i)| < \epsilon \tag{3.1.3}$$

for every set of $n > 0$ non-overlapping intervals (t_i^*, t_i), $0 \leqslant t_i < t_i^* \leqslant T$.

DEFINITION 3.1.5 The members of a set of functions $[z(\tau)_0^T]$ defined over $0 \leqslant \tau \leqslant T$ are *absolutely equicontinuous* if there is a δ for every $\epsilon > 0$ such that (3.1.2) implies (3.1.3) for every set of $n > 0$ non-overlapping intervals (t_i^*, t_i), $0 \leqslant t_i < t_i^* \leqslant T$, and all $z(\tau) \in [z(\tau)_0^T]$.

DEFINITION 3.1.6 Let $[z(\tau)_0^T]$ be a set of absolutely continuous functions defined over the real interval $0 \leqslant \tau \leqslant T$ and let $W(\tau, z, \dot{z})$ be a real function which is Lebesgues-integrable along every $z(\tau) \in [z(t)_0^T]$. Then the L-integral

$$\int_0^T W(\tau, z, \dot{z}) \mathrm{d}\tau \tag{3.1.4}$$

is upper semi-continuous in $[z(\tau)_0^T]$ if there is a δ for every $z^*(\tau) \in [z(\tau)_0^T]$ and $\epsilon > 0$ such that

$$\int_0^T \left\{ W(\tau, z, \dot{z}) - W(\tau, z^*, \dot{z}^*) \right\} \mathrm{d}\tau < \epsilon \tag{3.1.5}$$

for all $z(\tau) \in [z(\tau)_0^T]$ which satisfy

$$| z(\tau) - z^*(\tau) | < \delta, \qquad 0 \leqslant \tau \leqslant T.$$

3.2 Bibliography

CINQUINI, S., 'Sopra l'esistenza dell'estremo assoluto per gli integrali estesi a intervalli infiniti', *Atti Accad. naz Lincei Rc.*

CINQUINI, S., 'Une nova estensione dei moderni metodi del calcolo delle variazioni', *Annali Scu. norm. sup., Pisa,* Series II, No. 9, pp 253-261 (1940).

CINQUINI, S., 'Sopra le condizioni necessarie per la semicontinuità degli integrali dei problemi variazionali di ordine *n', ibid.,* Series II, No. 6, pp 149-178 (1937).

DARBO, G., 'L'estremo assoluto per gli integrali su intervallo infinito', *Rc. semin. mat. Univ. Padova,* V 22 (1953).

FEADO, S., 'Il calcolo delle variazioni per gli integrali su un intervallo infinito', *Commentat. pontif. Acad. Scient.,* V 8, pp 319-421 (1944).

FEADO, S., 'Il calcolo delle variazioni per gli integrali estesi a intervalli infiniti', *Annali Scu. norm. sup., Pisa,* Series II, No. 7, pp 91-132 (1953).

TONELLI, L., 'Fondamenti di calcolo delle variazioni', Volumes I and II, edited by NICOLA ZANICELLI, Bologna (1921).

Paper 2

CASE OF A CONSTANT TECHNOLOGY

INTRODUCTION

In his very stimulating paper "On the concept of optimal economic growth" [K], Koopmans states two basic theorems concerning the feasibility of Utility Maximization over Infinite Time (UMIT) in the case of a constant technology.

The first theorem assumes that the utility of future consumption is not discounted at all. This theorem is particularly interesting because it provides a first integral of Euler's equation. The second theorem assumes that the utility of future per capita consumption is discounted at a positive and constant rate. The statements and the proofs of the two theorems given in [K] contain, however, some small lacunae. It is the purpose of this paper to fill the latter.

A rather surprising side result of the following analysis is the discovery that it may no longer be possible to select an optimal growth program according to a given utility index if the initial capital stock exceeds a certain high, though still historically conceivable, value.

OBJECTIVE

Derive a set of conditions under which UMIT is feasible in the case of a constant technology.

PLAN

1. The growth model
2. The utility index
3. No time discounting

4. Positive time discounting
5. Conclusion

1. THE GROWTH MODEL

1.1 The variables

x – capital stock per worker, i.e. per labor unit
y – production flow per worker
c – consumption flow per worker
L – labor force
P – population

1.2 The general growth assumptions

1.2.1 At any given instant of time, i.e. at any given level of technology, the production flow per worker is a twice continuously differentiable function of the capital stock per worker only:

$$y = f(x), \qquad 0 \leqslant x < +\infty.$$

The law of decreasing returns requires that this function be strictly concave:

$$f'(x) > 0 \text{ and } f''(x) < 0, \qquad 0 \leqslant x < +\infty.$$

Moreover, no production can take place without some amount of capital:

$$f(0) = 0.$$

1.2.2 Labor and population grow autonomously and proportionally at the constant and positive rate λ:

$$L = L_0 \exp[\lambda\tau] \text{ and } P = P_0 \exp[\lambda\tau], \qquad 0 \leqslant \tau < +\infty$$

where $L_0 > 0, P_0 > 0$ and $\lambda > 0$ are given.

1.2.3 The flow of investment per worker $(\lambda x + \dot{x})$ is a piece-wise continuous function of time over $0 \leqslant \tau < +\infty$.

1.2.4 The economy is closed in the sense that there is no net long-term capital transfer. In other words, consumption is the difference between production and investments:

$$c = f(x) - \lambda x - \dot{x}, \qquad 0 \leqslant \tau < +\infty$$

at all points of continuity of $\dot{x}(\tau)$.

1.3 The set of feasible growth paths

In view of the fact that the general growth assumptions, Section 1.2, associate one and only one growth path $[x(\tau), y(\tau), c(\tau)]$ with every path $x(\tau)$, the set of feasible growth paths can be stated in terms of x only. We denote this set by $\{x(\tau)\}$ and define it as the set of all $x(\tau)$, $0 \leqslant \tau < +\infty$, which start from the historically given capital stock per worker x_0, satisfy the general growth assumptions and, moreover, always maintain the consumption flow per worker c above some given *starvation* level $c_s \geqslant 0$.

More precisely, given $x_0 > 0$, $\lambda > 0$, $c_s \geqslant 0$ and $f(x)$, where $f(x)$ satisfies Assumption 1.2.1, $x(\tau) \in \{x(\tau)\}$ if:

(i) $x(0) = x_0$;

(ii) $x(\tau)$ is defined positive and piece-wise continuously differentiable over $0 \leqslant \tau < +\infty$;

(iii) $-\infty < \dot{x}(\tau) < f[x(\tau)] - \lambda x(\tau) - c_s$, with $0 \leqslant \tau < +\infty$, at all points of continuity of $\dot{x}(\tau)$.

It will furthermore be convenient to call a path $x(\tau)$ *feasible* over $0 \leqslant \tau \leqslant T$ if it coincides over $0 \leqslant \tau \leqslant T$ with a member of $\{x(\tau)\}$.

2. THE UTILITY INDEX

2.1 The general preference assumptions

2.1.1 The national preference pattern with respect to instantaneous consumption can be described by any linear transformation of a thrice differentiable function of the consumption flow per capita or, since L/P = constant, of the consumption flow per worker. This *utility* function $U(c)$ is defined for consumption-per-worker flows greater than the non-negative *starvation* level c_s and may or may not be bounded from above or from below. It is, however, strictly concave:

$$U'(c) > 0 \text{ and } U''(c) < 0, \qquad c_s < c < +\infty$$

and satisfies

$$\lim_{c \to c_s} U'(c) = +\infty. \tag{2.1.1}$$

2.1.2 The national preference pattern for postponed consumption can be accounted for by a non-negative and constant time discount rate i. More precisely, the utility at time t_0 of a consumption flow c at time t_1 can be described by

$$U[c(t_1)]\exp[-i(t_1 - t_0)], \qquad 0 \leqslant t_0 < t_1 < +\infty.$$

2.1.3 The nation prefers the feasible path $x^*(\tau)$ to the feasible path $x(\tau)$ if there is a $T^* \geqslant 0$ such that

$$I[x^*(\tau)_0^T] - I[x(\tau)_0^T] > 0, \qquad T \geqslant T^*$$

where

$$I[x(\tau)_0^T] = \int_0^T U[c(\tau)]\exp[-i\tau]\mathrm{d}\tau$$

i.e. if the sum over time of the discounted utilities of consumption per capita is ultimately greater along $x^*(\tau)$ than along $x(\tau)$–(Weiszäcker's overtaking principle [W]). A feasible path $x^*(\tau)$ is called UMIT-optimal if it is preferred to all other feasible paths in the above sense. By definition, UMIT is achieved along such a most preferred path.

3. NO TIME DISCOUNTING

The first theorem (Theorem 3.1 here) is essentially established by Koopmans in [K], but, as already mentioned, the statement presented therein is incomplete. It does not sufficiently restrict the class of admissible $U(c)$. In fact, it only assumes $U' > 0$, $U'' < 0$, $0 \leqslant c < +\infty$, and

$$\lim_{c\to 0} U(c) = -\infty.$$

Now, depending on the value of the initial capital stock, Theorem 3.1 tells us that one more condition must be imposed on $U(c)$. A sufficient condition is

$$\lim_{c\to+\infty} (cu'/u) = \text{negative constant} \tag{3.1}$$

where, as always hereafter, $u = U'$. (Note that the necessary and sufficient condition is that $G(c)$, as defined by (3.14), approaches c_s as $c \to +\infty$. Another sufficient condition is that $u \to 0$ as $c \to +\infty$ (see Fig. 2). This latter condition implies (3.1), granted only that (cu'/u) approaches a constant as $c \to +\infty$.)

Economically speaking (3.1) is a rather weak condition. Indeed, the limit on the left-hand side of (3.1) must reasonably be a constant which, furthermore, has to be non-positive by virtue of the concavity of U. We are thus only eliminating one economically relevant possibility, namely that this limit tends to 0.

We now prepare the statement of Theorem 3.1 with the definition of some notations.

DEFINITION 3.1 Let $f(x)$ and $U(c)$ satisfy Assumptions 1.2.1 and 2.1.1. Let x_- and $x_+ > x_-$ denote respectively the greatest and the smallest solution of

$$f(x) - \lambda x = c_s.$$

Moreover, let $\bar{x}$ denote the so-called Golden Rule value of x defined by

$$f'(\bar{x}) = \lambda + i, \qquad \bar{x} > 0.$$

Lemma 3.1 follows then from the strict concavity of both $f(x)$ and $U(c)$.

LEMMA 3.1 The $x_-, \bar{x}$ and x_+ defined by Definition 3.1 exist and satisfy

$$x_- < \bar{x} < x_+$$

provided

$$f'(0) > \lambda + i \tag{3.2}$$

$$\lim_{x \to +\infty} f'(x) < \lambda + i \tag{3.3}$$

and

$$\bar{c} = f(\bar{x}) - \bar{x}$$
$$> c_s. \tag{3.4}$$

The meaning of x_- and x_+ is simple: only values of x which lie in the interval $x_- < x < x_+$ can be indefinitely sustained. In fact, $0 \leqslant x_0 \leqslant x_-$ condemns the economy to short-term starvation, while $x_0 > x_+$ is historically inconceivable. Thus, given $x_- < x_0 < x_+$, all indefinitely feasible $x(\tau)$ satisfy $x_- < x(\tau) < x_+$, $0 \leqslant \tau < \infty$.

The meaning of $\bar{x}$ is also simple and well known: it yields the highest sustainable value of c, namely the Golden Rule value (3.4) [P1].

THEOREM 3.1 Let $\{x(\tau)\}$ and $I[x(\tau)_0^T]$ be, respectively, defined by Sections 1.3 and 2.1 under the additional conditions of (3.2), (3.3) and (3.4):

$$i = 0 \text{ and } x_- < x_0 < x_+$$

where $x_-, \overline{x}$ and x_+ satisfy Definition 3.1. Moreover, in case $x_0 > \overline{x}$, let (3.1) also hold true. Then there exists a UMIT-optimal path in $\{x(\tau)\}$. This path, say $\hat{x}(\tau)$, satisfies the first-order differential equation

$$\dot{x}U'(c) = U(\overline{c}) - U(c), \qquad 0 \leqslant \tau < +\infty. \tag{3.5}$$

If $x_0 = \overline{x}$, then

$$\hat{x}(\tau) = \overline{x}, \qquad 0 \leqslant \tau < +\infty. \tag{3.6}$$

If $x_0 \neq \overline{x}$, then

$$\lim_{\tau \to +\infty} \hat{x}(\tau) = \overline{x} \tag{3.7}$$

$$\lim_{\tau \to +\infty} \hat{c}(\tau) = \overline{c} \tag{3.8}$$

and

$$\dot{\hat{x}}(\tau)\, \dot{\hat{c}}(\tau) > 0, \qquad 0 \leqslant \tau < +\infty. \tag{3.9}$$

In short, Theorem 3.1 tells us that, both in terms of x and c, the UMIT-optimal path either coincides from the start with the Golden Rule path or tends strictly monotonically to it as τ tends to $+\infty$. Moreover, $\hat{c}(\tau)$ is smaller, equal or greater than $\overline{c}$ depending on whether $\hat{x}(\tau)$ is itself smaller, equal or greater than $\overline{x}$.

It should be noted that $x_0 > \overline{x}$ constitutes a situation which is hardly ever encountered in practice. Indeed $x_0 > \overline{x}$ implies that the initial capital-output ratio κ_0 is greater than the elasticity α of production with respect to capital divided by the labor growth rate λ. Now, assuming $\alpha \geqslant 1/4$ and $\lambda \leqslant 4\%$, one still gets $\kappa_0 > 6$.

Proof of Theorem 3.1 We follow the same over-all strategy as applied in [K] and show successively that:

(i) every indefinitely fluctuating $x(\tau) \in \{x(\tau)\}$ is worse than some other $x^*(\tau) \in \{x(\tau)\}$ which has at the most one relative extremum;

(ii) every $x(\tau) \in \{x(\tau)\}$ which does not satisfy (3.7) is worse than one which does;

(iii) Equation (3.5) has a UMIT-optimal solution in $\{x(\tau)\}$ which satisfies (3.6) if $x_0=\bar{x}$ and (3.7), (3.8) and (3.9) if $x_0 \neq \bar{x}$.

Proof of (i) We first state a lemma.

LEMMA 3.2 Let $\{x(\tau)\}$ and $I[x(\tau)_0^T]$ be respectively defined by Sections 1.3 and 2.1, both $x_1(\tau)$ and $x_2(\tau)$ belong to $\{x(\tau)\}$ and $x_1(\tau)$ be twice continuously differentiable. Then,

$$I[x_2(\tau)_0^T] - I[x_1(\tau)_0^T]$$
$$= \int_0^T (x_2 - x_1) \{(\dot{u}_1/u_1) + f_1' - (i+\lambda)\} u_1 \exp[-i\tau]d\tau$$
$$- (x_2 - x_1) u_1 \exp[-i\tau] \Big|_0^T + \int_0^T M(\tau)d\tau$$

where $M(\tau)$ is positive and piece-wise continuous over $0 \leqslant \tau < +\infty$.

Proof $U(c)$ has continuous second-order partial derivatives with respect to x and $\dot{x}$. We may thus apply Taylor's formula up to the second-order derivatives:

$$[U(c_2) - U(c_1)] = \left[(x_2 - x_1)\frac{\partial}{\partial x} + (\dot{x}_2 - \dot{x}_1)\frac{\partial}{\partial \dot{x}}\right] U(c_1)$$
$$+\frac{1}{2}\left[(x_2 - x_1)\frac{\partial}{\partial x} + (\dot{x}_2 - \dot{x}_1)\frac{\partial}{\partial x}\right]^2 U(c_\Theta) \tag{3.10}$$

where

$$c_\Theta = f[x_1 + \Theta(x_2 - x_1)] - \lambda[x_1 + \Theta(x_2 - x_1)] - [\dot{x}_1 + \Theta(\dot{x}_2 - x_1)]$$

and $\Theta = \Theta(\tau)$ is a continuous function of time which satisfies

$$0 \leqslant \Theta(\tau) \leqslant 1, \qquad 0 \leqslant \tau < +\infty.$$

The second term on the right-hand side of (3.10) is a negative and continuous function of time which may be written $-M(\tau)\exp[i\tau]$. This follows from the fact that

$$a^2 \frac{\partial^2}{\partial x^2} U + 2ab \frac{\partial^2}{\partial x \partial \dot{x}} U + b^2 \frac{\partial^2}{\partial \dot{x}^2} U =$$

$$= a^2[u'(f' - \lambda)^2 + uf''] - 2abu'(f' - \lambda) + b^2u'$$

$$= u'[a(f' - \lambda) - b]^2 + a^2uf''$$

$$< 0, \qquad 0 \leqslant \tau < +\infty.$$

The product of $\exp[-i\tau]$ and the first term on the right-hand side of (3.10) can be integrated by parts:

$$\int_0^T [(x_2 - x_1)\, u_1(f'_1 - \lambda) - (\dot{x}_2 - \dot{x}_1)\, u_1] \exp[-i\tau]\mathrm{d}\tau$$

$$= \int_0^T (x_2 - x_1)\, [(\dot{u}_1/u_1) + f'_1 - (i + \lambda)]\, u_1 \exp[-i\tau]\mathrm{d}\tau$$

$$- (x_2 - x_1)\, u_1 \exp[-i\tau] \,|_0^T.$$

q.e.d.

Assume now that $x(\tau) \in \{x(\tau)\}$ fluctuates indefinitely. Starting from $x(\tau)$ we can construct an $x^{**}(\tau) \in \{x(\tau)\}$ which has at the most one extremum by the following process: over all intervals $\omega \leqslant \tau \leqslant \omega^*$, $\omega \geqslant 0$, such that $x(\omega) = x(\omega^*)$, and either $x(\tau) > x(\omega) \geqslant \bar{x}$, $\omega < \tau < \omega^*$, or $x(\tau) < x(\omega) \leqslant \bar{x}$, $\omega < \tau < \omega^*$, we replace $x(\tau)$ by $x(\omega)$.

Now, from Lemma 3.2 and the fact that $(f' - \lambda)(\bar{x} - x) > 0$ if $x \neq \bar{x}$,

$$\int_\omega^{\omega^*} \{U[c(\tau)] - U[c(\omega)]\}\, \mathrm{d}\tau$$

$$< \int_\omega^{\omega^*} [x(\tau) - x(\omega)]\{f'[x(\omega)] - \lambda\}\, u[c(\omega)]\mathrm{d}\tau$$

$$< 0.$$

It follows that $x^{**}(\tau)$ is better than $x(\tau)$.

Proof of (ii) By virtue of (i), it is sufficient to prove (ii) for $x(\tau) \in \{x(\tau)\}$ which do not fluctuate indefinitely. Thus let

$$\lim_{\tau \to +\infty} x(\tau) = x_{+\infty} \neq \bar{x}$$

and let $x^*(\tau)\in\{x(\tau)\}$ satisfy both (3.7) and $c^*(\tau)\geqslant c_s^*, 0\leqslant\tau<+\infty$, for some $c_s^*> c_s$. Then, (see the proof of Lemma 3.2)

$$\int_0^T \{U(c)-U(c^*)\}\,\mathrm{d}\tau < \int_0^T \{(f-\lambda x)-(f^*-\lambda x^*)\}u^*\mathrm{d}\tau - \int_0^T (\dot{x}-\dot{x}^*)\,u^*\mathrm{d}\tau. \tag{3.11}$$

Now

$$\lim_{\tau\to+\infty}\{f-\lambda x)-(f^*-\lambda x^*)\}<0$$

and, consequently, the first integral on the right-hand side of (3.11) tends to $-\infty$ with T to $+\infty$. The second integral, on the other hand, remains bounded. Indeed,

$$\left|\int_0^T (\dot{x}-\dot{x}^*)\,u^*\mathrm{d}\tau\right| \leqslant u(c_s^*)\,|x(T)-x^*(T)| \leqslant u(c_s^*)\,x_+.$$

Hence, $x^*(\tau)$ is infinitely better than $x(\tau)$.

Proof of (iii) By (i), (ii) and Lemma 3.2 an indefinitely feasible x-path will be UMIT-optimal if it satisfies both (3.7) and Euler's equation:

$$(\dot{u}/u)+f'-\lambda=0 \tag{3.12}$$

over $0\leqslant\tau<+\infty$. Now, time differentiation of (3.5) yields (3.12). Thus every solution of (3.5) satisfies (3.12). To prove (iii), it will therefore be sufficient to show that (3.5) has a solution in $\{x(\tau)\}$ which satisfies (3.7).

If $x_0=\bar{x}$, this solution is obviously (3.6). We need therefore only consider the case $x_0\neq\bar{x}$. For this purpose, write (3.5) in the form

$$f(x)-\lambda x=G(c) \tag{3.13}$$

where

$$G(c)=\frac{U(\bar{c})-U(c)}{u(c)}+c. \tag{3.14}$$

We notice first that

$$G'(c)=-\frac{U(\bar{c})-U(c)}{u(c)}\cdot\frac{u'(c)}{u(c)}.$$

Thus, $G(c)$ increases strictly over $c_s < c < \bar{c}$ and decreases strictly over $\bar{c} < c < +\infty$. Moreover, the absolute and strict maximum at $c = \bar{c}$ is equal to $G(\bar{c}) = \bar{c}$.

We notice next that

$$\lim_{c \to c_S} G(c) = c_S.$$

This is obvious if $U(c_s)$ is finite. Otherwise it follows from Fig.1.

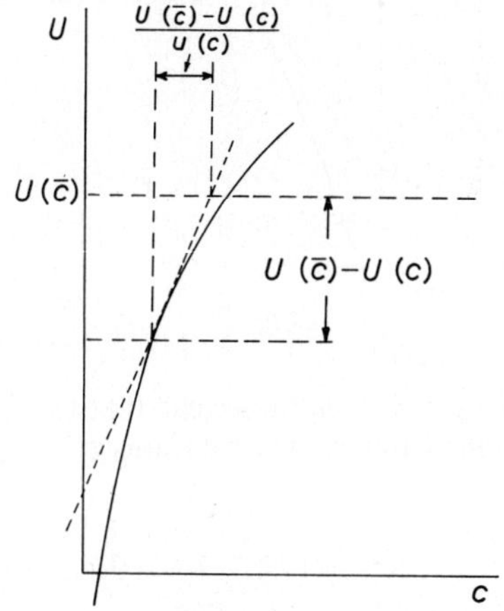

Fig. 1

Finally, we notice that (3.1) implies

$$\lim_{c \to +\infty} G(c) = \lim_{c \to +\infty} \frac{U(c)}{u(c)} \left\{ \frac{U(\bar{c})}{U(c)} - [1 - \frac{cu(c)}{U(c)}] \right\} \tag{3.15}$$

$$= \text{negative constant or} -\infty.$$

Indeed, if U has a finite upper bound over $c_S < c < +\infty$, then $(cu/U) \to 0$ and $[U(\bar{c})/U(c)] \to$ constant < 1 as $c \to +\infty$. If U is not upper-bounded, then $[U(\bar{c})/U(c)] \to 0$ as $c \to +\infty$ and

$$\lim_{c \to +\infty} \frac{cu(c)}{U(c)} = \lim_{c \to +\infty} \left(1 + \frac{cu'}{u}\right), \text{ using l'Hospital's Rule} \tag{3.16}$$

$$< 1, \text{ using (3.1)}$$

(see Fig. 2).

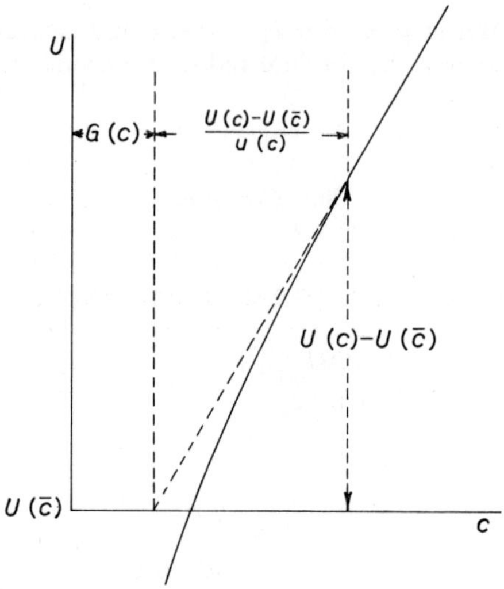

Fig. 2

Granted (3.1) and if $x_0 > \overline{x}$, it is thus clear that (3.13) has, for every $\hat{x}$ in $x_- < x < x_+$ different from $\overline{x}$, two solutions $c > c_s$, one of which, say $\hat{c} = \hat{c}(\hat{x})$, satisfies

$$(\hat{c} - \overline{c})(\hat{x} - \overline{x}) > 0. \tag{3.17}$$

(This is no longer necessarily true if (3.1) does not obtain. Consider, for instance, $U = (2\, c/\overline{c}) - (\overline{c}/c)$. Then $G \to \overline{c}/2$ as $c \to +\infty$ and (3.13) has no solution $\hat{c}$ for $x^* < \hat{x} < x_+$, where $f(x^*) - \lambda x^* = \overline{c}/2$, $x^* > \overline{x}$. Notice that U satisfies the assumptions of [K].) Moreover, with every value of $\hat{c}$, (3.5) associates, in turn, a unique value

$$\dot{\hat{x}} = G[\hat{c}(\hat{x})] - \hat{c}(\hat{x}) \tag{3.18}$$

which satisfies

$$(\hat{c} - \overline{c})\,\dot{\hat{x}} < 0, \qquad \hat{c} \neq \overline{c}$$

and, by (3.17) and (3.12), also

$$(\hat{x} - \overline{x})\,\dot{\hat{x}} < 0, \qquad \hat{x} \neq \overline{x} \tag{3.19}$$

and

$$(\hat{c} - \overline{c})\,\dot{\hat{c}} < 0, \qquad \hat{c} \neq \overline{c}, \text{ i.e. } \hat{x} \neq \overline{x}. \tag{3.20}$$

Now it can easily be verified by applying the rules of implicit differentiation to (3.13) that $\hat{c}(\hat{x})$ and, consequently, also the right-hand side of (3.18) are continuously differentiable with respect to $\hat{x}$ over $x_- < \hat{x} < x_+$. This is known to ensure the existence in the small of a unique and continuously differentiable solution $\hat{x}(\tau - t^*; x^*)$ through every value x^* in $x_- < x^* < x_+$ at time t^*. Moreover, $\hat{x}(\tau - t^*; x^*)$ can be extended before and after t^* as long as it remains both greater than x_- and smaller than x_+. (See also Observation 1 in the proof of Theorem 4.1.)

It follows that no solution of (3.18) other than (3.6) can take on the value $\bar{x}$ at any time $\tau \geqslant 0$. Thus $\hat{x}(\tau; x_0)$ and $\hat{c}(\hat{x}) = \hat{c}(\tau; x_0), x_0 \neq \bar{x}$, must satisfy (3.18), (3.19) and (3.20) over $0 \leqslant \tau + \infty$. Hence, $\hat{x}(\tau; x_0)$ belongs to $\{x(\tau)\}$, satisfies (3.9) as well as

$$\lim_{\tau \to +\infty} \hat{x}(\tau; x_0) = x_{+\infty}, \qquad x_- < x_{+\infty} < x_+ \tag{3.21}$$

where, by (3.5), $x_{+\infty} = \bar{x}$. In turn, this implies (3.8) by (3.13).

q.e.d.

4. POSITIVE TIME DISCOUNTING

We now extend Theorem 3.1 to the case $i > 0$. This extension is also dealt with by Koopmans in [K]. In this case, however, he does not establish a point which a mathematician is likely to consider as rather important. The elimination of this lacuna turns out to be far from trivial. (See below point C of the proof of Theorem 4.1.)

THEOREM 4.1 Let $\{x(\tau)\}$ and $I[x(\tau)_0^T]$ be defined by Sections 1.3 and 2.1 under the additional conditions (3.2), (3.3) and (3.4),

$$i > 0, \qquad x_- < x_0 < x_+$$

where $x_-, \bar{x}$ and x_+ satisfy Definition 3.1. Moreover, in case $x_0 > \bar{x}$, let also (3.21) hold true. Then there exists a UMIT-optimal path in $\{x(\tau)\}$. This path, say $\hat{x}(\tau)$, satisfies Euler's equation

$$(\dot{u}/u) + f'(x) - (\lambda + i) = 0, \qquad 0 \leqslant \tau < +\infty. \tag{4.1}$$

If $x_0 = \bar{x}$, it satisfies (3.6); if $x_0 \neq \bar{x}$, it satisfies (3.7), (3.8) and (3.9).

Proof of Theorem 4.1 In order to explain the general outline of the proof, it is convenient to begin with some preliminary observations.

Observation 1 Euler's equation (4.1) defines a second-order autonomous differential equation in x of the form

$$\ddot{x} = h(\dot{x}, x) \tag{4.2}$$

where

$$h(\dot{x}, x) = (f' - \lambda)\,[(u/u') + \dot{x}] - i(u/u') \tag{4.3}$$

has continuous partial first-order derivatives with respect to x and $\dot{x}$ in the region

$$R:\; 0 < x < +\infty, \qquad -\infty < \dot{x} < f(x) - \lambda x - c_s.$$

This is known to ensure that Euler's equation (4.1) has, for every point of time t^* and point $(x^*, \dot{x}^*)$ in R, a unique and twice continuously differentiable solution, say, $\tilde{x}(\tau - t^*; x^*, \dot{x}^*)$ which satisfies

$$\tilde{x}(0; x^*, \dot{x}^*) = x^*$$

and

$$\dot{\tilde{x}}(0; x^*, \dot{x}^*) = \dot{x}^*$$

and exists before and after t^* as long as $(\tilde{x}, \dot{\tilde{x}})$ lies in R. Moreover $\tilde{x}$ depends continuously on τ, x^* and $\dot{x}^*$ over its interval of existence. Given $x_0 > 0$, it will be convenient to denote by $\{ \tilde{x} \}$ the set of all initially feasible $\tilde{x}(\tau; x_0, \dot{x}_0)$, respectively defined over their entire interval of feasible existence.

Observation 2 It follows from the said uniqueness of Euler's solution through any feasible point $(t^*, x^*, \dot{x}^*)$, on the one hand, and the autonomy of (4.2), i.e. the independence of h on τ, on the other hand, that a member of $\{ \tilde{x} \}$ which is feasible over $0 \leqslant \tau < +\infty$ is necessarily monotonic everywhere. Thus, for such an $\tilde{x}$,

$$\lim_{\tau \to +\infty} \tilde{x} = x_{+\infty} \tag{4.4}$$

exists. Moreover, it can easily be deduced from Euler's equation that $x_{+\infty}$ can only be equal to either $\bar{x}$ or x_+.

Observation 3 No two members of $\{ \tilde{x} \}$ can ever meet again after $\tau = 0$, not even asymptotically. Otherwise, by Lemma 3.2 there would exist two members of $\{ \tilde{x} \}$ which would be strictly better than each other over some finite or infinite time interval! In short, $\{ \tilde{x} \}$ constitutes a so-called "central field."

Observation 4 $\tilde{x} = \bar{x}$ and $\dot{\tilde{x}} = 0$ at $\tau = t^*$ implies $\tilde{x} = \bar{x}$ over $t^* \leqslant \tau < +\infty$. This follows at once from Euler's equation (4.1) and the definition of $\bar{x}$ (Definition 3.1). Thus, in particular, $\tilde{x} = \tilde{x}(\tau; \bar{x}, 0)$ *is a solution* and, from our second observation, *the only solution which is feasible over* $0 \leqslant \tau < +\infty$ *in the case* $x_0 = \bar{x}$. In what follows, we need therefore only consider the case $x_0 \neq \bar{x}$.

Observation 5 If $x_0 \neq \bar{x}$, and $\tilde{x}$ exists over $0 \leqslant \tau < +\infty$, then $\tilde{x}$ is strictly monotonic everywhere. Indeed, Euler's equation (4.1) implies [see also (4.2) and (4.3)]

$$(\tilde{x} - \bar{x})\ddot{\tilde{x}} > 0, \text{ whenever } \dot{\tilde{x}} = 0 \text{ and } \tilde{x} \neq \bar{x}. \tag{4.5}$$

Together with Observation 2 this implies that $\tilde{x}$ must be strictly monotonic until, if at all, it reaches $\tilde{x} = \bar{x}$. Now $\tilde{x}$ cannot reach $\bar{x}$ at a finite time $t^* > 0$, since from Observation 1 and Observation 4,

$$\tilde{x}(\tau - t^*; \bar{x}, 0) = \tilde{x}(\tau; \bar{x}, 0) \neq \tilde{x}(\tau; x_0, 0), \qquad x_0 \neq \bar{x}.$$

General outline of the proof for $x_0 \neq \bar{x}$ A. The set $\{\tilde{x}\}$ can be divided into three mutually exclusive sets denoted by $\{\tilde{x}\}_1$, $\{\tilde{x}\}_2$ and $\{\tilde{x}\}_3$, where $\{\tilde{x}\}_3$ contains, if any, the only $\tilde{x}$ which is feasible over $0 \leqslant \tau < +\infty$ and satisfies (4.4) for $x_{+\infty} = \bar{x}$ (see Observations 2 and 3).

B. Unless one of them is empty, $\{\tilde{x}\}_1$ and $\{\tilde{x}\}_2$ partition the interval $-\infty < \dot{x}_0 < f(x_0) - \lambda x_0 - c_s$ of feasible $\dot{x}_0$ into two abutting and open intervals. Thus, the common end-point of these two intervals, say $\dot{x}_0^*$, cannot belong to either one of the latter. Hence, if neither $\{\tilde{x}\}_1$ nor $\{\tilde{x}\}_2$ are empty, $\tilde{x}(\tau; x_0, \dot{x}_0^*)$ exists and is the unique member of $\{\tilde{x}\}_3$ (Observation 5).

C. Under the assumptions of Theorem 4.1 neither $\{\tilde{x}\}_1$ nor $\{\tilde{x}\}_2$ can be empty. (This is not established by Koopmans [K].)

D. If $x_0 \neq \bar{x}$, $\tilde{x} \in \{\tilde{x}\}_3$ satisfies (3.7), (3.8) and (3.9).

E. $\tilde{x} \in \{\tilde{x}\}_3$ is UMIT-optimal in $\{x(\tau)\}$.

Proof of A We adopt the following definitions: $\{\tilde{x}\}_1$ is the set of all $\tilde{x} \in \{\tilde{x}\}$ which never reach the value $\bar{x}$, not even asymptotically. More preciseiy, it is the set of all $\tilde{x} \in \{\tilde{x}\}$ which neither satisfy

$$\tilde{x}(T; x_0, \dot{x}_0) = \bar{x} \tag{4.6}$$

for some $T > 0$, nor (4.4) for $x_{+\infty} = \bar{x}$.

$\{\tilde{x}\}_2$ is the set of all $\tilde{x} \in \{\tilde{x}\}$ which "cross" $\bar{x}$, i.e. for which there is a $T > 0$ such that both (4.6) and

$$\dot{\tilde{x}}(T; x_0, \dot{x}_0) \neq 0$$

hold true.

$\{x\}_3$ contains, as already said, at the most one member. It is, if it exists, the $\tilde{x} \in \{\tilde{x}\}$ which satisfies (4.4) for $x_{+\infty} = \bar{x}$.
For the sake of definitiveness, we now distinguish between $x_0 < \bar{x}$ and $x_0 > \bar{x}$.

Case of $x_0 < \bar{x}$ $\{\tilde{x}\}_1$ is then also the set of all $\tilde{x} \in \{\tilde{x}\}$ which have a maximum $\tilde{x}(T; x_0, \dot{x}_0) < \bar{x}$ at some time $T \geqslant 0$ and which increase strictly over $0 \leqslant \tau \leqslant T$ and decrease strictly to $\tilde{x} = 0$ over $T < \tau < T^*$, where T^* denotes the end-point of the interval of feasible existence of the $\tilde{x}$ in question (dotted lines on Fig. 3). This follows from (4.5), Observation 2 and the fact that Euler's equation (4.1) implies

$$\dot{\tilde{c}}(\bar{x} - \tilde{x}) > 0, \text{ whenever } \tilde{x} \neq \bar{x}. \tag{4.7}$$

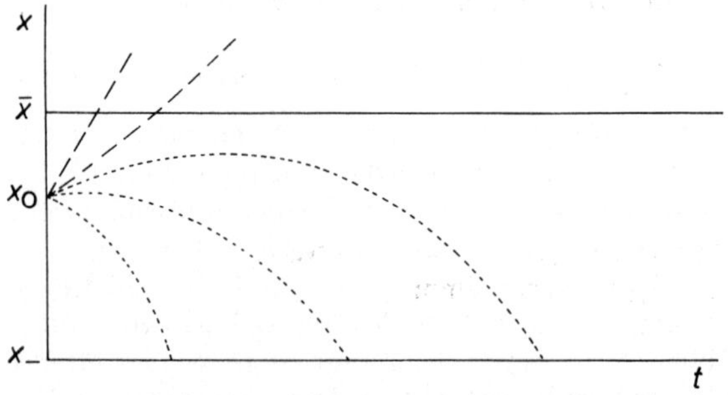

Fig. 3

If $x_0 < \bar{x}$, $\{\tilde{x}\}_2$ is also the set of all $\tilde{x} \in \{\tilde{x}\}$ which are strictly increasing over their respective intervals of feasible existence, say $0 \leqslant \tau < T^*$, and which "cross" $\bar{x}$ from below at some T in $0 < T < T^*$ (dashed lines in Fig. 3). Thus every $\tilde{x} \in \{\tilde{x}\}_2$ exists and is feasible over some interval after the time T of "crossing" $\bar{x}$. This follows from (4.5) and (4.7) (remember that $\tilde{c}$ is continuous from Observation 1).

If $x_0 < \bar{x}$, the only member of $\{x\}_3$, if any, is strictly monotonically increasing over $0 \leqslant \tau < +\infty$ (Observation 5).

Case of $x_0 > \bar{x}$ Then $\{\tilde{x}\}_1$ is also the set of all $\tilde{x} \in \{\tilde{x}\}$ which have a minimum $\tilde{x}(T; x_0, \dot{x}_0) > \bar{x}$ at some time $T \geqslant 0$ and which decrease strictly over $0 \leqslant \tau \leqslant T$ and increase strictly over $T < \tau < T^*$, where $T^* > T$ denotes, as before, the end-point of the interval of feasible existence of the $\tilde{x}$ in question (dotted lines in Fig. 4). This follows from (4.5) and the fact that

$$f(x) - \lambda x > c_s, \qquad \bar{x} < x < x_+. \tag{4.8}$$

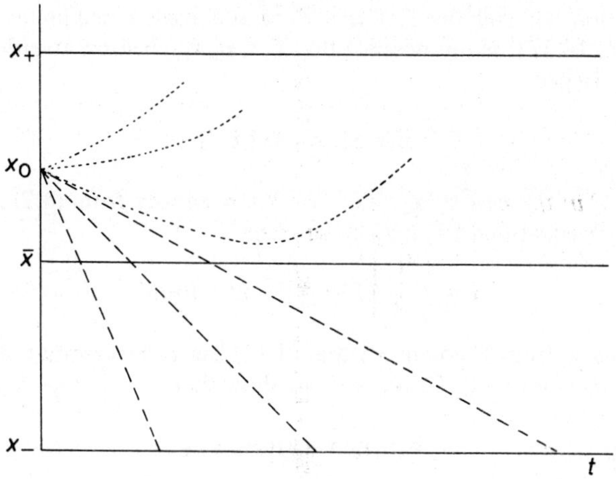

Fig. 4

If $x_0 > \bar{x}$, $\{\tilde{x}\}_2$ is also the set of all $\tilde{x} \in \{\tilde{x}\}$ which are strictly decreasing from $\tilde{x} = x_0$ to $\tilde{x} = 0$ over some finite interval $0 \leqslant \tau \leqslant T^*$. They consequently "cross" $\bar{x}$ from above at some time $T < T^*$ (dashed lines in Fig. 4). By virtue of Observation 5 it is also seen that the only member of $\{\tilde{x}\}_3$, if any, is a strictly decreasing function over $0 \leqslant \tau < +\infty$.

Proof of B in the case of $x_0 < \bar{x}$ All $\tilde{x} \in \{\tilde{x}\}$ which satisfy $\dot{\tilde{x}}(0; x_0, \dot{x}_0) = \dot{x}_0 \leqslant 0$ are strictly decreasing from $\tilde{x} = x_0$ to $\tilde{x} = 0$ by virtue of (4.3). They belong, therefore, to $\{\tilde{x}\}_1$ which is not empty. Moreover, if $\tilde{x}(\tau; x_0, \dot{x}_{01})$ belongs to $\{\tilde{x}\}_1$, then also all $\tilde{x}(\tau; x_0, \dot{x}_0)$ where $\dot{x}_0 < \dot{x}_{01}$. This follows from the fact that $\{\tilde{x}\}$ is a central field (Observation 3). Similarly, if $\tilde{x}(\tau; x_0, \dot{x}_{02})$ belongs to $\{\tilde{x}\}_2$, then also all $\tilde{x}(\tau; x_0, \dot{x}_0)$ where $\dot{x}_0 < \dot{x}_{02}$.

If $\{\tilde{x}\}_2$ is not empty, it follows that $\sup(\dot{x}_0;\ \tilde{x} \in \{\tilde{x}\}_1) = \inf(\dot{x}_0;\ \tilde{x} \in \{\tilde{x}\}_2) = \dot{x}_{03}$ exists and is positive. Hence, neither $\{\tilde{x}\}_1$ nor $\{\tilde{x}\}_2$ can be closed, i.e.

$$\tilde{x}(\tau; x_0, \dot{x}_{03}) \in \{\tilde{x}\}_3 \qquad \text{(see Observation 1).}$$

Proof of B in the case of $x_0 > \bar{x}$ $\{\tilde{x}\}_1$ is not empty since, by virtue of (4.5), all $\tilde{x} \in \{\tilde{x}\}$ which satisfy $\dot{\tilde{x}}(0; x_0, \dot{x}_0) = \dot{x}_0 \geqslant 0$ are strictly increasing over their interval of feasible existence. Now if $\{\tilde{x}\}_2$ is not empty.

$$\dot{x}_{03} = \inf\,[\dot{x}_0; \tilde{x}(\tau; x_0, \dot{x}_0) \in \{\tilde{x}\}_1]$$

exists. By virtue of the continuous dependence of $\tilde{x}$ on $\dot{x}_0$ and on τ (Observation 1), and the fact that $\tilde{x}$ cannot have a maximum above $\bar{x}$ because of (4.5) it is not possible that $\tilde{x}(\tau; x_0, \dot{x}_{03})$ belongs to either $\{\tilde{x}\}_1$ or $\{\tilde{x}\}_2$. Hence

$$\tilde{x}(\tau; x_0, \dot{x}_{03}) \in \{\tilde{x}\}_3.$$

Proof of C in the case of $x_0 < \bar{x}$ We know already from (4.2) and (4.3) that Euler's equation (4.1) may be written

$$\ddot{x} = (f' - \lambda)\,[(u/u') + \dot{x}] - i(u/u'). \tag{4.9}$$

We know also from Theorem 3.1 that (4.12) has, *ceteris paribus*, a solution $\hat{x}^*(\tau) \in \{x(\tau)\}$ for $i = 0$. To prove C, we show that

$$\tilde{x}[\tau; x_0, \hat{\dot{x}}^*(0)] \in \{\tilde{x}\}_2. \tag{4.10}$$

Writing $\bar{x}^*$ for the value of $\bar{x}$ if $i = 0$, i.e. for the solution of $f'(\bar{x}^*) = \lambda$, we first notice that $\bar{x}^* > \bar{x}$. We next observe that $[-i(u/u')] > 0$ and, consequently,

$$\tilde{\dot{x}}[0; x_0, \hat{\dot{x}}(0)] > \hat{\dot{x}}^*(0). \tag{4.11}$$

Hence, from the continuity of both $\tilde{\dot{x}}$ and $\hat{\dot{x}}^*$, either (4.10) holds true or $\tilde{x}[\tau; x_0, \hat{\dot{x}}^*(0)]$ crosses $\hat{x}^*(\tau)$ before $\hat{x}^* = \bar{x}$. In the latter case, there must be a first time $T > 0$ such that

$$\tilde{x}[T; x_0, \dot{x}^*(0)] = \hat{x}^*(T)$$

$$\tilde{x}[\tau; x_0, \hat{\dot{x}}^*(0)] > \hat{x}^*(T). \qquad 0 < \tau < T$$

Writing shortly $\tilde{x}^* = \tilde{x}[\tau; x_0, \hat{\dot{x}}^*(0)]$, this implies, however,

$$\int_0^T [U(\hat{c}^*) - U(\tilde{c}^*)]\mathrm{d}\tau$$

$$< i\int_0^T (\hat{x}^* - \tilde{x}^*)\mathrm{d}\tau$$

$$< 0$$

contrary to the definition of $\hat{x}^*(\tau)$. Thus (4.10) must obtain.

Proof of C in the case of $x_0 > \bar{x}$ For this case, it will be convenient to express Euler's equation (4.9) in the form

$$\ddot{\kappa} = (1-\alpha)\left(1 - \lambda\kappa - \frac{\dot{\kappa}}{1-\alpha}\right)\left\{\frac{u}{cu'}[f' - (\lambda + i)] + \frac{\dot{\kappa}}{\kappa}\left[\frac{\alpha}{1-\alpha} - \frac{\lambda\kappa}{(1-\lambda\kappa) - \dot{\kappa}/(1-\alpha)}\right]\right\} \tag{4.12}$$

where $\alpha = xf'/f$ denotes the elasticity of production with respect to capital and $\kappa = x/f$ the capital-output ratio. We show that (4.12) has a solution $\tilde{\kappa}(\tau;\ \kappa_0,\ \dot{\kappa}_0)$ which decreases in a strictly concave way to $\tilde{\kappa} = \bar{\kappa}$. The corresponding $\tilde{x}(\tau; x_0, \dot{x}_0)$ then belongs to $\{\ \tilde{x}\ \}_2$.

To begin with, notice that

$$\alpha^* = \min\left\{\alpha(x); \bar{x} \leqslant x \leqslant x_+\right\}$$

exists and satisfies $0 < \alpha^* < 1$. Hence, if $\dot{\kappa} < 0$ and $\bar{x} \leqslant x \leqslant x_+$, the expression between the braces in (4.12) is smaller than

$$\frac{2(\lambda + i)}{\nu} + \frac{\dot{\kappa}}{\bar{\kappa}} \cdot \frac{\alpha^*}{1-\alpha^*} + \lambda \tag{4.13}$$

where $-\nu$ denotes the negative constant in (3.1). Now (4.13) and, consequently, $\ddot{\kappa}$ will be negative if

$$\dot{\kappa} < -\left[\lambda + \frac{2(\lambda + i)}{\nu}\right]\frac{\kappa_+(1-\alpha^*)}{\alpha^*}. \tag{4.14}$$

Choosing $\dot{\kappa}_0$ negative enough to satisfy (4.14) it is seen that $\tilde{\kappa}(\tau;\ \kappa_0,\ \dot{\kappa}_0)$ decreases in a strictly concave way from κ_0 to $\bar{\kappa}$.

q.e.d.

5. CONCLUSION

It has been seen that more severe conditions must be imposed on the utility function $U(c)$ in the case $x_0 > \bar{x}$ than in the case $x_0 < \bar{x}$. As already mentioned in the introduction, this is a very surprising result. It means that a given utility index $I[x(\tau)_0^T]$ may or may not determine a UMIT-optimal policy depending on whether the initial wealth of the economy does or does not exceed a certain value (expressed in terms of x). In other words, whether or not an economy characterized by a certain production process and by certain growth preferences can launch a UMIT-optimal growth program, may depend on past history in a way which is contrary to intuition.

This is not the first instance where the specification of the growth model imposes some restrictions on the specification of the utility index $I[x(\tau)_0^T]$. It is known, indeed, that the existence of a UMIT-optimal path may require the time discount rate i to be no smaller than some positive constant depending on the rate of technological progress (see Papers 1 and 3). What is especially surprising in the present case, however, is that additional wealth may impose an additional constraint on the preference pattern of an economy which wants to apply the UMIT criterion.

Paper 3

PARTICULAR CASE OF A PROGRESSING TECHNOLOGY

INTRODUCTION

In a noteworthy contribution [K] to the literature on optimal growth, Koopmans has stated two basic theorems that establish the feasibility of Utllity Maximization over Infinite Time under a constant technology. It is the purpose of this paper to show that these two theorems can be easily extended to the case of a progressing technology in a particular, but important case.

OBJECTIVES

(1) Granted that Utility Maximization over Infinite Time (UMIT) is feasible under a constant technology, give a very simple proof that UMIT is also feasible under positive technological progress in the case of a Cobb-Douglas production function and a marginal utility function of the Bernoulli vintage.

(2) Show that UMIT under technological progress is only feasible if the utility of future consumption is discontinued at a rate i not smaller than some given minimum value i_0 which may be positive.

(3) Discuss the essential features of the optimal path ascertained under (1).

PLAN

1. The growth assumptions
2. The preference assumptions
3. No technological progress and no time discounting
4. Technological progress and minimum time discounting under no Bliss

5. No technological progress and positive time discounting under Bliss
6. Technological progress and arbitrarily large time discounting
7. Discussion of the results
8. A numerical illustration
9. Post-scriptum on the UMIT savings path

1. THE GROWTH ASSUMPTIONS

1.1 The variables

x – capital stock per worker, i.e. per labor unit
y – production flow per worker
c – consumption flow per worker
L – labor force
P – population

1.2 The growth model

1.2.1 At any given instant of time, i.e. at any given level of technology, the production flow per worker is a Cobb-Douglas function of the capital stock per worker only:

$$y = \exp[\rho\tau]x^{\alpha}, \qquad 0 \leqslant \tau < +\infty, 0 \leqslant x < +\infty$$

where $0 < \alpha < 1$.

1.2.2 Technology progresses autonomously at the constant rate $\rho \geqslant 0$ (see Section 1.2.1 above).

1.2.3 Labor and population grow autonomously and proportionally at the constant and positive rate λ:

$$L = L_0 \exp[\lambda\tau], P = P_0 \exp[\lambda\tau], \qquad 0 \leqslant \tau < +\infty$$

where $L_0 > 0$, $P_0 > 0$ and $\lambda > 0$ are given.

1.2.4 The flow of investment per worker $(\lambda x + \dot{x})$ is a piece-wise continuous function of time over $0 \leqslant \tau < +\infty$.

1.2.5 The economy is closed in the sense that there is no net long-term capital transfer. In other words, consumption is the difference between production and investment.

$$c = \exp[\rho\tau]x^{\alpha} - \lambda x - \dot{x}, \qquad 0 \leqslant \tau < +\infty$$

at all points of continuity of $\dot{x}(\tau)$.

1.3 The set of feasible growth paths

In view of the fact that the growth assumptions, Section 1.2, associate one and only one growth path $[x(\tau), y(\tau), c(\tau)]$ with every path $x(\tau)$, the set of feasible growth paths can be stated in terms of x only. We denote this set by $\{x(\tau)\}$ and define it as the set of all $x(\tau)$, $0 \leqslant \tau < +\infty$, which start from the historically given capital stock per worker x_0, satisfy the assumptions of Section 1.2 and, moreover, always maintain the consumption flow per worker c above zero.

More precisely, given $x_0 > 0$, $\rho \geqslant 0$, $\lambda > 0$ and $0 < \alpha < 1$, one has

$$x(t) \in \{x(\tau)\}$$

if *(i)* $x(0) = x_0$, *(ii)* $x(\tau)$ is defined positive and piece-wise continuously differentiable over $0 \leqslant \tau < +\infty$ and *(iii)* $-\infty < \dot{x}(\tau) < \exp[\rho\tau]x^{\alpha}(\tau) - \lambda x(\tau)$, $0 \leqslant \tau < +\infty$, at all points of continuity of $\dot{x}(\tau)$.

2. THE PREFERENCE ASSUMPTIONS

2.1 The utility index

2.1.2 The national preference pattern with respect to instantaneous consumption can be described by any linear transformation of a function of the consumption flow per worker (remember that L/P is constant). This "utility" function $U(c)$ satisfies

$$U'(c) = c^{-\nu}, \qquad \nu < 0$$

where ν is constant.

2.1.2 The national preference pattern for postponed consumption can be accounted for by a non-negative and constant time discount rate i. More precisely, the utility at time t_0 of a consumption flow c at time t_1 can be described by

$$U[c(t_1)]\exp[-i(t_1 - t_0)], \qquad 0 \leqslant t_0 < t_1 < +\infty.$$

2.1.3 The nation prefers the feasible path $x^*(\tau)$ to the feasible path $x(\tau)$ if there is a $T^* \geqslant 0$ such that

$$I[x^*(\tau)_0^T] - I[x(\tau)_0^T] > 0, \qquad T \geqslant T^*$$

where

$$I[x(\tau)_0^T] = \int_0^T U[c(\tau)]\exp[-i\tau]\mathrm{d}\tau$$

i.e. if the sum over time of the discounted utilities of consumption per capita is ultimately greater along $x^*(\tau)$ than along $x(\tau)$ (Weisszäcker's overtaking principle [W]). A feasible path $x^*(t)$ is called UMIT-optimal if it is preferred to all other feasible paths in the above sense. By definition, Utility Maximization over Infinite Time is achieved along such a most preferred path, if any.

2.2 The form of the utility function

Depending on whether $\nu \neq 1$ or $\nu = 1$, integration of the marginal utility $c^{-\nu}$ gives any linear transformation of

$$U(c) = c^{1-\nu}/(1-\nu) \tag{2.1}$$

$$U(c) = \ln c. \tag{2.2}$$

Thus $U(c)$ has a finite upper-band *(Bliss level)* if, and only if, $\nu > 1$.

3. NO TECHNOLOGICAL PROGRESS AND NO TIME DISCOUNTING

This is the first of Koopmans' two theorems (Theorem 3.1 in Paper 2) and is of special interest, because it gives a first integral of Euler's equation. In other words, it states a first (and not only second) order differential equation which the UMIT-optimal path has to satisfy [see (3.2) below].

THEOREM 3.1 Let $\{x(\tau)\}$ and $I[x(\tau)_0^T]$ be respectively defined by Sections 1.3 and 2.1 under the additional conditions $\rho = i = 0$ and

$$0 < x_0 < (1/\lambda)^{1/(1-a)}. \tag{3.1}$$

Then there exists a UMIT-optimal path in $\{x(\tau)\}$. This path, say $\hat{x}(\tau)$, satisfies the first-order differential equation,

$$\dot{x}U'(c) = U(\bar{c}) - U(c), \qquad 0 \leqslant \tau < +\infty. \tag{3.2}$$

where

$$\bar{c} = (1-\alpha)\bar{x}^a$$

denotes the so-called "Golden Rule" value of c defined by

$$\bar{x} = (\alpha/\lambda)^{1/(1-a)}. \tag{3.3}$$

Moreover,

$$\lim_{\tau \to +\infty} \hat{x}(\tau) = \bar{x} \tag{3.4}$$

$$\lim_{\tau \to +\infty} \hat{c}(\tau) = \bar{c} \tag{3.5}$$

and

$$\dot{\hat{x}}(\tau)\,\dot{\hat{c}}(\tau) > 0, \qquad t \leqslant \tau < +\infty, \tag{3.6}$$

whenever $\hat{x}(t) \neq \bar{x}$, $t \geqslant 0$.

4. TECHNOLOGICAL PROGRESS AND MINIMUM TIME DISCOUNTING UNDER NO BLISS

We now extend Theorem 3.1 to the case of technological progress under no Bliss ($\nu \leqslant 1$). It is convenient to distinguish between $\nu < 1$ and $\nu = 1$, i.e. between the utility functions (2.1) and (2.2) [Theorems 4.1 and 4.1a].

THEOREM 4.1 Let $\{x(\tau)\}$ and $I[x(\tau)_0^T]$ be defined by Sections 1.3 and 2.1, where

$$\left.\begin{aligned} &\nu < 1, \quad \rho > 0 \\ &i = (1-\nu)\gamma, \gamma \equiv \rho/(1-\nu) \\ &0 < x_0 < [1/(\lambda + \gamma)]^{1/(1-a)} \end{aligned}\right\}. \tag{4.1}$$

Then there exists a UMIT-optimal path $\hat{x}(\tau)$ which satisfies

$$(1-\nu)(\dot{x} - \gamma x) = c^{\nu}[(\bar{c}\exp[\gamma\tau])^{1-\nu} - c^{1-\nu}], \quad 0 \leqslant \tau < +\infty \tag{4.2}$$

where

$$\bar{x} = \left(\frac{\alpha}{\lambda + \gamma}\right)^{1/(1-a)} \tag{4.3}$$

and

$$\bar{c} = (1-\alpha)\bar{x}^{a}.$$

Moreover,

$$\lim_{\tau \to +\infty} \hat{x}(\tau)/\exp[\gamma\tau] = \overline{x} \tag{4.4}$$

$$\lim_{\tau \to +\infty} \hat{c}(\tau)/\exp[\gamma\tau] = \overline{c} \tag{4.5}$$

and

$$[(\dot{\hat{x}}/\hat{x}) - \gamma]\ [(\dot{\hat{c}}/\hat{c}) - \gamma] > 0, \qquad t \leqslant \tau < +\infty \tag{4.6}$$

whenever $\hat{x}(t) \neq \overline{x}\exp[\gamma t]$, $t \geqslant 0$.

Proof The proof follows at once from Theorem 3.1. Indeed, the case assumed by Theorem 4.1 is formally identical to the case defined by

$$\rho^* = i^* = 0,$$

$$\lambda^* = \lambda + \gamma \tag{4.7}$$

$$x^* = x\exp[-\gamma\tau] \tag{4.8}$$

$$\begin{aligned} c^* &= x^{*a} - \lambda^* x^* - \dot{x}^* \\ &= (\exp[\rho\tau]x^a - \lambda x - \dot{x})\exp[-\gamma\tau] \\ &= c\exp[-\gamma\tau] \end{aligned} \tag{4.9}$$

$$U^* = c^{*(1-\nu)}/(1-\nu). \tag{4.10}$$

It is easily verified that, in terms of the starred variables and parameters, (4.1)-(4.6) become, respectively, (3.1)-(3.6).

As we see in Section 6, no UMIT-optimal path can exist under the growth and preference assumptions of Sections 1.3 and 2.1 if

$$i < (1-\nu)\rho/(1-\alpha).$$

This is why

$$i_0 = (1-\nu)\rho/(1-\alpha)$$

has been referred to as the minimum time discount rate.

THEOREM 4.1a Let $\{ x(\tau) \}$ and $I[x(\tau)_0^T]$ be respectively defined by Sections 1.3 and 2.1 and the additional conditions

$$\nu = 1, \rho > 0, i = 0$$

and (4.1). Then there exists a UMIT-optimal path $\hat{x}(\tau) \in \{x(\tau)\}$ which satisfies

$$(\dot{x} - \gamma x) = c[\ln(\bar{c}/c) + \gamma\tau], \qquad 0 \leqslant \tau < +\infty$$

where $\bar{c}$ is defined as in Theorem 4.1. Moreover, $\hat{x}(\tau)$ satisfies (4.4), (4.5) and (4.6).

Proof With the change of variables (4.7), (4.8), (4.9) and

$$U^*(c^*) = \ln c^* \tag{4.11}$$

one gets

$$I[x(\tau)_0^T] = \int_0^T [\ln c^* + \gamma\tau]\, d\tau$$
$$= I[x^*(\tau)_0^T] + \tfrac{1}{2}\gamma T^2.$$

Hence, for two feasible paths $x_1(\tau)$ and $x_2(\tau)$,

$$I[x_1(\tau)_0^T] - I[x_2(\tau)_0^T] = I[x_1^*(\tau)_0^T] - I[x_2^*(\tau)_0^T].$$

As in the proof of Theorem 4.1, we are thus back to a case to which Theorem 3.1 does apply.

q.e.d.

5. NO TECHNOLOGICAL PROGRESS AND POSITIVE TIME DISCOUNTING

This is the second of Koopmans' two theorems mentioned in Paper 2. It differs from the first because it does not provide a first integral of Euler's equation. This seems to be impossible if $i < (1-\nu)\rho/(1-\alpha)$.

THEOREM 5.1 Let $\{x(\tau)\}$ and $I[x(\tau)_0^T]$ be defined by Sections 1.3 and 2.1 under the additional conditions

$$\rho = 0, i \geqslant 0$$

and (3.1). (If $i = 0$, we then have the stronger Theorem 3.1.) Then there exists a UMIT-optimal path in $\{x(\tau)\}$. This path, say $\hat{x}(\tau)$, satisfies Euler's equation

$$-(\dot{u}/u) = (\alpha/x^{1-\alpha}) - (\lambda + i), \qquad 0 \leqslant \tau < +\infty \tag{5.1}$$

as well as (3.4), (3.5) and (3.6), where $\bar{x}$ and $\bar{c}$ this time denote the, say, Golden Utility Values

$$\bar{x} = \left(\frac{\alpha}{\lambda + i}\right)^{1/(1-a)} \tag{5.2}$$

and

$$\bar{c} = (1 - \bar{s})\bar{x}^a$$

where $$\bar{s} = \alpha\lambda/(\lambda + i).$$

6. TECHNOLOGICAL PROGRESS AND ARBITRARILY LARGE TIME DISCOUNTING

We can now extend Theorems 4.1 and 4.1a to the case of an arbitrary large time discount rate.

THEOREM 6.1 Let $\{ x(\tau) \}$ and $I[x(\tau)_0^T]$ be defined by Sections 1.3 and 2.1 under the additional conditions

$$\rho > 0, i \geqslant \max\left\{0, i_0\right\}, i_0 = (1 - \nu)\gamma \tag{6.1}$$

and (4.1). (In regard to the second of these, if $i = i_0 \geqslant 0$ we have the stronger Theorems 4.1 and 4.1a.) Then there exists a UMIT-optimal path $\hat{x}(\tau)$ which satisfies Euler's equation

$$+ \nu(\dot{c}/c) = \frac{\alpha \exp[\rho\tau]}{x^{1-a}} - (\lambda + i), \qquad 0 \leqslant \tau < +\infty \tag{6.2}$$

as well as (4.4), (4.5) and (4.6); here $\bar{x}$ and $\bar{c}$ this time denote the "Golden Utility" values

$$\bar{x} = \left(\frac{\alpha}{\lambda + \gamma + i - i_0}\right)^{1/(1-a)} \qquad i_0 \equiv (1 - \nu)\gamma \tag{6.3}$$

and

$$\bar{c} = (1 - \bar{s})\bar{x}^a$$

where

$$\bar{s} = \alpha(\lambda + \gamma)/(\lambda + \gamma + i - i_0).$$

Proof It is perfectly similar to the proof of Theorem 4.1. By the same change of variables (4.7), (4.8), (4.9) and (4.10) or (4.11), the case considered by Theorem 6.1 is brought back to a case which satisfies the conditions of Theorem 5.1 for

$$\rho^* = 0$$

and

$$i^* = i - i_0. \tag{6.4}$$

q.e.d.

It is interesting to see that Theorem 6.1 no longer holds true if, *ceteris paribus*,

$$i < i_0, \qquad i = (1 - \nu)\gamma. \tag{6.5}$$

THEOREM 6.2 Let $\{ x(\tau) \}$ and $I[x(\tau)_0^T]$ be defined by Sections 1.3 and 2.1 under the conditions $\rho > 0$, (4.1) and (6.5). Then there does not exist a UMIT-optimal path in $\{ x(\tau) \}$.

Proof It is known that the satisfaction of Euler's equation

$$\frac{\partial}{\partial x}\left\{U(c)\exp[-i\tau]\right\} - \frac{\mathrm{d}}{\mathrm{d}\tau}\frac{\partial}{\partial \dot{x}}\left\{U(c)\exp[-i\tau]\right\} = 0, \qquad 0 < \tau < +\infty \tag{6.6}$$

constitutes a necessary condition for the UMIT-optimality of $\hat{x}(\tau)$. Under our assumptions, this implies (6.2) which reads, in terms of the starred variables and parameters,

$$\nu(\dot{c}^*/c^*) = \frac{\alpha}{x^{*(1-a)}} - (\lambda^* + i^*). \tag{6.7}$$

It can be shown (see, for instance, Paper 2), on the other hand, that (6.7) requires

$$\lim_{\tau \to +\infty} \hat{x}^*(\tau) = x^*_{+\infty} \tag{6.8}$$

where either

$$x^*_{+\infty} = \left(\frac{\alpha}{\lambda^* + i^*}\right)^{1/(1-a)} \tag{6.9}$$

or

$$x^*_{+\infty} = (1/\lambda^*)^{1/(1-a)}. \tag{6.10}$$

Now both (6.9) and (6.10) imply that the capital stock per worker $\hat{x}^*(\tau)$ is from some time $T^* > 0$ on indefinitely maintained above its Golden Rule value $(\alpha/\lambda^*)^{1/(1-a)}$. As known [P2], this is inefficient in the sense that there exists another path $\hat{x}(\tau) \in \{x(\tau)\}$ such that both

$$\hat{\hat{c}}(\tau) \geqslant \hat{c}(\tau), \qquad 0 \leqslant \tau < +\infty$$

and

$$\hat{\hat{c}}(t) > \hat{c}(t)$$

for some $t \geqslant 0$, i.e. such that

$$I[\hat{x}(\tau)_0^{+\infty}] - I[\hat{\hat{x}}(\tau)_0^{+\infty}] < 0,$$

contrary to the UMIT-optimality of $\hat{x}(\tau)$.

q.e.d.

Thus, there is a value of i, namely i_0, below which it becomes inefficient to apply Euler's condition (6.6). In other words, it is absurd to apply the UMIT criterion if $i < i_0$. Thus, under the assumption of no Bliss, there does not exist any UMIT-optimal solution for $i < 0$, even if one allows a negative i in the definition of Section 2.1.3 of the UMIT index $I[x(\tau)_0^T]$. Under Bliss, however, $i_0 = (1-\nu)\gamma < 0$ and a UMIT-optimal solution exists for negative values of i not smaller than i_0.

7. DISCUSSION OF THE RESULTS

We now turn to the discussion of the results established by Theorems 4.1, 4.1a and 6.1. For this purpose, it is convenient to distinguish between $0 < x_0 < \bar{x}$, $x_0 = \bar{x}$ and $\bar{x} < x_0 < x_+$, where, as before

$$\bar{x} = \left(\frac{\alpha}{\lambda + \gamma + i - i_0}\right)^{1/(1-a)}, \qquad i_0 = \gamma(1-\nu) \qquad \gamma = \rho/(1-\alpha) \tag{7.1}$$

and

$$x_+ = [1/(\lambda + \gamma)]^{1/(1-a)}. \tag{7.2}$$

Case of $x_0 = \bar{x}$ The UMIT-optimal path coincides with the Golden Utility path:

$$\hat{x} = \bar{x}\exp[\gamma\tau] \tag{7.3}$$

$$\bar{c} = (1-\bar{s})\bar{x}^{a}\exp[\gamma\tau] \tag{7.4}$$

$$\hat{s} = \bar{s}\,.$$

Case of $x_0 \neq \bar{x}$ The UMIT-optimal x and c paths, i.e. $\hat{x}(\tau)$ and $\hat{c}(\tau)$, tend, in relative terms, strictly monotonically to their respective Golden Utility paths (7.3) and (7.4).

Case of $0 < x_0 < \bar{x}$ The growth rates of both $\hat{x}(\tau)$ and $\hat{c}(\tau)$ (dashed lines in Figs 1 and 2) are always greater than γ. This means that per capita, consumption always grows faster than technology. This is very satisfactory.

Case of $\bar{x} < x_0 < x_+$ Both $\hat{x}(\tau)$ and $\hat{c}(\tau)$ always grow at a smaller rate than γ and initially may even decrease (dotted lines in Figs 1 and 2). As a matter of fact, $\hat{c}(\tau)$ decreases if (and only if)

$$x_0 > \left(\frac{\alpha}{\lambda + i}\right)^{1/(1-a)} \tag{7.5}$$

This is much less satisfactory.

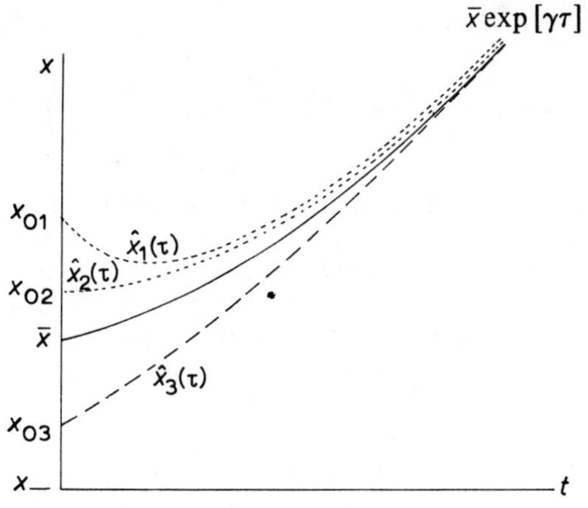

Fig. 1

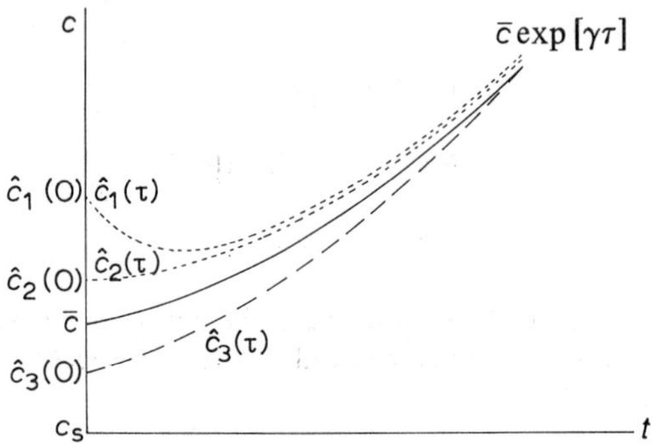

Fig. 2

Notice, however, that the initial situation $x_0 > \bar{x}$ can only arise "historically" if a UMIT-unoptimal growth policy has been previously followed. Indeed, granted our growth assumptions, the capital stock must be historically accumulated out of savings, i.e. there must have been a time when the capital-output ratio $\kappa = x/y$ had a smaller value than the Golden Utility value

$$\bar{\kappa} = \alpha/(\lambda + \gamma + i - i_0).$$

Now, no UMIT-optimal $\hat{\kappa}(\tau)$ can ever cross $\bar{\kappa}$ in a finite period of time, i.e. accumulate a capital stock per worker x_0 at time $\tau = 0$ greater than the Golden Utility stock

$$\bar{x} = \left(\frac{\alpha}{\lambda + \gamma + i - i_0}\right)^{1/(1-a)} = \left(\frac{\alpha}{\lambda + i + \nu\gamma}\right)^{1/(1-a)}$$

and, *a fortiori,* greater than the right-hand side of (7.5).

Within the present framework, *an initially decreasing UMIT-optimal c-path must therefore be considered as the best way to dispose of a "wrongly" accumulated great "surplus" of capital.* The initial slope of this decrease is steeper, the greater the national impatience to consume, i.e. the greater the time discount rate i. This follows from Euler's equation (6.2) for $\tau = 0$.

A nation which inherits such a "surplus" capital stock is naturally better off at any time in the future than a nation which does not (Fig. 2). This does not alter the fact, however, that an initially decreasing consumption per capita path can hardly be regarded as an attractive proposition by a real policy maker, especially in a situation of capital "surplus".

Another unsatisfactory aspect of an initially decreasing UMIT path is that, in practice, the prescribed rate of capital disinvestment may exceed what is feasible under the condition that disinvestment can only take place through natural depreciation or the consumption of stocks.

We come to the conclusion therefore that, if at all, the *UMIT criterion applies only to the case*

$$x_0 \leqslant [\alpha/(\lambda + i)]^{1/(1-a)}. \tag{7.6}$$

Now this conclusion has a very important consequence. Indeed, (7.6) and the condition $i \geqslant i_0$ imply together

$$(\alpha/x_0^{1-a}) - \lambda \geqslant i \geqslant i_0 = (1-\nu)\gamma \tag{7.7}$$

i.e. that there is not only a lower, but also an upper limit to the value of i. The question whether or not (7.7) will generally be satisfied, must therefore be raised. Notice that it is certainly satisfied if both

$$x_0 \leqslant \left(\frac{\alpha}{\lambda + \gamma}\right)^{1/(1-a)} \tag{7.8}$$

and

$$\gamma \geqslant i \geqslant (1-\nu)\gamma \tag{7.9}$$

obtain. Since, as we see below, (7.4) generally applies in practice, (7.9) shows that a reasonable UMIT-optimal solution generally exists for some value of i.

It is true that the range of admissible values of i defined by (7.7) and *a fortiori* by (7.9) may be very small. Granted the assumption of a constant time discount rate, however, (7.7) may not be as restrictive as it appears to be at first sight. Indeed, it may be argued that the value of a time discount rate to which a nation is going to adhere for the whole of the future should not be chosen on the basis of the present level of consumption, but rather on the grounds that this level tends to grow exponentially after, at the most, some initial period of time. Loosely speaking, the level of per capita consumption will be extremely high over most of the future. It may thus be argued that one should choose i equal to its minimum value i_0. However, this argument of, say, "minimum impatience", rests on the assumption of a constant time discount rate i. Now, this assumption constitutes certainly an important weakness of the UMIT criterion. This aspect of the UMIT criterion, as well as the meaning of i_0 is discussed in detail elsewhere (see Part 1, Sections 3.41 and 3.42).

Let us next turn to another important question that must be raised in connection with the UMIT criterion. We know by now that $\dot{\hat{c}}(\tau)$ is positive over $0 < \tau < +\infty$ if $x_0 \leqslant \bar{x}$. We do not know, however, whether or not $\hat{c}(0)$ is too "low", i.e. whether or not the optimal savings policy $\hat{s}(\tau)$ is initially too "high" to be practically enforceable. All we know is that

$$0 < \hat{c}(0) \leqslant \bar{c}$$

i.e. that

$$1 - (\bar{c}/x_0^\alpha) \leqslant \hat{s}(0) < 1.$$

This is not much, indeed. What is worse, we cannot even answer the question of whether $\hat{s}(\tau)$ is monotonic or not, since this implies some knowledge of $\ddot{\hat{x}}(\tau)$ which we do not possess. [Meanwhile, I was able to show that $\hat{s}(\tau)$ approaches $\bar{s}$ monotonically from above if $(x_0 - \bar{x})(1 - \alpha\nu) < 0$, and from below if $(x_0 - \bar{x})(1 - \alpha\nu) > 0$.]

According to some previous investigations by Tinbergen and Bos, under different growth assumptions, $\hat{s}(\tau)$ may very well exceed the values which are generally considered as reasonable [TB]. We therefore computed a numerical solution, which is explained in the next section. The results turn out to be quite reasonable.

To complete this section, let us show that (7.8), i.e.

$$\alpha/\kappa_0 \geqslant \lambda + \gamma$$

is generally satisfied in practice, at least by economies which can be expected to fulfill our growth assumptions (Section 1.2).

If the traditional ranges of values ¼ to ⅓ for α and 3 to 5 for κ are accepted, the following table of values for the marginal product of capital α/κ results.

TABLE 7.1 Marginal product of capital, α/κ

α	α/κ, %, for κ equal to		
	3	4	5
¼	8	6	5
⅓	11	8	6.7

Now, according to the statistical yearbook of the United Nations, there is no (non-communist) economy which has sustained a net per capita growth rate higher than 8% over any period of, say 10 years. Furthermore, even if Japan, Germany and Italy have made an extremely good showing over the '50s, it is rather doubtful whether any one of these economies or, in general, any economy at all could sustain a 6% per capita growth rate in the very long run. Or, if this should be proved possible, as I would very much like it to be, it would most probably indicate that technological progress is not as independent of the savings ratio as Section 1.2 assumes. In other words, it is probable that Section 1.2 would no longer apply to such high growth-rate economies. One may therefore conclude that the bulk of the economies which satisfy the growth assumptions of Section 1.2 also satisfy (7.9).

8. A NUMERICAL ILLUSTRATION

We consider an economy which satisfies the growth and performance assumptions of Sections 1.2 and 2.1 for $\nu = 1$. Thus

$$x/y_0 = (\kappa/\kappa_0)^{a/(1-a)}\exp[\gamma\tau]$$

and

$$U(c) = \ln c\,.$$

The values of the growth parameters and the initial conditions are chosen to fit, *grosso modo,* the US economy:

$$\begin{aligned}&\alpha = 1/3,\ \rho = 4/300,\ \lambda = 1/100\\ &\kappa_0 = 3.5 \text{ years},\ y_0 = 2{,}400 \text{ US \$}.\end{aligned} \tag{8.1}$$

Hence, for

$$i = 6.5\% \tag{8.2}$$

the UMIT-optimal κ and c paths are the balanced growth paths

$$\kappa_1(\tau) = \kappa_0\exp[\gamma\tau], \qquad 0 \leqslant \tau < +\infty$$

$$\hat{c}_1(\tau) = [1 - (\lambda + \gamma)\kappa_0]\kappa_0^{a/(1-a)}\exp[\gamma\tau], \qquad 0 \leqslant \tau < +\infty$$

where

$$(\lambda + \gamma)\kappa_0 = \hat{s}_1 = 10.5\%.$$

Now, 10.5% is roughly the net long-term post-war savings ratio of the US. In other words, the behaviour of the US economy would not be very different from what it actually is (dashed lines on Fig. 3), if:

(a) it really satisfied the growth assumptions of Section 1.2 for the values (8.1) of the parameters and initial conditions;

(b) it really applied the UMIT criterion defined by Section 2.1, (2.2) and (8.2).

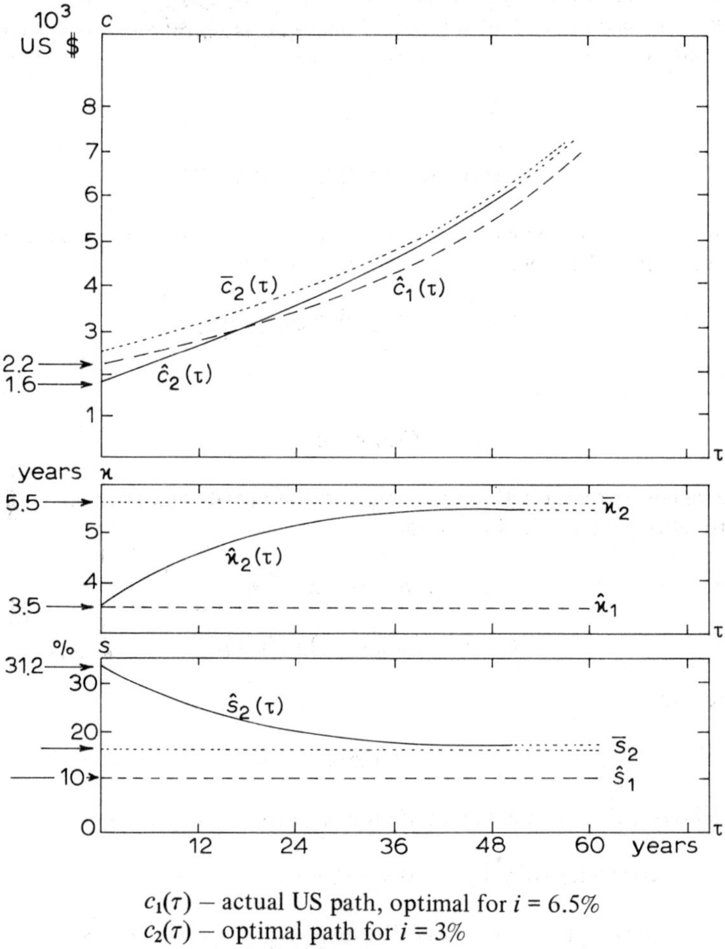

$c_1(\tau)$ – actual US path, optimal for $i = 6.5\%$

$c_2(\tau)$ – optimal path for $i = 3\%$

$$\lim_{\tau\to+\infty} \frac{\hat{c}_2(\tau)}{\bar{c}_2(\tau)} = 1; \frac{\bar{c}_2(\tau)}{\hat{c}_1(\tau)} \approx 1.16.$$

Fig. 3

Granted (a), it is interesting to see the nature of the UMIT-optimal US path, *ceteris paribus,* for a lower time discount rate, say $i = 3\%$. This path (full lines in Fig. 3) has been graciously tabulated by Bull Netherlands N.V.

It is seen that the optimal capital-output ratio, say $\hat{k}_2(\tau)$, increases monotonically from 3.5 years to the asymptotic value of 5.55 years (dotted line in Fig. 3). The savings ratio decreases monotonically from the initial value of 31.2% to the asymptotic value of 16.7% (dotted line in Fig. 3). *The optimal savings path is thus nowhere excessively high.* It is likely, however, that the initial value of the savings ratio would be much higher for a lower discount rate.

It can also be seen that the optimal c-path, $\hat{c}_2(\tau)$, starts off at the relatively high level of 1,600 US \$ and "catches up" with $\hat{c}_1(\tau)$ only after 13 years. Thereafter, $\hat{c}_2(\tau) > \hat{c}_1(\tau)$.

Moreover,

$$\lim_{t \to +\infty} \frac{\hat{c}_2(\tau)}{\hat{c}_1(\tau)} = 1.16.$$

Thus, over "most" of the future, path 2 yields a consumption flow about 15% higher than path 1.

The interesting fact is that the initial consumption loss is more than compensated for during the average lifetime of a citizen. This seems to indicate that 6.5% is a rather high value for i and that, within the framework of this "logical experiment" the US economy would do well to increase its saving ratio. (It must be stressed that this is not meant to be a practical advice. The "logical experiment" in question rests on too many hypothetical assumptions.)

9. POST-SCRIPTUM ON THE UMIT SAVINGS PATH

After this book was completed, I established the following theorem.

THEOREM 9.1 Let $\{x(\tau)\}$ and $I[x(\tau)_0^{+\infty}]$ be defined by Sections 1.3 and 2.1 under the additional conditions

$$\begin{gathered} i \geqslant \max\{0, i_0\}, \qquad i_0 = (1 - \nu)\gamma \\ \nu \leqslant 1/\alpha. \end{gathered} \tag{9.1}$$

Then, the UMIT-optimal savings path $\hat{s}(\tau)$ satisfies both

$$[\hat{s}(\tau) - \bar{s}]\,(x_0 - \bar{x}) < 0, \qquad 0 \leqslant \tau < +\infty \tag{9.2}$$

$$\dot{\hat{s}}(\tau)\,(x_0 - \bar{x}) \geqslant 0, \qquad 0 \leqslant \tau < +\infty. \tag{9.3}$$

Proof Writing $\kappa = x/y = x^{1-\alpha}\exp[-\rho\tau]$ and using the identity

$$\dot{\kappa}/\kappa = [(s/\kappa) - (\gamma + \lambda)]\,(1 - \alpha).$$

Euler's equation (6.2) can be put in the form

$$-\frac{\dot{s}}{1-s} = \left(\frac{1}{\nu} - \alpha\right)\left[\frac{\alpha}{\kappa} - (\gamma + \lambda)\right] + (\alpha - \bar{s})\frac{\alpha}{\kappa} - \frac{1}{\nu}(i - i_0) + (\bar{s} - s)\frac{\alpha}{\kappa} \tag{9.4}$$

where $\bar{s} = (\gamma + \lambda)\bar{\kappa}$. We know from Theorem 6.1, on the other hand, that

$$\frac{\alpha}{\hat{\kappa}} - [\gamma + \lambda + i - i_0]\begin{cases} > 0 \text{ if } x_0 < \bar{x} \\ < 0 \text{ if } x_0 > \bar{x} \end{cases} \tag{9.5}$$

obtains over $0 \leqslant \tau < +\infty$, and that

$$\lim_{\tau \to +\infty} \hat{s}(\tau) = \bar{s} = \frac{\gamma + \lambda}{\gamma + \lambda + i - i_0}. \tag{9.6}$$

Now (9.1), (9.4) and (9.5) imply

$$-\frac{\dot{\hat{s}}}{1-\hat{s}} > \left(\frac{1}{\nu} - \alpha\right)(i - i_0) + \alpha(i - i_0) - \frac{1}{\nu}(i - i_0) + (\bar{s} - \hat{s})$$

$$= (\bar{s} - \hat{s}), \qquad 0 \leqslant \tau < +\infty \tag{9.7}$$

provided only that $x_0 < \bar{x}$. Similarly $x_0 > \bar{x}$ implies

$$-\frac{\dot{\hat{s}}}{1-\hat{s}} < (\bar{s} - \hat{s}), \qquad 0 \leqslant \tau < +\infty. \tag{9.8}$$

It therefore follows that $[\hat{s}(t) - \bar{s}]\,(x_0 - \bar{x}) > 0$ implies $\dot{\hat{s}}(\tau)\,(x_0 - \bar{x}) < 0$, $t \leqslant \tau < +\infty$, which is contrary to (9.6). This establishes (9.2).

We notice next that (9.4) is an *autonomous* first-order differential equation of the form

$$\dot{s} = h(s, \kappa).$$

It follows that $\hat{s}(\hat{\kappa})$ is a monotonic function of $\hat{\kappa}$ over $\kappa_0 \leqslant \hat{\kappa} \leqslant \bar{\kappa}$, respectively $\bar{\kappa} \leqslant \hat{\kappa} \leqslant \kappa_0$. Since, by Theorem 6.1 $\hat{\kappa}(\tau)$ is monotonic, $\hat{s}(\tau)$ must therefore also be monotonic (over $0 \leqslant \tau < +\infty$). By (9.2) this implies (9.3).

q.e.d.

Paper 4

AN EXPLICIT SOLUTION

INTRODUCTION

Present day theory of optimal economic growth is essentially based on the criterion known as Utility Maximization over Infinite Time, or, shortly, UMIT. This states that a nation should maximize the sum of the instantaneous utilities of per capita consumption over the infinite future.

Research on the UMIT criterion can be and has been directed along three main lines:

(1) the establishment of necessary and sufficient conditions for the existence of a UMIT-optimal solution;

(2) the derivation of the general properties of the UMIT criterion on the basis of the conditions established under (1);

(3) the inference of the general properties of the UMIT criterion on the basis of some particular explicit UMIT solution(s).

This paper follows approach (3). An important advantage of this approach lies in the fact that it yields some crucial information on the UMIT-optimal savings path. Another advantage of an explicit UMIT solution is that it enables us to determine at least in a particular case, how much relative utility is lost by following any other non-optimal growth policy. We exploit both these advantages in this paper.

OBJECTIVES

(1) Derive an explicit UMIT-optimal solution in a particular, but theoretically important case. The general assumptions are that the economy is a closed Cobb-Douglas economy characterized by a constant non-negative rate of technological progress and an exponentially growing and fully employed labor force. The particular assumptions are that the time discount rate has the minimum value at which UMIT is feasible [under our

assumptions, this value will be positive if and only if the rate of technological progress is positive (see Paper 3)] and both the elasticity of production with respect to capital and the elasticity of the marginal utility of per capita consumption (Frisch's flexibility) are equal to ½.

(2) Draw some general conclusions from the particular results established under (1), especially as to the form of the UMIT-optimal savings path.

(3) Compare the sum of the instantaneous utilities of per capita consumption under the UMIT-optimal savings policy and under the constant savings policy (constant savings ratio) towards which the UMIT policy is known to tend asymptotically. [The UMIT-optimal savings path is known to tend to a well defined constant value (see Paper 3).]

PLAN

1. The growth assumptions
2. The preference assumptions
3. An explicit UMIT-optimal solution
4. Sharpness of the UMIT optimum
5. Interpretation of the results

1. THE GROWTH ASSUMPTIONS

1.1 The variables

x – capital stock per worker, i.e. per labor unit
y – production flow per worker
c – consumption flow per worker
L – labor force

1.2 The equations

1.2.1 At any given level of technology Q, the production process satisfies the Cobb-Douglas function

$$y = Qx^{\alpha}, \qquad 0 \leqslant x < +\infty$$

where α is a constant and $0 < \alpha < 1$.

1.2.2 Technology progresses autonomously at the constant and non-negative rate ρ. Thus, setting $Q(0) = 1$.

$$Q = \exp[\rho\tau], \qquad \rho \geqslant 0, 0 \leqslant \tau < +\infty.$$

1.2.3 Labor grows autonomously at the constant and non-negative rate λ. Thus,

$$L = L_0 \exp[\lambda\tau], \qquad L_0 > 0, 0 \leqslant \tau < +\infty.$$

1.2.4 The flow of investment per worker

$$\lambda x + \dot{x}$$

is a piece-wise continuous function of time over $0 \leqslant \tau < +\infty$.

1.2.5 The economy is closed in the sense that there is no long-term capital transfer with the rest of the world. In other words, consumption is the difference between production and investment, i.e.

$$c = y - (\lambda x + \dot{x})$$

at all points of continuity of $\dot{x}(\tau)$.

1.2.6

$$\rho + \lambda > 0.$$

(Note that no UMIT-optimal path exists if $\rho = \lambda = 0$ [K].)

1.3 The set of feasible growth paths

Here feasible means indefinitely feasible in the sense of Part I.

In view of the fact that the growth assumptions, Section 1.2, associate one and only one growth path $x(\tau), y(\tau), c(\tau)$ with every path $x(\tau)$, the set of feasible growth paths can be stated in terms of x only. We shall therefore denote this set by $\{ x(\tau)_0^{+\infty} \}$ and define it as the set of all $x(\tau)$, which start from the historically given capital stock per worker x_0, and are defined positive over $0 \leqslant \tau < +\infty$ and satisfy everywhere the assumptions of Section 1.2. More precisely, given $x_0 > 0$, $\rho \geqslant 0$, $\lambda \geqslant 0$, $\rho + \lambda > 0$, then $x(\tau) \in \{ x(\tau)_0^{+\infty} \}$ if and only if the following hold.

1.3.1 $x(0) = x_0$.

1.3.2 $x(\tau)$ is defined positive and piece-wise continuously differentiable over $0 \leqslant \tau < +\infty$.

1.3.3 $-\infty < \dot{x}(\tau) < \exp[\rho\tau]\, x^a - \lambda x$; $0 \leqslant \tau < +\infty$, at all points of continuity of $\dot{x}(\tau)$.

2. THE PREFERENCE ASSUMPTIONS

2.1 Instantaneous consumption

The national preference pattern with respect to instantaneous consumption can be described by any linear transformation of the utility function

$$U(c) = c^{1-\nu}/(1-\nu), \qquad 0 < \nu < 1, \quad 0 < c < +\infty$$

where ν is a given constant.

2.2 Postponed consumption

The national preference pattern for postponed consumption can be accounted for by a non-negative and constant time discount rate

$$i = (1-\nu)\rho/(1-\alpha).$$

More precisely, the utility at time t_0 of a consumption flow c at time t_1 can be described by

$$U[c(t_1)]\exp\left[-\frac{1-\nu}{1-\alpha}\rho(t_1-t_0)\right], \qquad 0 \leqslant t_0 < t_1 < +\infty.$$

2.3 Feasible path preference

The nation prefers the feasible path $x^*(\tau)$ to the feasible path $x(\tau)$ if there is an $\Omega \geqslant 0$ such that

$$\left\{I[x^*(\tau)_0^T] - I[x(\tau)_0^T]\right\} > 0, \qquad \Omega \leqslant T < +\infty$$

where

$$I[x(\tau)_0^T] = \int_0^T U(c)\exp[-i\tau]d\tau$$

i.e., if the sum over time of the (discounted) utilities of consumption per worker is ultimately greater along $x^*(\tau)$ than along $x(\tau)$. A feasible path $x^*(\tau)$ is called UMIT-optimal if it is preferred to every other feasible $x(\tau)$.

3. AN EXPLICIT UMIT-OPTIMAL SOLUTION

THEOREM 3.1 Let the growth and preference assumptions of Sections 1 and 2 obtain under the specification that

$$\alpha = \nu = \tfrac{1}{2}.$$

Denote respectively by κ_0 and

$$\bar{\kappa} = 1/\, 2(\lambda + 2\rho)$$

the initial and asymptotic (Golden Rule) values of the capital-output ratio $\kappa = x/y = x^{1/2}$. Then, the UMIT-optimal x-, y-, c- and s-paths, say $\hat{x}(\tau)$, $\hat{y}(\tau)$, $\hat{c}(\tau)$ and $\hat{s}(\tau)$ are

$$\hat{x}(\tau) = \bar{\kappa}^2 \left\{1 - m\exp[-(\lambda + 2\rho)\tau]\right\}^2 \exp[2\rho\tau]$$

$$\hat{y}(\tau) = \bar{\kappa} \left\{1 - m\exp[-(\lambda + 2\rho)\tau]\right\} \exp[2\rho\tau]$$

$$\hat{c}(\tau) = \tfrac{1}{2}\bar{\kappa} \left\{1 - m\exp[-(\lambda + 2\rho)\tau]\right\} \exp[2\rho\tau]$$

and

$$\hat{s}(\tau) = \tfrac{1}{2} \left\{1 + m\exp[-(\lambda + 2\rho)\tau]\right\} \tag{3.1}$$

where

$$m \equiv 1 - (\kappa_0/\bar{\kappa}).$$

Proof We first notice that the case $\rho > 0$ can be formally brought back to the case $\rho = 0$ by the change of variables. [This change has already been used in Paper 3.]

$$\hat{x}^*(\tau) = x(\tau)/\exp[2\rho\tau]$$

$$\hat{y}^*(\tau) = y(\tau)/\exp[2\rho\tau]$$

$$\hat{c}^*(\tau) = c(\tau)/\exp[2\rho\tau]$$

$$\lambda^* = \lambda + 2\rho > 0$$

$$i^* = 0.$$

It is therefore sufficient to prove the theorem for $\rho = 0, \lambda > 0$. Now, under the assumptions of the theorem in the case $\rho = 0$, Koopmans shows [K] that a necessary and sufficient condition for $x(\tau)$ to be UMIT-optimal is to satisfy the equation

$$\dot{x} = [U(\bar{c}) - U(c)]/U'(c), \qquad 0 \leqslant \tau < +\infty \tag{3.2}$$

where

$$\bar{c} = a(\bar{x})$$

$$a(x) = x^{1/2} - \lambda x. \tag{3.3}$$

In our case, $U(c) = 2c^{1/2}$. Hence, (3.2) becomes

$$\dot{x} = 2[(\bar{c}c)^{1/2} - c]\,. \tag{3.4}$$

On the other hand, by definition,

$$\dot{x} = -c + a(x). \tag{3.5}$$

Substituting (3.5) for $\dot{x}$ in (3.4) one gets

$$c - 2(\bar{c}c)^{1/2} + a = 0$$

and, consequently,

$$c^{1/2} = \bar{c}^{1/2} \mp (\bar{c} - a)^{1/2}$$

or

$$c = 2\bar{c} - a \mp 2[\bar{c}(\bar{c} - a)]^{1/2}$$

i.e.

$$\dot{x} = 2\left\{\pm\ [\bar{c}(\bar{c} - a)]^{1/2} - (\bar{c} - a)\right\} \tag{3.6}$$

where, as always hereafter, the upper and lower signs refer, respectively, to the case $x_0 < \bar{x}$ and $x_0 > \bar{x}$. Now (3.6) can be integrated explicitly. Indeed, (3.6) yields

$$2\tau = \int_{x_0}^{x_\tau} (1/\{(\bar{c} - a)^{1/2}[\pm\bar{c}^{1/2} - (\bar{c} - a)^{1/2}]\})\mathrm{d}x$$

$$= \int_{a(x_0)}^{a(x_\tau)} (1/\{a'(\bar{c} - a)^{1/2}[\pm\bar{c}^{1/2} - (\bar{c} - a)^{1/2}]\})\mathrm{d}a \tag{3.7}$$

where, as shown presently, $a'(x)$ can be expressed in terms of $a(x)$, $\bar{c}$ and λ only.

We first notice that the definition (3.3) of $a(x)$ implies

$$x^{1/2} = [1 \mp (1 - 4a\lambda)^{1/2}]/2\lambda. \tag{3.8}$$

It follows that

$$\begin{aligned} a'(x) &= (1/2x^{1/2}) - \lambda \\ &= \left\{\lambda/[1 \mp (1 - 4a\lambda)^{1/2}]\right\} - \lambda \\ &= \lambda(1 - 4a\lambda)^{1/2}/[\pm 1 - (1 - 4a\lambda)^{1/2}] \\ &= \lambda(\bar{c} - a)^{1/2}[\pm \bar{c}^{1/2} - (\bar{c} - a)^{1/2}]. \end{aligned} \tag{3.9}$$

Substitution of (3.9) for a' in (3.7) gives

$$\begin{aligned} -2\lambda\tau &= \int_{a(x_0)}^{a(x_\tau)} \mathrm{d}(\bar{c} - a)/(\bar{c} - a) \\ &= \ln\left\{[\bar{c} - a(x_\tau)]/[\bar{c} - a(x_0)]\right\} \end{aligned}$$

i.e.

$$a(x) = \bar{c} - [\bar{c} - a(x_0)]\exp[-2\lambda\tau]. \tag{3.10}$$

Finally, substituting (3.10) into (3.8) after squaring both sides of (3.8),

$$\begin{aligned} 4\lambda^2 x &= 1 + \left[1 - \frac{a(x_0)}{\bar{c}}\right]\exp[-2\lambda\tau] \mp 2\left[1 - \frac{a(x_0)}{\bar{c}}\right]^{1/2}\exp[-\lambda\tau] \\ &= \left\{1 \mp \left[1 - \frac{a(x_0)}{\bar{c}}\right]^{1/2}\exp[-\lambda\tau]\right\}^2 \\ &= \left\{1 \mp [1 - 4\lambda\kappa_0(1 - \lambda\kappa_0)]^{1/2}\exp[-\lambda\tau]\right\}^2 \\ &= \left\{1 - (1 - 2\lambda\kappa_0)\exp[-\lambda\tau]\right\}^2 \\ &= (1 - m\exp[-\lambda\tau])^2 \end{aligned}$$

i.e. (3.1) for $\rho = 0$. The rest of the theorem for $\rho = 0$ follows at once from the definitions $y = x^{1/2}$, $s = (\lambda x + \dot{x})/y$ and $c = (1 - s)y$. *q.e.d.*

4. SHARPNESS OF THE UMIT-OPTIMUM

THEOREM 4.1 Let the growth and preference assumptions of Sections 1 and 2 obtain, and let

$$\kappa_0 < \bar{\kappa}, \qquad \bar{\kappa} \equiv \alpha/\lambda.$$

Denote the feasible path resulting from the indefinitely constant savings policy

$$s^* = \bar{s} = \alpha$$

by a star and, as before, the UMIT-optimal path by a hat. Then

$$\lim_{\tau\to+\infty} \frac{\hat{c}(\tau)}{c^*(\tau)} = 1 \tag{4.1}$$

$$\lim_{T\to+\infty} \frac{I[\hat{x}(\tau)_0^T]}{I[x^*(\tau)_0^T]} = 1 \tag{4.2}$$

and

$$\max_{0<T<+\infty} \frac{I[\hat{x}(\tau)_0^T]}{I[x^*(\tau)_0^T]} \leqslant \max_{0<\tau<+\infty} \left[\frac{\hat{c}(\tau)}{c^*(\tau)}\right]^{1-\nu} \tag{4.3}$$

If, moreover, $\alpha = \nu = ½$, then

$$\lim_{T\to 0} \frac{I[\hat{x}(\tau)_0^T]}{I[x^*(\tau)_0^T]} = \left[\frac{\kappa_0}{\bar{\kappa}}\right]^{½} \tag{4.4}$$

$$\hat{c}(0)/c^*(0) = \kappa_0/\bar{\kappa} \tag{4.5}$$

and

$$\hat{c}(\tau)/c^*(\tau) < 1, 2, \qquad 0 \leqslant \tau < +\infty. \tag{4.6}$$

Furthermore,

$$I[\hat{x}(\tau)_\omega^\Omega]/I[x^*(\tau)_\omega^\Omega] < 1, 1 \tag{4.7}$$

for any two points of time ω and Ω, $0 \leqslant \omega < \Omega < +\infty$.

Proof It follows from the definitions

$$\kappa^* = x^*/y^*$$

and

$$s^* = \left(\lambda + \frac{\rho}{1-\alpha}\right)\kappa^* + \frac{\dot{\kappa}^*}{1-\alpha} = \alpha$$

that

$$\kappa^*(\tau) = \overline{\kappa}(1 - m\exp[-\{\lambda(1-\alpha) + \rho\}\tau])$$

and consequently,

$$c^*(\tau) = (1-\alpha)\overline{\kappa}^{a/(1-a)}(1 - m\exp[-\{\lambda(1-\alpha)+\rho\}\tau])^{a/(1-a)} \times \exp[\rho\tau/(1-\alpha)]. \quad (4.8)$$

Hence,

$$\lim_{\tau\to+\infty} c^*(\tau)\exp[-\rho\tau/(1-\alpha)] = (1-\alpha)\overline{\kappa}^{a/(1-a)}.$$

Since it is known (Theorem 4.1 in Paper 3) that

$$\lim_{\tau\to+\infty} \hat{c}(\tau)\exp[-\rho\tau/(1-\alpha)] = (1-\alpha)\overline{\kappa}^{a/(1-a)}$$

(4.1) follows. Notice, on the other hand, that (4.8) implies

$$\lim_{T\to+\infty}\left\{I\left[\overline{x}\exp[\rho\tau/(1-\alpha)]\,{}_0^T\right] - I[x^*(\tau)_0^T]\right\}$$

$$= \text{positive constant}, \qquad \overline{x}^{(1-a)} = \overline{\kappa}$$

and that $\hat{c}(\tau) < (1-\alpha)\overline{x}^a\exp[\rho\tau/(1-\alpha)]$, $0 \leqslant \tau < +\infty$; see Theorem 4.1 in Paper 3. It follows that

$$\lim_{T\to+\infty}\left\{I[\hat{x}(\tau)_0^T] - I[x^*(\tau)_0^T]\right\} = \text{positive constant}$$

also, and since

$$\lim_{T\to+\infty}\int_0^T [c^*(\tau)]^{1-\nu}\exp[-i\tau]\mathrm{d}\tau = +\infty$$

$$i = (1-\nu)\rho/(1-\alpha)$$

that (4.2) must obtain. Moreover, $\hat{c}(0) < c^*(0)$, since $\hat{s}(0) > \alpha$ (Theorem 9.1 in Paper 3). By (4.1) the ratio $I[\hat{x}(\tau)_0^T]/I[x^*(\tau)_0^T]$ must therefore have a maximum. At the latter

$$\frac{I[\hat{x}(\tau)_0^T]}{I[x^*(\tau)_0^T]} = \frac{\mathrm{d}I[\hat{x}(\tau)_0^T]/\mathrm{d}T}{\mathrm{d}I[x^*(\tau)_0^T]/\mathrm{d}T}$$

$$= \left[\frac{\hat{c}(T)}{c^*(T)}\right]^{1-\nu}. \tag{4.9}$$

Now, (4.9) implies (4.3). If $\alpha = \nu = ½$, then it follows from Theorem 3.1 and (4.8) that

$$\frac{\hat{c}(\tau)}{c^*(\tau)} = \frac{\{1 - m\exp[-(\lambda + 2\rho)\tau]\}^2}{\{1 - m\exp[-(½\lambda + \rho)\tau]\}}. \tag{4.10}$$

This implies (4.5), since

$$(1 - m)^2/(1 - m) = 1 - m = \kappa_0/\kappa\,.$$

Now (4.5) implies (4.4) by l'Hospital's Rule. Indeed, the latter says that the first and third terms in (4.9) tend to the same limit as T tends to 0. On the other hand, (4.10) implies

$$\hat{c}(\tau)/c^*(\tau) = [1 - z^2]^2/[1 - m^{½}z]$$

$$< [1 - z^2]^2/[1 - z]$$

$$= (1 - z)(1 + z)^2$$

where

$$z \equiv m^{½}\exp[-(½\lambda + \rho)\tau].$$

Now it can easily be verified that the last term of (4.10) has an absolute maximum for $z = ⅓$. The value of this maximum is

$$32/27 < 1.2.$$

This proves (4.6).

Finally,

$$I[\hat{x}(\tau)_\omega^\Omega] = \int_\omega^\Omega 2[\hat{c}(\tau)]^{1/2}\exp[-\rho\tau]\mathrm{d}\tau$$

$$< 1.1\int_\omega^\Omega 2[c^*(\tau)]^{1/2}\exp[-\rho\tau]\mathrm{d}\tau$$

$$= I[x^*(\tau)_\omega^\Omega]1.1.$$

q.e.d.

5. INTERPRETATION OF THE RESULTS

This section infers a certain number of general properties of the UMIT criterion on the basis of the results established in the two preceding sections. The term "general" refers here to the growth and preference assumptions of Sections 1 and 2. More precisely, let us agree, once and for all, that all statements on the properties of the UMIT solutions are hereafter implicitly limited to the case defined by these assumptions.

Our conjectures about the general characteristics of the UMIT-optimal solution are best integrated in a description of these characteristics which is partly based on previously known facts. So that the reader may easily differentiate between the statements which are established facts and those which are only conjectures, all statements will be followed by either (fact) or (conjecture). [For the facts, see Paper 3, and all statements followed by (conjecture) become facts for $\alpha = \nu = ½$.]

Since the UMIT criterion is closely related to the so-called "Golden Rule of Capital Accumulation", it is also convenient to express the UMIT-optimal growth path with respect to the Golden Rule or, shortly, GR path. As a matter of fact, granted our growth and preference assumptions, the UMIT criterion tells us essentially that the GR path should be monotonically approached and ultimately reached.

Recall that the GR growth path is the consumption dominant member of the set of all *a priori* feasible balanced growth paths, i.e. of all balanced growth paths

$$x = x_0\exp[\lambda\tau], \qquad \lambda \equiv \rho/(1-\alpha)$$

$$y = x_0^a\exp[\lambda\tau]$$

$$c = [x_0^a - (\lambda+\gamma)x_0]\exp[\lambda\tau]$$

$$s = (\lambda+\gamma)x_0^{1-a}$$

which are feasible for some value of x_0. The GR value $\bar{x}$ of x_0 is naturally the value of x which maximizes the function

$$a(x) = x^a - (\lambda + \gamma)x.$$

As known, $a(x)$ is a positive and strictly concave function over $0 < x < [1/(\lambda + \gamma)]^{1/(1-a)}$ which has a strict maximum $a(\bar{x}) = \bar{c}$ at

$$\bar{x} = [\alpha/(\lambda + \gamma)]^{1/(1-a)}. \tag{4.11}$$

The GR growth path, say

$$(\bar{x}\exp[\gamma\tau], \bar{y}\exp[\gamma\tau], \bar{c}\exp[\gamma\tau], \bar{s}) \tag{4.12}$$

i.e. thus defined by (4.11) and

$$\bar{y} = \bar{x}^a$$

$$\bar{c} = \bar{x}^a - (\lambda + \gamma)\bar{x} = (1 - \alpha)\bar{y}$$

$$\bar{s} = \alpha.$$

This enables us to give a very simple description of the essential features of the UMIT-optimal growth path:

$$[\hat{x}(\tau), \hat{y}(\tau), \hat{c}(\tau), \hat{s}(\tau)]. \tag{4.13}$$

If $x_0 = \bar{x}$, the UMIT-optimal growth path coincides with the Golden Rule growth path (4.12) (fact). Hence, once reached, the GR growth path becomes UMIT-optimal for the rest of the future (fact). If $x_0 \neq \bar{x}$, the UMIT-optimal x-, y-, c- and s-paths tend not only relatively (fact), but also absolutely (conjecture for x, y, c; fact for s) and strictly monotonically (fact, except for the strictness of the monotonicity of s) to their respective GR paths. More precisely, the essential features of $\hat{x}(\tau)$, $\hat{y}(\tau)$, $\hat{c}(\tau)$ are summarized in Tables 4.1, 4.2 and 4.3. These tables contain an interesting new result which deserves further comment. That result is that $\hat{s}(\tau)$ decreases strictly over time from sone initial value $\hat{s}(0) > \alpha$ to

TABLE 4.1

$x_0 < \bar{x}$	$\hat{x}$	$\hat{y}$	$\hat{c}$	$\hat{s}$
$\rho = 0$	$\dot{\hat{x}} > 0$	$\dot{\hat{y}} > 0$	$\dot{\hat{c}} > 0$	$\dot{\hat{s}} < 0$
$\rho > 0$	$\dot{\hat{x}} > \gamma\hat{x}$	$\dot{\hat{y}} > \gamma\hat{y}$	$\dot{\hat{c}} > \gamma\hat{c}$	$\dot{\hat{s}} < 0$

TABLE 4.2

$x_0 = \bar{x}$	$\hat{x}$	$\hat{y}$	$\hat{c}$	$\hat{s}$
$\rho = 0$	$\hat{x} = x_0$	$\hat{y} = x_0^a$	$\hat{c} = (1-\alpha)x_0^a$	$\hat{s} = \alpha$
$\rho > 0$	$\hat{x} = x_0 \exp[\gamma\tau]$	$\hat{y} = x_0^a \exp[\gamma\tau]$	$\hat{c} = (1-\alpha)x_0 \exp[\gamma\tau]$	$\hat{s} = \alpha$

TABLE 4.3 $\gamma = \rho/(1-\alpha)$

$x_0 > \bar{x}$	$\hat{x}$	$\hat{y}$	$\hat{c}$	$\hat{s}$
$\rho = 0$	$\dot{\hat{x}} < 0$	$\dot{\hat{y}} < 0$	$\dot{\hat{c}} < 0$	$\dot{\hat{s}} > 0$
$\rho > 0$	$\dot{\hat{x}} < \gamma\hat{x}$	$\dot{\hat{y}} < \gamma\hat{y}$	$\dot{\hat{c}} < \gamma\hat{c}$	$\dot{\hat{s}} > 0$

$\hat{s}(+\infty) = \alpha$ whenever $x_0 < \bar{x}$, i.e. in all cases which are of practical importance. [This last assertion is explained in detail in Paper 3.] Now, α is generally believed to lie somewhere between ¼ and ⅓, which is already a rather high value for the savings ratio. This raises the question of whether or not $\hat{s}(0)$ is generally too high to be practically enforceable. If $\alpha = \nu = \frac{1}{2}$, Theorem 3.1 tells us that

$$\hat{s}(0)/\alpha = 2 - (\kappa_0/\bar{\kappa}), \qquad \kappa = x/y.$$

Hence, if $\alpha = \nu = \frac{1}{2}$ and

$$\kappa_0/\bar{\kappa} = 1.00, \quad 0.70, \quad 0.50, \quad 0.30.$$

Then, respectively,

$$\hat{s}(0)/\alpha = 1.00, \quad 1.30, \quad 1.50, \quad 1.70.$$

Table 4.4 indicates the range of values of $\bar{\kappa}$ which are compatible with the usual values of α, ρ and λ. Since κ_0 ranges generally between, say, 2.5 and 5.5, it is seen that $\kappa_0/\bar{\kappa} \leqslant 0.6$ does not constitute an exceptional situation.

TABLE 4.4 Values of $\bar{x} = \alpha/(\lambda + \gamma)$, actual values of α, λ and $\gamma \equiv \rho/(1-\alpha)$

$\lambda + \gamma$	2%	3%	4%	5%	6%	7%	8%
$\alpha = ¼$	12.5	8.3	6.3	5.0	4.2	3.6	3.1
$\alpha = ⅓$	16.7	11.1	8.3	6.7	5.6	4.8	4.2

Taking the values $\hat{s}(0)/\alpha$ for $\alpha = \nu = \frac{1}{2}$ as an order of magnitude, it follows that, in practice, $\hat{s}(0)$ may very well approach and even exceed, say, 0.45 (conjecture). In other words, $\hat{s}(0)$ may often be "unduly" hard on the initial (planning) generation (conjecture) at least if, as we have assumed,

$$i = \rho(1-\nu)/(1-\alpha) \tag{4.14}$$

i.e. if i is chosen at the minimum level at which UMIT is feasible. [UMIT is not feasible if $i < \rho(1-\nu)/(1-\alpha)$; see Paper 3.]

It appears, therefore, that a "fair" welfare distribution over the generations, if at all possible, is only compatible with the UMIT criterion when the time discount rate i is chosen sufficiently high. The choice of a higher value of i raises, however, an almost unsolvable problem. Indeed, if one drops what I have called elsewhere the "Principle of Minimum Impatience", i.e. if one does not choose the lowest feasible value of i, (4.14), one must find some other way to determine i. Now the UMIT time discount rate i can hardly be assimilated to the so-called "social" time discount rate, since the first is assumed to be constant, while the latter is quite universally believed to be a decreasing function of the state of "wealth" of the economy. Clearly, it would make no sense to equate forever the UMIT time discount rate i with the "social" time discount rate of the generation which, by some historical accident, happened to initiate the UMIT-optimal program. The ideal solution is, of course, to make i dependent on, say, $\hat{c}(\tau)$. This can be shown, however, to be logically inconsistent with UMIT.

Another new result which follows from Theorem 3.1 is the previously mentioned conjecture that the UMIT-optimal growth path (4.13) tends not only relatively, but also absolutely to the GR growth path (4.12). This result shows that the UMIT-optimal growth path practically reaches the GR growth path in a finite period of time. More precisely, given any $\epsilon > 0$, however small, there is a T such that the respective absolute differences between the x-, y-, c- and s-components of the UMIT growth path (4.13) and the GR growth path (4.12) become all smaller than ϵ for $\tau \geqslant T$. From this result and the above discussed behaviour of $\hat{s}(\tau)$, one may conclude that it is "practically" UMIT-optimal to reach the GR growth path in a relatively short period of time and to apply initially a rather "hard" savings policy if $x_0 < \bar{x}$ (conjecture). It is interesting to see that the UMIT criterion prescribes (conjecture) an optimal policy which may be considered to be an application of the "turnpike" theorem to the case of an infinite time horizon and a "GR final state".

We now turn to the discussion of the results of Section 4. The latter constitutes a first answer to the question of whether it is really "worthwhile" for a nation to impose the "hardships" of UMIT planning on its poorer generations, i.e. on generations characterized by a capital-output ratio smaller than, say, 0.6 of the GR ratio $\bar{\kappa}$.

For the purpose of answering this question, it is convenient to consider the growth path

$$[x^*(\tau), y^*(\tau), c^*(\tau), s^*]$$

defined by the indefinitely constant savings policy

$$s^* = \alpha.$$

As a matter of fact, Theorem 4.1 tells us that

$$\lim_{T \to +\infty} \frac{I[x^*(\tau)_0^T]}{I[\hat{x}(\tau)_0^T]} = 1.$$

Thus, in relative terms, the UMIT-optimal savings policy $\hat{s}(\tau)$ is not "better" than the constant savings policy $s^* = \alpha$. This policy already casts some serious doubts on the value of the short term prescriptions of the UMIT criterion. One may, indeed, argue that what really matters in the choice between two growth paths, say $x_1(\tau)$ and $x_2(\tau)$, is the ratio between $I[x_1(\tau)_0^{+\infty}]$ and $I[x_2(\tau)_0^{+\infty}]$ and not their difference.

In addition to $\alpha = \nu = \frac{1}{2}$, Theorem 4.1 tells us that there is no period of time during which the relative gain of utility along $\hat{c}(\tau)$, in comparison to $c^*(\tau)$, is greater than 10% (4.7). It also tells us that the initial relative loss of utility along $\hat{c}(\tau)$, in comparison to $c^*(\tau)$, is of the order of $[1-(\kappa_0/\bar{\kappa})^{\frac{1}{2}}]$ (4.4), i.e. easily of the order of 20% (we have seen that $(\kappa_0/\bar{\kappa}) \leqslant 0.6$ is not exceptional). In terms of consumption, the maximum relative gain for any generation is smaller than 20% (4.6), while the relative loss for the initial generation will be of the order of $[1-(\kappa_0/\bar{\kappa})]$, i.e. easily of 40% (4.5).

We infer tentatively from these results that the UMIT-optimum is rather "flat" and that a relatively important initial departure from the UMIT-optimal policy does not much affect the total welfare of the nation over infinite time. It may therefore be argued that the UMIT criterion is not satisfactory in the sense that the sacrifice it imposes on the poorer generations can be avoided without great loss to the later and much richer generations.

Paper 5

ABSOLUTE VERSUS RELATIVE UTILITY MAXIMIZATION

INTRODUCTION

There has been a growing feeling of discomfort about the optimality criterion known as Utility Maximization over Infinite Time or UMIT. The trouble lies in the fact that no UMIT-optimal solution is known to exist unless either one of the three following conditions are satisfied:

(i) consumption per capita c is known never to exceed some maximum value $\bar{\bar{c}}$;

(ii) the utility $u(c)$ of per capita consumption c cannot exceed a finite upper bound $\bar{\bar{u}}$, however great c;

(iii) the utility of future consumption is discounted at a rate i greater than some well defined positive minimum value i_0.

Now, condition (i) is only fulfilled under a constant technology and both (ii) and (iii) impose rather severe restrictions on the admissible preference pattern of an economy.

There are still other unsatisfactory aspects to UMIT. Let us only mention one: if the utility function $u(c)$ is not bounded from above and technology is progressing at a positive rate, the UMIT-optimal savings ratio is generally higher, the poorer the economy. In other words, it generally prescribes a glaringly unfair distribution of welfare among the different generations (Paper 4). In short, UMIT does not seem to be an appropriate criterion in the case of a progressing technology.

Does this mean that there is something intrinsically wrong with the principle of UMIT itself? The answer depends on the particular properties of the assumed growth model. As a matter of fact, it is the purpose of this paper to show that the above difficulties can be avoided in a particular, but very important case.

OBJECTIVES

1. Assuming a closed Cobb-Douglas economy and constant growth rates of both labor and technology, define and explain an interpretation of the principle of UMIT, which avoids the conceptual pitfalls of the traditional interpretation. The resulting criterion is called Relative UMIT or RUMIT.

2. Assuming furthermore a Bernoulli utility function, show that the RUMIT-optimal savings path is likely to be decreasing, constant or increasing depending on whether ν is smaller, equal or greater than $1/\alpha$, where ν and α denote respectively the elasticity of marginal utility and the elasticity of production with respect to capital.

PLAN

1. The growth model
2. The RUMIT index
3. The RUMIT solution

1. THE GROWTH MODEL

1.1 The variables

x–capital stock per capita, i.e. per labor unit
y–production flow per capita
c–consumption flow per capita
L–labor force
P–population

1.2 The growth assumptions

1.2.1 At any given instant of time, i.e. at any given level of technology, the production flow per worker is a Cobb-Douglas function of the capital stock per worker only,

$$y = \exp[\rho\tau]\, x^{a}, \qquad 0 \leqslant \tau < +\infty,\ 0 \leqslant x < +\infty$$

where $0 < \alpha < 1$.

1.2.2 Technology progresses autonomously at the constant rate $\rho < 0$ (see above).

1.2.3 Labor and population grow autonomously and proportionally at the constant and positive rate λ. Units are chosen so that

$$L = P = P_0 \exp[\lambda\tau], \qquad 0 \leqslant \tau < +\infty.$$

1.2.4 The flow of investment per worker is non-negative and continuous over $0 \leqslant \tau < +\infty$,

$$\lambda x + \dot{x} \geqslant 0.$$

1.2.5 The economy is closed in the sense that there is no net long-term capital transfer. In other words, consumption is the difference between production and investment.

$$c = \exp[\rho\tau]\, f(x) - \lambda x - \dot{x}, \qquad 0 \leqslant \tau < +\infty.$$

1.3 The set of feasible growth paths

Here feasible means indefinitely feasible in the sense of Part I.

In view of the fact that the growth assumptions of Section 1.2 associate one and only one growth path $[x(\tau), y(\tau), c(\tau)]$ with every path $x(\tau)$, the set of feasible growth paths can be stated in terms of x only. We denote this by $\{x(\tau)\}$ and define it as the set of all $x(\tau)$, $0 \leqslant \tau < +\infty$, which start from the historically given capital stock per worker x_0 and satisfy the assumptions of Section 1.2.

More precisely, given x_0 in $0 < x_0 < 1/(\gamma + \lambda)^{1/(1-a)}$, $\gamma = \rho/(1-\alpha)$, $\rho > 0$ and $\lambda > 0$, $x(\tau) \in \{x(\tau)\}$ if

(i) $x(0) = x_0$;

(ii) $x(\tau)$ is defined and continuously differentiable over $0 \leqslant \tau < +\infty$;

(iii) $-\lambda x(\tau) \leqslant \dot{x}(\tau) < \exp[\rho\tau] x^a(\tau) - \lambda x(\tau)$, $0 \leqslant \tau < +\infty$.

1.4 The upper limit of *a priori* feasible consumption

THEOREM 1.1 Every $x(\tau) \in \{x(\tau)\}$ satisfies

$$0 < x(\tau) < x_+(\tau), \qquad 0 \leqslant \tau < +\infty$$

where

$$x_+(\tau) = [1/(\gamma + \lambda)]^{1/(1-a)} \exp[\gamma\tau], \qquad \gamma = \rho/(1-\alpha).$$

Moreover, for every $t^* \geqslant 0$ and $\epsilon > 0$ there is an x_0 in $0 < x < x_+(0)$ such that

$$x_+(t^*) - x(t^*) < \epsilon$$

for some $x(\tau) \in \{x(\tau)\}$.

(Proof below)

It follows that, whatever x_0 in $0 < x < x_+(0)$,

$$c(\tau) \leqslant y(\tau) < y_+(\tau) < [1/(\gamma + \lambda)]^{\alpha/(1-\alpha)} \exp[\gamma\tau], \qquad 0 \leqslant \tau < +\infty$$

along every feasible growth path. In other words, the generation living at time t can never enjoy a c-level as high as $y_+(t)$. Depending on the past history of investments, $c(t)$ may, however, become closer to $y_+(t)$ than any pre-assigned difference. This is why $y_+(t)$ is called the (never reachable) *upper limit of* a priori *feasible consumption.*

Proof of Theorem 1.1 It is known that s = constant $\leqslant 1$, $0 \leqslant \tau < +\infty$, implies that

$$\kappa = \kappa_{+\infty} + (\kappa_0 - \kappa_{+\infty}) \exp[-\{\rho + (1-\alpha)\lambda\}\tau], \qquad 0 \leqslant \tau < +\infty$$

where $\kappa_{+\infty} = s/(\gamma + \lambda)$. This establishes the theorem, since we have assumed that $0 < \kappa_0 < 1/(\gamma + \lambda)$.

q.e.d.

2. THE RUMIT INDEX

2.1 The concept of relative consumption

It seems to be an often forgotten truism that rules of rational behavior can only be defined with respect to a given game, or at the most, to a given set of similar games. This remains true for games played with Nature and, in particular, for games of optimal economic growth. In short, an optimal growth criterion can only be defined with respect to the properties of a given growth model.

Now, as shown in Section 1.4, one of the properties of the growth model defined in Section 1.2 is that every *a priori* feasible c-path satisfies

$$0 < c(\tau) < y_+(\tau), \qquad 0 \leqslant \tau < +\infty.$$

Notice that, at any given point of time τ, some *a priori* feasible c-path comes nearer to $y_+(\tau)$ than any pre-assigned distance. No *a priori* feasible c-path, however, can reach the value $y_+(\tau)$ at any finite τ. According to the rules of the game defined by the growth assumptions, Section 1.2, the interval of *a priori* feasible c-values is finite and well defined at every point of time τ. Now this very important feature of the growth model, Section 1.2, i.e. of the growth models which are mostly considered, is not properly taken into account by the usual definition of UMIT. This is, in this case, the real cause of the difficulties pointed out in the introduction.

As a matter of fact, it has hitherto been assumed that the same utility function $U(c)$ holds true for all generations, at least over their respective intervals of *a priori* feasible c-levels. It does not seem to have been clearly recognized that, in the case of a progressing technology, this procedure introduces an extremely strong bias in favor of future generations: these are given greater weight simply because they are potentially capable of attaining higher levels of consumption. Given technological progress, the assumption of a common utility function gives potentially wealthier generations more "voting rights" in the determination of the optimal path.

The bias in favor of the future may easily be so important that the total weight given to the welfare of the generations living within any finite future becomes completely negligible. This means that any two feasible c-paths are equally "UMIT-good", provided only that they grow ultimately fast enough to infinity, namely at the asymptotic balanced growth rate $\rho/(1-\alpha)$. Mathematically speaking, it means that the UMIT-integral

$$\int_0^{+\infty} U(c_\tau)\mathrm{d}\tau \tag{2.1}$$

diverges to $+\infty$ even if the so-called Ramsey device is applied.

The surprising thing is that the divergence of the integral (2.1) is generally misinterpreted. I must admit that for quite some time, I myself had hardly questioned the commonly expressed belief that the maximization of this integral satisfies the ethical principle of neutrality with respect to the welfare of different generations. Sticking to this belief, most economists seem to deduce that the divergence of integral (2.1) implies that it is fortunately impossible to apply this ethical principle to the maximization of total welfare over infinite time.

They therefore reluctantly accept the imposition either of a finite upper limit to the utility function $U(c)$ or of the introduction of a time discount rate i in the UMIT-integral, i.e. replace (2.1) by

$$\int_0^{+\infty} U(c_\tau)\exp[-i\tau]\mathrm{d}\tau \tag{2.2}$$

Both devices are, however, most unsatisfactory.

An upper limit to $U(c)$, say $\bar{\bar{U}}$, obviously sets an upper limit to the weight given to any future generation. It therefore decreases the importance of the bias in favor of the future introduced by a common utility function $U(c)$. It can, however, never completely eliminate this bias, since future generations are potentially richer and can *a priori* approach the upper limit $\bar{\bar{U}}$ more closely.

The maximization of integral (2.2) instead of integral (2.1) raises the question, on the other hand, of both the value and economic interpretation of i. In fact, i must not only be constant, but also at least equal to the minimum value

$$i_0 = (1 - \bar{\nu})\rho/(1 - \bar{\alpha})$$

where

$$\bar{\nu} = \lim_{c \to +\infty} \frac{cu'(c)}{u(c)} \qquad u(c) = U'(c).$$

If $U(c)$ has no finite upper bound, then $\bar{\nu}$ cannot exceed 1 and, consequently, i_0 is positive except in the limiting case $\bar{\nu} = 1$. Now the two conditions that i must be constant and not smaller than a positive i_0 are very difficult to reconcile with the idea that i should express the "social" time discount rate of the economy.

The latter is quite generally believed to be a strictly monotonically decreasing function of the general level of wealth or, in this context, of consumption per capita c. The only way to maintain a social interpretation of i is consequently to identify i with the lower limit i_{00} towards which the social time discount rate of the economy is expected to tend for infinitely great values of c. This presupposes, however, that i_0 is not greater than i_{00}, which is a perfectly unwarranted assumption.

Little else, therefore, remains but to consider i as a pure control variable of the distribution of welfare among the different generations. This distribution then becomes arbitrary unless some rule can be found to decide upon the value of i. The only rule I can think of is to choose $i = i_0$, i.e. to apply what I have called elsewhere the Principle of Minimum Impatience (see 3.4.2, Part I). As we shall see below, this comes nearest to the democratic principle that every generation should have an equal voting right in the determination of the optimal path.

The best way to eliminate the above explained bias in favor of future generations is naturally to eliminate its cause, i.e. the assumption that the same utility function $U(c)$ applies to all generations. This is what we do presently.

Since a generation living at time τ can only expect a c-level somewhere between 0 and $y_+(\tau)$, it makes no sense to endow it with a preference pattern with respect to c-levels greater than $y_+(\tau)$. It follows that the range of definition of its utility function, say $U_\tau(c)$, should logically extend, and only extend, over the interval $0 < c < y_+(\tau)$. On the other hand, by the principle of equal voting rights, we shall give the same weight U_+ to $U_\tau[y_+(\tau)]$ for all τs (Fig. 1).

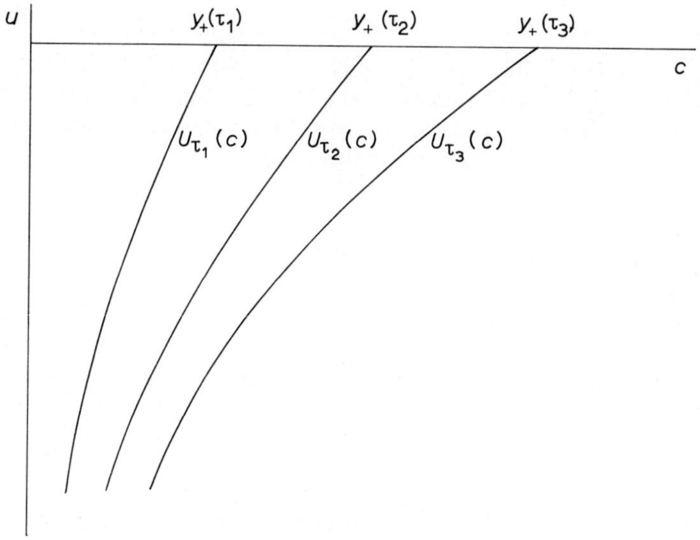

Fig. 1

The next step is to express the fact that, since all successive generations belong to the same society, they may be expected to have a similar, though not identical, preference pattern with respect to per capita consumption. Mathematically, this means that some relation should be defined between the different utility functions $U_\tau(c)$. Since, whatever τ,

$$-\infty < U_\tau(c) < U_+, \qquad 0 < c < y_+(\tau)$$

there is a c_2 in $0 < c < y_+(t_2)$ for every given c_1 in $0 < c < y_+(t_1)$ such that

$$-\infty < U_{t_2}(c_2) = U_{t_1}(c_1) < U_+. \tag{2.3}$$

The simplest way to establish a relation between the functions $U_\tau(c)$ is therefore to assume that (2.3) holds true if and only if

$$c_1/y_+(t_1) = c_2/y_+(t_2)$$

Then, whatever τ and c in $0 < c < y_+(\tau)$,

$$U_\tau(c) = U_\tau\left[\frac{c}{y_+(\tau)} y_+(\tau)\right]$$

$$\cdot = U[c/y_+(\tau)] .$$

The similarity between the preference patterns of the different generations is thus very simply expressed by assuming that they all have the same preference scaling with respect to $c/y_+(\tau)$, i.e. to what we call *relative per capita consumption* and denote by z.

2.2 The general preference assumptions

2.2.1 The national preference pattern with respect to instantaneous consumption can be described by any linear transformation of a thrice differentiable function of relative per capita consumption $z = c/y_+$. This "utility" function $U(z)$ is defined over $0 < z < 1$ and is strictly concave

$$u(z) > 0, \qquad u'(z) < 0, \qquad 0 < z < 1, \qquad u(z) = U'(z).$$

2.2.2 The nation prefers the feasible path $x^*(\tau)$ to the feasible path $x(\tau)$ if there is a $T^* \geqslant 0$ such that

$$\int_0^T \left\{U[z^*(\tau)] - U[z(\tau)]\right\} d\tau > 0, \qquad T^* \leqslant T < +\infty$$

i.e. if the sum over time of the utilities of relative consumption per capita is ultimately greater along $x^*(\tau)$ than along $x(\tau)$. A feasible path $x^*(\tau)$ is called RUMIT-optimal if it is preferred to all other paths in the above sense.

2.3 The particular preference assumptions

2.3.1 The conditions of Section 2.2 are fulfilled.

2.3.2 The marginal utility function is

$$u(z) = A/z^\nu, \qquad 0 < z < 1$$

where ν and A are respectively a given and an arbitrary positive constant.

3. THE RUMIT SOLUTION

3.1 Existence

As in the case of UMIT, necessary and sufficient conditions for the existence of a RUMIT-optimal growth path are that it (1) satisfies Euler's equation and (2) is efficient in the sense of Definition 3.1.

DEFINITION 3.1 If two feasible c-paths $c_1(\tau)$ and $c_2(\tau)$ satisfy

$$c_1(\tau) \geqslant c_2(\tau), \qquad 0 \leqslant \tau < +\infty$$

and, for some $t^* \geqslant 0$, also

$$c_1(t^*) > c_2(t^*)$$

then $c_1(\tau)$ *dominates* $c_2(\tau)$. Any c-path dominated by another feasible c-path is *inefficient.* A feasible c-path which is not inefficient is *efficient.*

Under the present growth model, a known sufficient condition for efficiency is that there is a T such that

$$s(\tau) \leqslant \alpha, \qquad T \leqslant \tau < +\infty. \tag{3.1}$$

This is the complement of Phelps' Golden Rule of Capital Accumulation [P1].

As regards Euler's equation, it can be easily derived from our growth and preference assumptions. It reads

$$-\Phi(c/y_+)\,[(\dot{c}/c) - \gamma] = (\alpha/\kappa) - (\gamma + \lambda) \tag{3.2}$$

where

$$\Phi(z) = zu'(z)/u(z).$$

Under the particular preference assumptions of Section 2.3,

$$\Phi(z) = -\nu < 0, \qquad 0 < z < 1. \tag{3.3}$$

In this case, a theorem derived by T. C. Koopmans ([K], see also Paper 2) can be used to obtain a first integral of (3.2). Depending on whether $\nu \neq 1, \nu > 0$, or $\nu = 1$, the integration yields, respectively,

$$(1-\nu)(\dot{x} - \gamma x) = c^{\nu}\,[(\bar{c}\exp[\gamma\tau])^{1-\nu} - c^{1-\nu}] \tag{3.4}$$

and

$$(\dot{x} - \gamma x) = c\,[\ln(\overline{c}/c) + \gamma\tau] \qquad\qquad (3.5)$$

where

$$\overline{c} = (1-\alpha)[\alpha/(\gamma + \lambda)]^{a/(1-a)}.$$

These two first integrals of Euler's equation can be shown to always have a solution which is unique and efficient, i.e. RUMIT-optimal in $\{x(\tau)\}$. In terms of z, this solution tends monotonically to the asymptotic Golden Rule value (see Paper 3):

$$\overline{z} = (1-\alpha)\alpha^{a/(1-a)}.$$

3.2 Explicit solutions

THEOREM 3.1   If Φ is constant and

$$\nu = 1/\alpha$$

the RUMIT-optimal solution, denoted by a hat, is

$$\hat{s} = \alpha$$

$$\hat{\kappa} = \overline{\kappa} + (\kappa_0 - \overline{\kappa})\exp[-(1-\alpha)(\gamma + \lambda)\tau]$$

$$\overline{\kappa} = \alpha/(\gamma + \lambda)$$

$$\hat{c} = (1-\alpha)\hat{\kappa}^{a/(1-a)}\exp[\gamma\tau].$$

(Proof below)

THEOREM 3.2   If $\nu \neq 1$, $\nu > 0$, then the initial RUMIT-optimal savings ratio satisfies

$$[\hat{s}(0) - \alpha]\,(x_0 - \overline{x})\,(1 - \alpha\nu) < 0.$$

(Proof below)

THEOREM 3.3   If $\alpha = \nu = \frac{1}{2}$, then the RUMIT-optimal solution is
$$\hat{s} = \frac{1}{2}\left\{1 + m\exp[-(\gamma + \lambda)\tau]\right\}$$
$$\hat{\kappa} = \overline{\kappa}\left\{1 - m\exp[-(\gamma + \lambda)\tau]\right\}$$
$$\hat{c} = \frac{1}{2}\overline{\kappa}\left\{1 - m\exp[-(\gamma + \lambda)\tau]\right\}\exp[\gamma\tau]$$

where $\gamma = 2\rho$ and $m = 1 - (\kappa_0/\overline{\kappa})$, $\overline{\kappa} = 1/[2(2\rho + \lambda)]$.

(Proof in Paper 4, Theorem 3.1)

Proof of Theorem 3.1 If $s = \alpha$, $0 \leqslant \tau < \infty$, then

$$c = (1-\alpha)\kappa^{\alpha/(1-\alpha)}\exp[\gamma\tau]$$

where

$$\kappa = \overline{\kappa} + (\kappa_0 - \overline{\kappa})\exp[-(1-\alpha)(\gamma+\lambda)] \qquad \overline{\kappa} = \alpha/(\gamma+\lambda).$$

Hence,

$$(\dot{c}/c) - \gamma = [\alpha/(1-\alpha)](\dot{\kappa}/\kappa) = [(\alpha/\kappa) - (\gamma+\lambda)]\alpha.$$

For $\alpha\nu = 1$, this is Euler's equation (3.2). By (3.1), this solution is efficient, hence RUMIT-optimal.

q.e.d.

Proof of Theorem 3.2 Granted Theorem 3.1, it is sufficient to show that $\hat{c}(0)$ increases or decreases, depending whether $x_0 < \overline{x}$ or $x_0 > \overline{x}$, as ν increases and α is fixed. Now $\hat{c}(0)$ satisfies (3.4) for $\tau = 0$ and $\nu \neq 1$, i.e.

$$[x_0^a - (\gamma+\lambda)x_0](1-\nu) + \nu\hat{c} - \overline{c}^{1-\nu}\hat{c}^{\nu} = 0.$$

Hence,

$$\frac{\nu}{\hat{c}}\frac{d\hat{c}}{d\nu} = \frac{1}{(\nu-1)}\left\{1 + \frac{\ln m}{1-m}\right\}$$

where $m = (\overline{c}/\hat{c})^{\nu-1}$

Now $1 + [\ln m/(1-m)] > 0$ if $m > 1$ and < 0 if $m < 1$.

It follows that

$$\frac{d\hat{c}}{d\nu}\begin{cases} >0 \text{ if } \hat{c} < \overline{c} \\ <0 \text{ if } \hat{c} > \overline{c}. \end{cases}$$

Now it is known that $\hat{c} < \bar{c}$ if $x_0 < \bar{x}$ and $\hat{c} > \bar{c}$ if $x_0 > \bar{x}$ ([K] or Paper 2).

q.e.d.

3.3 Conclusion

The three theorems above seem to indicate that, if $\alpha\nu \neq 1$, the RUMIT-optimal savings path approaches its asymptotic value α in a strictly monotonic way, from below if $(\bar{x} - x_0)(1 - \alpha\nu) < 0$ and from above, if $(\bar{x} - x_0)(1 - \alpha\nu) > 0$. Now, if one considers that a higher savings ratio should not be imposed on poorer generations, this means that in the case where $x_0 < \bar{x}$, RUMIT is only acceptable if $\nu > 1/\alpha > 1$. For $\alpha = 1/3$, ν would have to be at least equal to 3.

Notice, however, that the condition $\alpha\nu > 1$ has been derived under the particular assumption of a constant $\Phi(z)$. It is to be expected that, more generally, $\Phi(z)$ is a monotonically increasing function of z over its range of definition. A simple assumption would be

$$U(z) = -(z - z_s)^{-(\nu-1)}, \qquad z_s < z < 1$$

i.e.

$$\Phi = -\nu z/(z - z_s), \qquad z_s < z < 1 \tag{3.6}$$

where $z_s > 0$ denotes the "starvation" level of relative per capita consumption. Such a form of $U(z)$ is likely to ensure that the savings ratio is the smaller the wealthier the generation, perhaps even in the case where $x_0 > \bar{x}$, provided only ν is chosen small enough in (3.6).

It is also important to realize that if some device for the econometric determination of $U(z)$ can be found, $U(z)$ need only be determined over $0 < z < 1$, i.e. over an interval of c-values which are perfectly within the range of experiences of the present generation. In this respect, as well as from the conceptual point of view, RUMIT seems to constitute a sensible improvement over UMIT.

One may naturally object that RUMIT has only been defined for the growth model of Section 1.2. It must be admitted that the generalization of RUMIT to other growth models is not straightforward. A certain specialization of the optimality criterion is perhaps the price to pay for reasonable results. As already pointed out, rules of optimal behavior can only be defined with respect to a well defined game.

MATHEMATICAL APPENDIX

A. PROOFS OF THEOREMS IN PART I

Proof of Theorem 1.5.2

We show that

(i) $\kappa(\tau)$ is uniquely determined over $0 \leqslant \tau < +\infty$ by the initial condition $\kappa(0) = \kappa_0 (> 0)$;

(ii) $\kappa(\tau)$ is bounded over $0 \leqslant \tau < +\infty$;

(iii) if

$$\lim_{\tau \to +\infty} \kappa(\tau) = \kappa_{+\infty}, \qquad \kappa_{+\infty} = \text{constant} \tag{M.1}$$

then

$$\kappa_{+\infty} = \overline{\kappa}$$

(iv) there is a $t_\delta > 0$ for every $\delta > 0$ such that $\kappa(\tau)$ has no extremum $> \overline{\kappa} + \delta$ or $< \overline{\kappa} - \delta$ for $\tau \geqslant t_\delta$.

It then follows that there is a $t \geqslant t_\delta$ for every $\delta > 0$, such that

$$|\kappa(\tau) - \overline{\kappa}| < \delta, \qquad \tau \geqslant t.$$

Proof of (i) From the tautological equation

$$\dot{x} = s(\tau)\exp[\rho\tau]f(x) - \lambda(\tau)x$$

and the continuity of $s(\tau)$, $\lambda(\tau)$ and $f(x)$, it follows that the initial condition $x(0) = x_0 > 0$ determines $x(\tau)$ over its interval of existence. The latter is infinite, since $0 < s(\tau) < 1$, $0 \leqslant \tau < +\infty$. From the definition $\kappa = x\exp[-\rho\tau]/f(x)$, it follows that (i) must hold true.

Proof of (ii) It follows from the tautological equation

$$s = (\gamma + \lambda)\kappa + [\dot{\kappa}/(1-\alpha)]$$

that $\dot{\kappa} \leqslant 0$ if $\kappa \geqslant s/(\gamma + \lambda)$. Hence, writing $g = \lambda + \gamma$ and g_{lb} for the g.l.b. of g in $0 < x < +\infty$,

$$\kappa(\tau) \leqslant \max\left\{\kappa_0, 1/g_{lb}\right\}.$$

Proof of (iii) If $\kappa_{+\infty} = 0$, then

$$\lim_{\tau \to +\infty} (\dot{x}/x) = (\bar{s}/\kappa_{+\infty}) - \bar{\lambda}$$

$$= +\infty.$$

If $\kappa_{+\infty} > 0$, then

$$\lim_{\tau \to +\infty} \frac{x}{f(x)} = \lim_{\tau \to +\infty} \kappa_{+\infty} \exp[\rho\tau] = +\infty.$$

Hence, in both cases

$$\lim_{\tau \to +\infty} x = +\infty.$$

It follows that

$$\lim_{\tau \to +\infty} \dot{\kappa}(t) = \lim_{\tau \to +\infty} (1-\alpha)(s - g\kappa)$$

$$= (1-\bar{\alpha})\,\bar{g}\,(\bar{\kappa} - \kappa_{+\infty})$$

where

$$\bar{g} = \bar{\lambda} + [\rho/(1-\bar{\alpha})]$$

and

$$\bar{\lambda} = \lim_{\tau \to +\infty} \lambda(\tau).$$

Now the existence of $\kappa_{+\infty}$ requires that this limit be zero, i.e. $\kappa_{+\infty} = \bar{\kappa}$.

Proof of (iv) Given δ, take $\epsilon = \delta\bar{g}/2$. Then there is a t_ϵ such that $|\bar{s} - s(\tau)| < \epsilon$ for $\tau \geqslant t_\epsilon$. Assume first that there is a $T \geqslant t$ for every $t \geqslant t_\epsilon$ such that $\dot{\kappa} = 0$ and $\kappa > \bar{\kappa} + \delta$. Then, at T,

$$(s - \bar{s}) + (\bar{s} - g\kappa) = 0$$

and, consequently,

$$|\bar{g}\bar{\kappa} - g\kappa| < \epsilon$$

i.e.

$$\begin{aligned} g/\bar{g} &< [\bar{\kappa} + (\epsilon/\bar{g})]/\kappa \\ &= [\bar{\kappa} + (\delta/2)]/(\bar{\kappa} + \delta). \end{aligned}$$

Since λ tends to $\bar{\lambda}$, it follows that there is a $\beta > 0$ and a $t_\beta \geqslant t_\epsilon$ such that $\alpha < \bar{\alpha} - \beta$ for $T \geqslant t_\beta$. Now this is contrary to $\alpha'(x) \leqslant 0$. If $\alpha'(x) \geqslant 0$, it implies $x(T) \leqslant x^*$ for some x^* and $T \geqslant t_\beta$, i.e. the absurd conclusion that

$$\begin{aligned} 0 < \bar{\kappa} &< \kappa(T) \\ &\leqslant [x^*/f(x^*)]\exp[-\rho T] \end{aligned}$$

however great $T \geqslant t_\beta$.

Assume next that there is a $T \geqslant t$ for every $t \geqslant t_\epsilon$ such that $\dot{\kappa} = 0$ and $\kappa < \bar{\kappa} - \delta$. Then,

$$g > \frac{\bar{\kappa} - (\delta/2)}{\bar{\kappa} - \delta}\bar{g}, \qquad T \geqslant t_\epsilon. \tag{M.2}$$

Since λ tends to $\bar{\lambda}$, (M.2) is contrary to $\alpha'(x) \geqslant 0$. If $\alpha'(x) \leqslant 0$, it implies $x(\tau) \leqslant x^*$ for some x^* and $T \geqslant t^* \geqslant t_\epsilon$. Hence,

$$\lim_{\tau \to +\infty} \kappa(\tau) = 0$$

which is impossible by (iii).

q.e.d.

Proof of Theorem 1.6.2

The proof follows at once from (ii) in the proof of Theorem 1.5.2.

q.e.d.

Proof of Theorem 3.1.1

It follows from the Q-EG and IG assumptions that, in terms of x, Euler's equation is a second-order differential equation of the form

$$x = h(\tau, \dot{x}, x)$$

where h is continuously differentiable with respect to t, $\dot{x}$ and x in the region $R: 0 \leqslant \tau < +\infty$, $0 < x < +\infty$, $-\infty < \dot{x} < \exp[\rho\tau]f(x) - \lambda x$. This implies that only one solution of Euler's equation can go through a given point $(t, \dot{x}_t, x_t)$ of R. In other words, the UMIT-optimal program must be self-consistent.

q.e.d.

Proof of Theorem 3.2.6

We know from Theorem 3.3.2 that $\hat{\kappa}(\tau)$ becomes monotonic from some point of time onwards. Since, from Theorem 1.6.2, $\hat{\kappa}(\tau) < \kappa_+$ from some point of time onwards, it follows that

$$\lim_{\tau \to +\infty} \hat{\kappa}(\tau) = \kappa_{+\infty}, \qquad \kappa_{+\infty} = \text{constant}.$$

Hence, by Euler's equation,

$$\lim_{\tau \to +\infty} (\dot{\hat{c}}/\hat{c}) = [(\alpha/\kappa_{+\infty}) - (i + \lambda)](1/\nu). \tag{M.3}$$

Now, by Theorem 1.5.2, the right-hand side of (M.3) can only be equal to γ. This implies

$$\kappa_{+\infty} = \alpha/[(\gamma + \lambda) + i - i_0], \qquad i_0 = (1 - \nu)\gamma$$

and, consequently, the theorem.

q.e.d.

Proof of Theorem 3.2.7

From Theorem 5.1 and 6.1 in Paper 3 and Observation 2 in Paper 2, an Eulerian program is UMIT-optimal if $i \geqslant i_0$. It is therefore also efficient if $i \geqslant i_0$. If $i < i_0$, it is inefficient from Theorems 3.2.5 and 3.2.6.

q.e.d.

Proof of Theorem 3.2.8

The proof follows from Theorem 3.2.7 and Theorems 5.1 and 6.1 of Paper 3.

q.e.d.

Proof of Theorem 3.2.11

Assume that $0 \leqslant i < i_0$ and that an indefinitely feasible Eulerian program $\tilde{\kappa}(\tau)$ exists along which the MC condition is satisfied. By Theorem 3.2.6,

$$\begin{aligned}\lim_{\tau \to +\infty} \tilde{s} &= \tilde{s}_{+\infty} \\ &> \alpha.\end{aligned}$$

Write $\kappa^*(\tau)$ for the indefinitely feasible program defined by

$$s^*(\tau) = \alpha, \qquad 0 \leqslant \tau < +\infty.$$

Then, for some $t > 0$

$$(c^* - \tilde{c}) > \tfrac{1}{2}[(1-\alpha)(\alpha/g)^{\alpha/(1-\alpha)} - (1-s_{+\infty})(s_{+\infty}/g)^{\alpha/(1-\alpha)}]\exp(\gamma\tau), \qquad \tau \geqslant t$$

where the term between square brackets is easily shown to be positive for $s_{+\infty} \neq \alpha$. Hence,

$$\begin{aligned}\int_0^{+\infty} (U^* - \tilde{U})\exp[-i\tau]\mathrm{d}\tau \\ &> \text{pos. const} \int_0^{+\infty} \exp[\{(1-\nu)\gamma - i\}\tau] \\ &= +\infty.\end{aligned}$$

The MC condition requires, consequently, $i \geqslant i_0$. But, then, every Eulerian program is UMIT-optimal by Theorem 6.1 in Paper 3.

q.e.d.

Proof of Theorem 3.2.12

Let $x^*(\tau)$ be the indefinitely feasible program defined by

$$s^*(\tau) = \tfrac{1}{2}.$$

Then,

$$\lim_{\tau \to +\infty} \frac{c^*(\tau)}{c(\tau)} = \lim_{\tau \to +\infty} \frac{\tfrac{1}{2}}{1 - s(\tau)} \frac{y^*(\tau)}{y(\tau)}$$

$$= +\infty$$

Indeed, $1 - s(\tau)$ tends to 0, while

$$\lim_{\tau \to +\infty} (y^*/y) = \text{constant}$$

since

$$\lim_{\tau \to +\infty} [(\dot{y}^*/y) - (\dot{y}/y)] = 0.$$

q.e.d.

Proof of Theorem 3.2.13

Along any indefinitely feasible program which satisfies $c(\tau) \to +\infty$ as $\tau \to +\infty$, one has

$$\int_0^{+\infty} U(c)\exp[-i\tau]d\tau > -A \int_0^{+\infty} \exp[-i\tau]d\tau$$

$$= -(A/i)$$

for some positive number A. On the other hand, denoting by $x_s(\tau)$ the indefinitely feasible program defined by $s_s(\tau) = 1$, $0 \leqslant \tau < +\infty$, one has

$$\int_0^{+\infty} [U(c) - U(y_s)]\exp[-i\tau]d\tau$$

$$< \int_0^{+\infty} u(y_s)(c - y_s)\exp[-i\tau]d\tau$$

$$< - \int_0^{+\infty} u(y_s)\dot{x}\exp[-i\tau]d\tau$$

$$= - u(y_s)x\exp[-i\tau]\big|_0^{+\infty}$$

$$- \int_0^{+\infty} ixu(y_s)\exp[-i\tau]d\tau$$

$$+ \int_0^{+\infty} xu'(y_s)\dot{y}_s\exp[-i\tau]d\tau$$

$$< u(y_0)x_0.$$

q.e.d.

Proof of Theorem 3.3.2

At an extremum, $\dot{\kappa} = 0$ and, by Euler's equation (3.2.3),

$$\ddot{\kappa} = (1-s)(1-\alpha)\left\{\gamma + (1/\Phi)\ [(\alpha/\kappa) - i - \lambda]\right\}.$$

Hence, $\dot{\kappa} = 0$ and $\kappa \geqslant \bar{\kappa}$ imply $\ddot{\kappa} > 0$. It follows that an indefinitely feasible Eulerian program $\tilde{\kappa}(\tau)$ cannot have a maximum $\geqslant \bar{\kappa}$. Moreover, it cannot have a minimum $\geqslant \bar{\kappa}$. Indeed, such a minimum would imply

$$\lim_{\tau \to +\infty} \tilde{\kappa}(\tau) = \kappa_{+\infty} > \bar{\kappa}.$$

Now, Euler's equation excludes any value for $\kappa_{+\infty}$ other than $1/(\gamma + \lambda)$. $\kappa_{+\infty} = 1/(\gamma + \lambda)$ implies, however,

$$\lim_{\tau \to +\infty} \tilde{s}(\tau) = 1$$

i.e. the inefficiency of $\tilde{\kappa}(\tau)$.

In order to prove the theorem, it is sufficient to show that $\tilde{\kappa}(\tau) \leqslant \bar{\kappa}$ cannot have a minimum at t_2 after a maximum at $t_1 < t_2$. Indeed, a maximum which is not followed by a minimum is excluded, since it would imply

$$\lim_{\tau \to +\infty} \tilde{\kappa}(\tau) = \kappa_{+\infty} < \bar{\kappa}$$

i.e. a condition which is contrary to Euler's equation.

Assume that $\tilde{\kappa}(\tau)$ does have a maximum at t_1 and a minimum at $t_2 > t_1$. Then,

$$\tilde{\kappa}(t_1) > \tilde{\kappa}(t_2)$$

$$\dot{\tilde{\kappa}}(t_1) = \dot{\tilde{\kappa}}(t_2) = 0$$

and

$$\ddot{\tilde{\kappa}}(t_1) < 0 < \ddot{\tilde{\kappa}}(t_2).$$

It follows that

$$\{(1/\Phi)[(\alpha/\kappa)-(i+\lambda)]\}_{\tau=t_1}<\gamma<\{(1/\Phi)[(\alpha/\kappa)-(i+\lambda)]\}_{\tau=t_2}$$

and, by Euler's equation, that

$$(\dot{c}/c)_{\tau=t_1}>(\dot{c}/c)_{\tau=t_2}. \tag{M.4}$$

On the other hand, Euler's equation implies also

$$\frac{\mathrm{d}}{\mathrm{d}\tau}\frac{\dot{c}}{c}=\frac{\mathrm{d}}{\mathrm{d}\tau}\frac{1}{-\Phi}\left[\frac{\alpha}{\kappa}-(i+\lambda)\right]$$

$$=\left|\frac{\Phi'}{\Phi}\right|\left(\frac{\dot{c}}{c}\right)^2 c-\frac{\alpha\dot{\kappa}}{\kappa^2\,|\,\Phi\,|}.$$

Since $\dot{\kappa}\leqslant 0$, $t_1\leqslant t_2$, it follows that

$$(\dot{c}/c)_{\tau=t_1}<(\dot{c}/c)_{\tau=t_2}$$

which is contrary to (M.4).

q.e.d.

Proof of Theorem 3.4.1

We know from Theorem 3.2.2 that $\hat{x}(\tau)$ and $\hat{\hat{x}}(\tau)$ must, respectively, satisfy over $t\leqslant\tau<+\infty$

$$\hat{\Phi}(\dot{\hat{c}}/\hat{c})+(\hat{\alpha}/\hat{\kappa})-\lambda=i[\hat{c}(0)]$$

and

$$\hat{\hat{\Phi}}(\dot{\hat{\hat{c}}}/\hat{\hat{c}})+(\hat{\hat{\alpha}}/\hat{\hat{\kappa}})-\lambda=i[\hat{c}(t)].$$

This implies the theorem.

q.e.d.

Proof of Theorem 3.4.2

If $\nu = 1 + \epsilon > 1$, then

$$[\ln u(c) c^{1+(\epsilon/2)}]' = (1/c)\,[\Phi + 1 + \tfrac{1}{2}\epsilon]$$

$$< 0$$

since $\Phi + \nu \leqslant 0$ by $\Phi' \geqslant 0$. It follows that the integral

$$U(c) - U(c_0) = \int_{c_0}^{c} u(c)\mathrm{d}c \tag{M.5}$$

converges as $c \to +\infty$. If $\nu = 1 - \epsilon < 1$, then

$$[\ln u(c) c]' = (1/c)\,[\Phi + 1]$$

$$> 0$$

for some $c^* > 0$. This implies that (M.5), i.e. $U(c)$, diverges.

q.e.d.

Proof of Theorem 4.3.2

In the UMIT case and under the Bernoulli assumption, Euler's equation reads

$$\nu(\dot{c}/c) = (1/\kappa_0) - \eta, \qquad \eta = i + \lambda. \tag{M.6}$$

The solution is

$$c = c_0 \exp[\{(1/\kappa_0) - \eta\}(t/\nu)]. \tag{M.7}$$

From (M.7) and

$$c = y - \lambda x - \dot{x}$$

$$= y - \lambda\kappa_0 y - \kappa_0 y$$

we get

$$y = y_0 \exp[\{(1/\kappa_0) - \lambda\}t]$$

$$-\frac{c_0 \exp[\{(1/\kappa_0) - \lambda\}t]}{\kappa_0} \int_0^t \exp\left[\left\{\left(\frac{1}{\kappa_0} - \eta\right)\frac{1}{\nu} - \left(\frac{1}{\kappa_0} - \lambda\right)\right\}\tau\right] \mathrm{d}\tau$$

$$= y_0 \exp[\{(1/\kappa_0) - \lambda\}t] - \left(\frac{c_0}{\kappa_0}\right)\frac{\nu \exp[\{(1/\kappa_0 - \lambda\}t]}{(i_0 - i)}\left\{\exp\left[(i_0 - i)\frac{t}{\nu}\right] - 1\right\}$$

$$= \left[y_0 + \frac{c_0 \nu}{\kappa_0 (i_0 - i)}\right] \exp[\{(1/\kappa_0) - \lambda\} t/\nu]$$

$$- \left(\frac{c_0}{\kappa_0}\right)\frac{\nu \exp[\{(1/\kappa_0) - \eta\}t]}{(i_0 - i)}. \tag{M.8}$$

Now $i \leqslant i_0$ implies

$$[(1/\kappa_0) - \eta](1/\nu) \geqslant (1/\kappa_0) - \lambda$$

and consequently, that y becomes negative from some point of time onwards. This proves the necessity of $i > i_0$.

Granted $i > i_0$, we determine c_0 by making c_0 as great as possible without making y negative. Thus from (M.8) we obtain

$$y_0 - (c_0 \nu/\kappa_0)[1/(i - i_0)] = 0.$$

Hence,

$$c_0 = (y_0 \kappa_0/\nu)(i - i_0)$$

and finally,

$$y = (x_0/\kappa_0)\exp[\{(1/\kappa_0) - \eta\}(t/\nu)]$$

$$x = x_0 \exp[\{(1/\kappa_0) - \eta\}(t/\nu)]$$

$$c = (x_0/\nu)(i - i_0)\exp[\{(1/\kappa_0) - \eta\}(t/\nu)].$$

This solution is UMIT-optimal, since for any other indefinitely feasible program $c^*(\tau)$, by Lemma 3.1, Paper 2,

$$I[c^*(\tau)_0^{+\infty}] - I[c(\tau)_0^{+\infty}] < \lim_{\tau \to +\infty} x c^{-\nu} \exp[-i\tau]$$

$$= 0.$$

This establishes the theorem, since it is easily verified that the MUEFT differential equation can only have an exponential solution.

q.e.d.

Proof of Theorem 4.4.1

It follows from (4.2.3) in Part I that $\hat{x}_\omega(\tau)$ satisfies

$$\int_t^{t+\omega} \left[\hat{u}_\omega \left(\frac{\partial \hat{y}_\omega}{\partial \hat{x}_\omega} - (i+\lambda) + \frac{\dot{\hat{u}}_\omega}{\hat{u}_\omega} \right) \right]_\tau [\hat{x}(\tau) - \hat{x}_\omega(\tau)]$$

$$\times \exp[-i(\tau - t)] \mathrm{d}\tau$$

$$= \int_t^{t+\omega} \left[\frac{\partial \hat{y}_\omega}{\partial \hat{x}_\omega} \hat{u}_\omega \right]_{\omega+\tau} [\hat{x}(\tau) - \hat{x}_\omega(\tau)]$$

$$\times \exp[-(i+\lambda)\omega - i(\tau - t)] \mathrm{d}\tau$$

$$< \max_{t \leqslant \tau \leqslant t+\omega} \left\{ \hat{x}(\tau) - \hat{x}_\omega(\tau) \right\} \int_{t+\omega}^{t+2\omega} \left(\frac{\partial \hat{y}_\omega}{\partial \hat{x}_\omega} \hat{u}_\omega \right)_\tau$$

$$\times \exp[-(i+\lambda)\omega - i(\tau - t - \omega)] \mathrm{d}\tau$$

$$< \max_{t \leqslant \tau \leqslant t+\omega} \left\{ \hat{x}(\tau) - \hat{x}_\omega(\tau) \right\} \exp[-i\omega] \int_{t+\omega}^{t+2\omega} \left(\frac{\partial \hat{y}_\omega}{\partial \hat{x}_\omega} \hat{u}_\omega \right)_\tau$$

$$\times \exp[-(i+\lambda)(\tau - t - \omega)] \mathrm{d}\tau$$

$$= \max_{t \leqslant \tau \leqslant t+\omega} \left\{ \hat{x}(\tau) - \hat{x}_\omega(\tau) \right\}$$

$$\times \exp[-i\omega] \hat{u}_\omega(t+\omega) \quad \text{(using Definition 2.5.1 in Part I).}$$

Using (2.4.32) in Paper 1, Part II, it follows further that

$$\int_t^{t+\omega} [U(\hat{c}) - U(\hat{c}_\omega)]\exp[-i(\tau - t)]\mathrm{d}\tau$$

$$< \exp[i\omega]\hat{u}_\omega(t+\omega)\left[\max_{t\leqslant\tau\leqslant t+\omega}\left\{\hat{x}(\tau) - \hat{x}_\omega(\tau)\right\} - \left\{\hat{x}(\omega+t) - \hat{x}_\omega(t+\omega)\right\}\right]$$

q.e.d.

Proof of Theorem 4.4.4

Let us respectively write $\hat{c}(\tau)$ and $\hat{c}^*(\tau)$ for the UMIT-optimal and MUEFT-optimal programs defined by the initial GU capital-output ratio

$$\kappa_0 = \overline{\kappa}_\omega = (1/2g)(1 - \exp[-g\omega]), \qquad g = 2\rho + \lambda. \qquad \text{(M.10)}$$

Then, by Theorem 3.1 in Paper 4,

$$I[\hat{c}(\tau)_t^{t+\omega}] = (\overline{\kappa}/2)^{½}\int_t^{t+\omega}\left\{1 - m\exp[-g(\tau - t)]\right\}\mathrm{d}\tau$$

$$= (\overline{\kappa}/2)^{½}[\omega + (m/g)(\exp[-g\omega] - 1)]$$

$$= (1/2g^{½})[\omega - (m/g)(1-m)]$$

where $\overline{\kappa} = ½g$ denotes the GU UMIT capital-output ratio and

$$m = 1 - (\kappa_0/\overline{\kappa})$$

$$= \exp[-g\omega]).$$

On the other hand, it follows at once from (M.10) and (4.3.2) that

$$I[\hat{c}_\omega(\tau)_t^{t+\omega}] = \kappa_0^{½}[1 - g\kappa_0]^{½}\omega$$

$$= (\omega/2g^{½})(1 - m^2)^{½}$$

Hence

$$\frac{I[\hat{c}_\omega(\tau)_t^{t+\omega}]}{I[\hat{c}(\tau)_t^{t+\omega}]} = \frac{g\omega(1-m^2)^{½}}{g\omega - m(1-m)}$$

$$= \frac{-(\ln m)(1-m^2)^{½}}{-(\ln m) - m(1-m)}.$$

q.e.d.

B. DICTIONARY OF NOTATIONS

B.1 Abbreviations

EG – Exponential Growth.
IG – Instantaneous Government.
MUEFT – Marginal Utility Equilibrium over Finite Time.
MUEIT – Marginal Utility Equilibrium over Infinite Time.
Q-EG – Quasi-exponential Growth.
Q-EG λ_0 – Quasi-exponential Growth under exponential labor growth.
RUMIT – Relative Utility Maximization over Infinite Time.
UMIT – Utility Maximization of Infinite Time.

B.2 "Unmarked" variables and parameters

B.2.1 Latin letters

c – consumption per labor unit.
g – $[\rho/(1-\alpha)] + \lambda$
i – time discount rate
L – labor force.
m – labor-population ratio L/P.
P – population.
Q – technological level.
s – net savings ratio $(\lambda x + \dot{x})/y$.
t – given point of time.
u – marginal utility of consumption per labor unit.
U – utility of consumption per labor unit.
x – capital per labor unit.
y – production per labor unit.
z – relative consumption per labor unit c/y_+.

B.2.2 Greek letters

α – elasticity of production with respect to capital: $xf'(x)/f(x)$.
γ – $\rho/(1-\alpha)$.
λ – growth rate of the labor force and of the total population, $\dot{L}/L = \dot{P}/P$.
ρ – technological progress, $\dot{Q}/Q$.
κ – capital-output ratio, x/y.
τ – time variable.
ξ – absolute value of the maximum rate of disinvestment of capital per labor unit: $\dot{x}/x \geqslant -\xi$.

B.3 "Marked" variables and parameters

B.3.1 General notations

A tilde ($\tilde{\ }$) on a variable means that the latter satisfies Euler's equation.

A hat ($\hat{\ }$) on a variable having no subscript ω, e.g. $\hat{x}(\tau)$, means that the variable denotes a UMIT-optimal program.

A hat ($\hat{\ }$) on a variable having a subscript ω, e.g. $\hat{x}_\omega(\tau)$, means that the variable denotes a MUEFT-optimal program.

A bar ($\bar{\ }$) on a variable (Latin letter) with no subscript ω, e.g. $\bar{x}$, denotes the asymptotic value of the variable divided by $\exp[\gamma\tau]$, as determined by an asymptotically constant and positive savings ratio $\bar{s}$. Thus, for instance

$$\bar{x} = \lim_{\tau\to+\infty} x(\tau)\exp[-\gamma\tau]$$

where $x(\tau)$ is determined by some given indefinitely feasible savings program satisfying

$$\lim_{\tau\to+\infty} s(\tau) = \bar{s}, \qquad 0 < \bar{s} \leqslant 1.$$

In particular, $\bar{s}$ may be the UMIT GU savings ratio

$$\bar{s} = \lim_{x\to+\infty} \left\{ \alpha g/(g + i - i_0) \right\}.$$

A bar ($\bar{\ }$) on a variable (Latin letter) with a subscript ω, e.g. $\bar{x}_\omega$, denotes the MUEFT-optimal asymptotic value of the variable divided by $\exp[\gamma\tau]$. Thus, for instance,

$$\bar{x}_\omega = \lim_{\tau\to+\infty} \hat{x}_\omega(\tau)\exp[-\gamma\{\hat{x}(\tau)\}\tau].$$

A bar ($\bar{\ }$) on a parameter (Greek letter) denotes the limit value of the parameter as its arguments tend to infinity. Thus,

$$\bar{\alpha} = \lim_{x\to+\infty} \alpha(x)$$

$$\bar{\gamma} = \rho/(1-\bar{\alpha})$$

$$\bar{\lambda} = \lim_{\tau\to+\infty} \lambda(\tau)$$

$$\bar{g} = \bar{\gamma} + \bar{\lambda}.$$

The subscript ω refers to the MUEFT strategy (see the above definition of hats on variables having a subscript ω; see also i_ω in Section B.3.2).

B.3.2 Particular marks on variables (Latin letters)

c_{lb} = non-negative lower bound of the interval $c_{lb} < c < +\infty$ over which $U(c)$ is defined.

c_s = starvation level of consumption. (A necessary condition for feasibility is $c > c_s$.)

i_0 $= (1-\nu)\rho/(1-\overline{\alpha})$.

i_{00} $= \lim\limits_{c \to +\infty} i(c)$ in case $i = i(c)$, $i'(c) \leqslant 0$.

i_ω $= \dfrac{\alpha_{T+\omega}}{\kappa_{T+\omega}} \cdot \dfrac{u_{T+\omega}}{u_T} \exp[-i\omega - \int\limits_t^{t+\omega} \lambda_{\tau'} d\tau']$

$s_s(\tau)$ $= 1$, $0 \leqslant \tau < +\infty$ (see Proof of Theorem 3.2.13 in Section A).

$x_1(\tau)$ = limit path in Paper 1.

x_m = minimum value of x in Paper 1.

x_0, x_t = initial values of x at $\tau = 0$ or $\tau = t$.

$x_s(\tau)$ = indefinitely feasible $x(\tau)$ defined by $s_s(\tau) = 1$, $0 \leqslant \tau < +\infty$ (see Proof of Theorem 3.2.13, Section A).

$x_d(\tau; \omega, a)$ = indefinitely feasible $x(\tau)$, $\omega \leqslant \tau < +\infty$ defined by $x(\omega) = a$ and $\dot{x}(\tau) = -\xi x(\tau)$, $\omega \leqslant \tau < +\infty$ (Paper 1).

$x_s(\tau; \omega, a)$ = indefinitely feasible $x(\tau)$, $\omega \leqslant \tau < +\infty$, defined by $x(\omega) = a$ and $c(\tau) = c_s$, $\omega \leqslant \tau < +\infty$ (Paper 1).

x_-, x_+ = minimum and maximum solutions of

$$\exp[\rho\tau] f[x(\tau)] - g_{lb} x(\tau) = c_s$$

$y_s(\tau)$ $= \exp[\rho\tau] f[x_s(\tau)]$ (see Proof of Theorem 3.2.13 in Section A).

$y_+(\tau)$ $= \exp[\rho\tau] f[x_+(\tau)]$; if $c_s = 0$ and $f(x) = x^a$, then (Paper 5)

$$y_+(\tau) = (1/g)^{a/(1-a)} \exp[\gamma\tau].$$

B.3.3 Particular marks on parameters (Greek letters)

κ_0, κ_t = initial values of $\kappa(\tau)$ at $\tau = 0$ or $\tau = t$.

B.4 Mathematical notations

A dot ($\dot{}$) on a variable, e.g. $\dot{c}$, denotes differentiation with respect to time. A prime ($'$) at the upper right side of a function of a single variable, e.g. $u'(c)$, denotes differentiation with respect to this variable. Accordingly, double primes denote second derivatives, and so on.

BIBLIOGRAPHY

Akerlof, G. A., "Stability, Marginal Products, Putty, and Clay", *Essays on the Theory of Optimal Economic Growth,* edited by K. Shell, The MIT Press (1967).

Arrow, K. J. and M. Nerlove, "Optimal Advertising Policy under Dynamic Conditions", *Economica, New Series,* Vol.29(114), pp 129-142 (May 1962).

Arrow, K. J., "Discounting and Public Investment Criteria", 1965 Western Resources Conference, Seminar in Water Resources Research (July 1965).

Atsumi, H., "Neoclassical Growth and the Efficient Program of Capital Accumulation", *Review of Economic Studies,* Vol.32(2), pp 127-136 (April 1965).

Bardhan, P. K., "Optimum Accumulation and International Trade", *ibid.,* Vol.32(3), pp 241-244 (July 1965).

Bardhan, P. K., "Optimum Foreign Borrowing", *Essays on the Theory of Optimal Economic Growth,* edited by K. Shell, The MIT Press (1967).

Bator, F. M., "On Capital Productivity, Input Allocation, and Growth", *Quarterly Journal of Economics,* Vol.71(1), pp 86-106 (February 1957).

Beals, R. and T. C. Koopmans, "Maximizing Stationary Utility in a Constant Technology", Cowles Foundation Discussion Paper No.229, Yale University, New Haven, Connecticut (1967).

Bellman, R. and S. E. Dreyfus, *Applied Dynamic Programming,* Princeton University Press (1962).

Black, J., "Optimum Savings Reconsidered or Ramsey without Tears", *Economic Journal,* Vol.72(286), pp 360-366 (June 1962).

Black, J., "Technical Progress and Optimum Savings", *Review of Economic Studies,* Vol.29(80), pp 238-240 (June 1962).

Boltyanskii, V. G., L. S. Pontryagin, R. V. Gamrelidze and E. F. Mischenko, "The Mathematical Theory of Optimal Processes", translated from the Russian, Interscience, New York and London (1962).

Bombach, H., "Optimales Wachstum und Gleichgewichwaschstum", *Schriften des Vereins für Socialpolitik,* Neue Folge, Band 27 (1962).

Bos, H. C. and J. Tinbergen, "The Optimum Rate of Development", *Mathematical Models of Economic Growth,* pp 24-31, McGraw-Hill (1962).

Bruno, M., "Optimal Accumulation in Discrete Capital Models", *Essays on the Theory of Optimal Economic Growth,* edited by K. Shell, The MIT Press (1967).

Bruno, M., "Optimal Patterns of Trade and Development", *Review of Economics and Statistics,* Vol.49(4), pp 545-554 (November 1967).

Carter, N. G., "A New Look at the Sandee Model", *Essays on the Theory of Optimal Economic Growth,* edited by K. Shell, The MIT Press (1967).

Cass, D., "Studies in the Theory of Optimal Economic Growth", Technical Report No.6, Department of Economics, University of Chicago (1965).

Cass, D., "Optimum Growth in an Aggregative Model of Capital Accumulation", *Review of Economic Studies,* Vol.32(3), pp 233-240 (July 1965).

Cass, D., "Optimum Growth in an Aggregative Model of Capital Accumulation: Turnpike Theorem", *Econometrica,* Vol.34(4), pp 833-885 (October 1966).

Cass, D. and M. E. Yarri, "Individual Saving, Aggregate Capital Accumulation, and Efficient Growth", *Essays on the Theory of Optimal Economic Growth",* edited by K. Shell, The MIT Press (1967).

Cerny, M. and J. Skolka, "Outline of an Optimum Long-term Plan Model", English Summary, European, Meeting of the Econometric Society, Warsaw (1966).

Chakravarty, S., "The Existence of an Optimum Saving Programme", *Econometrica,* Vol.30(1), pp 178-187 (January 1962).

Chakravarty, S., "Optimal Savings with Finite Planning Horizon", *International Economic Review,* Vol.3(1), pp 338-355 (September, 1962).

Chakravarty, S. and R. S. Eckhaus, *An Approach to Multi-sectoral Intertemporal Planning Model,* MIT Center for International Studies (April 1962; revised November 1962).

Chakravarty, S., "Optimal Investment and Technical Progress", *Review of Economic Studies,* Vol.31(3), pp 203-206 (June 1964).

Chakravarty, S., "Optimal Programme of Capital Accumulation in a Multisector Economy", *Econometrica,* Vol.33(3), pp 557-570 (July 1965).

Chakravarty, S., "Optimal Savings with Finite Planning Horizon: A Reply", *International Economic Review,* Vol.7(1), pp 119-123 (January 1966).

Chakravarty, S., "Alternative Preference Functions in Problems of Investment Planning on the National Level", *Activity Analysis in the Theory of Growth and Planning,* edited by E. Malinvaud and M. O. L. Bacharach, pp 150-169, Macmillan Company of Canada (1967).

Champernowne, D. C., "Some Implications of Golden Age Conditions When Savings Equal Profits", *Review of Economic Studies,* Vol.29(80), pp 235-237 (June 1962).

Chase, E. S., "Leisure and Consumption", *Essays on the Theory of Optimal Economic Growth,* edited by K. Shell, The MIT Press (1967).

Chenerey, H. B. and A. Macewan, "Optimal Patterns of Growth and Aid: The Case of Pakistan", *The Theory and Design of Economic Development,* edited by I. Adelman and E. Thorbecke, John Hopkins Press, Baltimore (1966).

Connors, M. and D. Teichroew, *Optimal Control of Dynamic Operations Research Models,* International Textbook Company, Scranton, Pennsylvannia (1967).

Desgupta, A., "A note on Optimum Savings", *Econometrica,* Vol.32(3), pp 431-432 (July 1964).

Datta-Chaudhuri, M., "Optimum Allocation of Investments and Transportation in a Two-region Economy", *Essays on the Theory of Optimal Economic Growth,* edited by K. Shell, The MIT Press (1967).

Desrousseaux, J., "Expansion stable et taux d'intéret optimal", *Annales de Mines,* pp 31-46 (November 1961).

Diamond, P. A., *Essays in the Theory of Economic Growth,* Doctoral Dissertation, Massachusetts Institute of Technology (1963).

Diamond, P. A., "Optimal Growth in a Model of Srinavasan", *Yale Economic Essays,* Vol.4(1), pp 273-277 (1964).

Diamond, P. A., T. C. Koopmans and R. E. Williamson, "Stationary Utility and Time Perspective", *Econometrica,* Vol.32(1-2), pp 82-100 (January-April 1964).

Diamond, P. A., "The Evaluation of Infinite Utility Streams", *ibid.,* Vol.33(1), pp 170-177 (January 1965).

Diamond, P. A., "Optimal Paths of Capital Accumulation under the Minimum Time Objective: A Comment", Institute of Business and Economic Research, University of California (April 1965).

Diamond, P. A., "National Debt in a Neoclassical Growth Model", *American Economic Review,* Vol.55(5), pp 1126-1150 (December, 1965).

Dixit, A. K., "Optimal Development in the Labour-surplus Economy", *Review of Economic Studies,* Vol. 35(101), pp 23-34 (January 1968).

Dobell, A. R., "Growth Models and Optimal Accumulation", Brief background notes prepared for the Research Conference on Uncertainty, Harvard University (August 1966).

Drandakis, E. M., "Properties of Efficient Accumulation Paths in a Closed Production Model", Cowles Foundation Discussion Paper No.153, Yale University, Connecticut (January 1963).

Drandakis, E. M. and S. C. Hu, "On Optimal Induced Technical Progress", memorandum, University of Rochester, Rochester, N.Y.

Dreyfus, S. E. and R. E. Bellman, *Applied Dynamic Programming,* Princeton University Press (1962).

Eckaus, R. S. and S. Chakravarty, *An Approach to Multi-sectoral Intertemporal Planning Model,* MIT Center for International Studies (April 1962, revised November 1962).

Eckaus, R. S. and K. S. Parikh, "Planning for Growth: Multi-sectoral Intertemporal Models Applied to India", MIT Center for International Studies (April 1966).

Eckstein, O., "Investment Criteria for Economic Development and the Theory of Intertemporal Welfare Economics", *Quarterly Journal of Economics,* Vol.71(1), pp 56-85 (February 1967).

Frisch, R., *New Methods of Measuring Marginal Utility,* J. C. B. Mohr (Paul Siebeck), Tübingen (1932).

Frisch, R., "Dynamic Utility", *Econometrica,* Vol.32(3), pp 418-424 (July 1964).

Furuya, H. and K. Inada, "Balanced Growth and Intertemporal Efficiency in Capital Accumulation", *International Economic Review,* Vol.3(1), pp 94-107 (January 1962).

Gale, D., "On Equilibrium for a Multi-sector Model of Income Propagation", *ibid.,* Vol.5(2), pp 185-200 (May 1964).

Gale, D., "Optimal Programs for a Multi-sector Economy with an Infinite Time Horizon", Technical Report No.1, Department of Mathematics, Brown University, Providence, R.I. (1965).

Gale, D., "On Optimal Development in a Multi-sector Economy", *Review of Economic Studies,* Vol.34(97), pp 1-18 (January 1967).

Galenson, W. and H. Leibenstein, "Investment Criteria, Productivity and Economic Development", *Quarterly Journal of Economics,* Vol.69(3), pp 343-370 (August 1955).

Gamrelidze, R. V., V. G. Boltyanskii, L. S. Pontrygin and E. F. Mischenko, "The Mathematical Theory of Optimal Processes", translated from Russian, Interscience, New York and London (1962).

Goldman, S. M., H. H. Ryder and H. Uzawa, "Optimum Patterns of Trade and Investment in a Two-sector Model of International Trade", Technical Report No.7, NSF: GS-420, Department of Economics, University of Chicago (January 1965).

Goldman, S. M., "Sequential Planning and Continual Planning Revision", Working Paper No.120, Institute of Business and Economic Research, Center for Research in Management Science, University of California (1967).

Goldman, S. M., "Optimal Growth and Continual Planning Revision", *Review of Economic Studies,* Vol.35(102), pp 145-154 (April 1968).

Goodwin, R. M., "The Optimal Growth Path for an Underdeveloped Economy", *Economic Journal,* Vol.71(284), pp 756-774 (December 1961).

Hall, R. E., "Inheritance and Economic Growth", memorandum, Massachusetts Institute of Technology (January 1967).

Hall, R. E., "Intertemporal Preferences with Variable Rates of Impatience", memorandum, Massachusetts Institute of Technology (April 1967).

Hamada, K., "Optimum Capital Accumulation of an Economy Facing an International Capital Market: The Case of an Imperfect World Capital Market", Technical Report No.4, Department of Economics, University of Chicago (November 1965).

Hamada, K., "On the Optimal Transfer and Income Distribution in a Growing Economy", *Review of Economic Studies,* Vol.34(99), pp 285-294 (July 1967).

Haque, W., "A pseudo-classical Dynamic Programming Model of Capital Accumulation", *International Economic Review,* Vol.6(1), pp 32-46 (January 1965).

Harrod, R. F., "Second Essay in Dynamic Theory", *Economic Journal,* Vol.70(278), pp 277-293 (June 1960).

Heertje, A., "On the Optimum Rate of Savings", *Weltwirtschaftliches Archiv,* Vol.90(1), pp 7-44 (1963).

Hirshleifer, J., "On the Theory of Optimal Investment Decision", *The Journal of Political Economy,* Vol.66(4), pp 329-352 (August 1958).

Hu, S. C. and E. M. Drandakis, "On Optimal Induced Technical Progress", memorandum, University of Rochester, Rochester, N.Y.

Hurwicz, L., "Programming Involving Infinitely Many Variables and Constraints", *Activity Analysis in the Theory of Growth and Planning,* edited by E. Malinvaud and M. O. L. Bacharach, pp 142-149, Macmillan Company of Canada (1967).

Inada, K. and H. Furuya, "Balanced Growth and Intertemporal Efficiency in Capital Accumulation", *International Economic Review,* Vol.3(1), pp 94-107 (January 1962).

Inagaki, M., "The Golden Utility Path", memorandum, Netherlands Economic Institute (April 1963).

Inagaki, M., "Critical Comments on Phelps' Second Golden Rule Essay", *De Economist,* Vol. 114(9/10), pp 534-539 (September/October 1966).

Inagaki, M., "Balanced Growth Under Factor Augmenting Technological Progress", *Zeitschrift für die Gesamte Staatswizzenschaft,* Vol.123(7), pp 1-8 (January 1967).

Inagaki, M., "Efficient, Inefficient and Critical Growth", *Towards Balanced International Growth,* edited by H. C. Bos, North-Holland (1968).

Intrilligator, M., "Essay on Productivity and Savings", Chapter 2, PhD dissertation, Massachusetts Institute of Technology (1963).

Johansen, L., "Savings and Growth in Long-term Programming Models", memorandum, Institute of Economics, University of Oslo, Norway (1964).

Johansen, L., "Stone Theoretical Properties of a Two-sector Model of Optimal Growth", *Review of Economic Studies*, Vol.34(97), pp 125-142 (January 1967).

Johansen, L., "Some Problems of Pricing and Optimal Choice of Factor Proportions in a Dynamic Setting", *Econometrica, New Series,* Vol.34(134), pp 133-152 (May 1967).

Kahn, A. E., "Investment Criteria in Development Programs", *Quarterly Journal of Economics,* Vol.65(1), pp 38-61 (February 1951).

Kaldor, N., "Capital Accumulation and Economic Growth", *The Theory of Capital,* edited by F. A. Lutz and D. C. Hague, pp 177-222, St. Martin's Press, New York (1961).

Koopmans, T. C., "Stationary Ordinal Utility and Impatience", *Econometrica,* Vol.28(2), pp 287-309 (April 1960).

Koopmans, T. C., P. A. Diamond and R. E. Williamson, "Stationary Utility and Time Perspective", *Econometrica,* Vol.32(1-2), pp 82-100 (January-April 1964).

Koopmans, T. C., "On the Concept of Optimal Economic Growth", *Semaine d'Etude sur le Role de l'Analyse Econométrique dans la Formation de Plans de Dévelopment,* Pontifical Academy of Sciences, Vatican City, Vol.1, pp 225-287 (1965).

Koopmans, T. C., "Structure of Preference Over Time", Cowles Foundation, Discussion Paper No.206, . Yale University, Connecticut (1966).

Koopmans, T. C., "Objectives, Constraints and Outcomes of Optimal Growth Models", *Econometrica,* Vol.35(1), pp 1-15 (January 1967).

Koopmans, T. C. and R. Beals, "Maximizing Stationary Utility in a Constant Technology", Cowles Foundation Discussion Paper No.229, Yale University, Connecticut (1967).

Kurz, M., "A Two-sector Extension of Swan's Model of Economic Growth: The Case of No Technical Change", *International Economic Review,* Vol.4(1), pp 68-69 (January 1963).

Kurz, M., "Optimal Paths of Capital Accumulation under the Minimum Time Objective", *Econometrica,* Vol.33(1), pp 42-66 (January 1965).

Kurz, M., "Optimal Economic Growth and Wealth Effects", Technical Report No.136, Institute for Mathematical Studies in the Social Sciences Stanford University, Stanford, California (1965).

Leibenstein, H. and W. Galenson, "Investment Criteria, Productivity and Economic Development", *Quarterly Journal of Economics,* Vol.69(3), pp 343-370 (August 1955).

Leitmann, G., et al., *Optimization Techniques,* Academic Press, New York (1962).

Leontief, W. W., "Theoretical Note on Time-preference, Productivity of Capital, Stagnation and Economic Growth", *American Economic Review,* Vol.48(2), pp 105-111 (March 1958).

Leontief, W. W., "Time-preference and Economic Growth", *ibid.,* Vol. 49(5), pp 1041-1043 (December 1959).

Levhari, D., "Essays on Optimal Economic Growth", unpublished dissertation, Massachusetts Institute of Technology (June, 1964).

Levhari, D. and N. Liviatan, "The Concept of the Golden Rule in the Case of More than One Consumption Good", *American Economic Review,* Vol.58(1), pp 100-119 (March 1968).

Liviatan, N. and D. Levhari, "The Concept of the Golden Rule in the Case of More than One Consumption Good", *ibid.,* Vol.58(1), pp 100-119 (March 1968).

Macewan, A. and H. B. Chenerey, "Optimal Patterns of Growth and Aid: The Case of Pakistan", *The Theory and Design of Economic Development,* edited by I. Adelman and E. Thorbecke, John Hopkins Press, Baltimore (1966).

Mackenzie, L. W., "Accumulation Programs of Maximum Utility and the von Neuman Facet", memorandum, University of Rochester, Rochester, New York (March 1967).

Malinvaud, E., "Capital Accumulation and Efficient Allocation of Resources", *Econometrica,* Vol.21(2), pp 233-267 (April 1953).

Malinvaud, E., "Programmes d'expansions et taux d'interet", *ibid.,* Vol.27(2), pp 215-227 (April 1959).

Malinvaud, E., "The Analogy between Atemporal and Intertemporal Theories of Resource Allocation", *Review of Economic Studies,* Vol. 28(3), pp 143-160 (June 1961).

Malinvaud, E., "Efficient Capital Accumulation: A corrigendum", *Econometrica,* Vol.30(3), pp 570-573 (July 1962).

Malinvaud, E., "Sur la détermination des croissances optimales", Institut National De La Statistique et des Etudes Economiques, Paris (March 1965).

Malinvaud, E., "Croissances optimales dans un modèle macroéconomique", *The Econometric Approach to Development Planning,* pp 301-384, Pontifical Academy of Sciences, Amsterdam (1965).

Maneschi, A., "Optimal Savings with Finite Planning Horizon: A Note", *International Economic Review,* Vol.7(1), pp 109-118 (January 1966).

Maneschi, A., "Optimal Savings with Finite Planning Horizon: A Rejoinder", *ibid.,* Vol.7(1), pp 124-126 (January 1966).

Marglin, S. A., "The Social Rate of Discount and the Optimal Rate of Investment", *Quarterly Journal of Economics,* Vol.77(1), pp 95-111 (February 1963).

Marglin, S. A., "The Rate of Interest and the Value of Capital with Unlimited Supplies of Labour", *Essays on the Theory of Optimal Economic Growth,* edited by K. Shell, The MIT Press (1967).

Marty, A. L., "The Neoclassical Theorem", *American Economic Review,* Vol.54(6), pp 1026-1029 (December 1964).

Meade, J. E., *Trade and Welfare, Mathematical Supplement,* Oxford University Press, London (1955).

Meade, J. E., "The Effect of Saving on Consumption in a State of Steady Growth", Review of Economic Studies, Vol.29(80), pp 227-234 (June 1967).

Meade, J. E., "Life-Cycle Savings, Inheritance and Economic Growth", *ibid.,* Vol.33(93), pp 61-78 (January 1966).

Mirrlees, J., "Optimal Planning for a Dynamic Economy", unpublished dissertation, Cambridge University (1963).

Mirrlees, J. A., "Optimum Growth when Technology is Changing", *Review of Economic Studies,* Vol.34(97), pp 95-124 (January 1967).

Mischenko, E. F., R. V. Gamrelidze, V. G. Boltyanskii and L. S. Pontryagin, "The Mathematical Theory of Optimal Processes", translated from the Russian, Interscience, New York and London (1962).

Nerlove, M. and K. J. Arrow, "Optimal Advertising Policy under Dynamic Conditions", *Economica, New Series,* Vol.29(114), pp 129-142 (May 1962).

Nordhaus, W. D., "The Optimal Rate and Direction of Technical Change", *Essays on the Theory of Optimal Economic Growth,* edited by K. Shell, The MIT Press (1967).

Parikh, K. S. and R. S. Eckhaus, "Planning for Growth: Multi-sectoral Intertemporal Models Applied to India", MIT Center for International Studies (April 1966).

Pearce, I., "The End of the Golden Age in Solovia", *American Economic Review,* Vol.52(5), pp 1088-1097 (December 1962). (See Phelps' "A Comment", *ibid.,* Vol.52(5), pp 1097-1099 (December 1962).

Phelps, E. S., "The Golden Rule of Accumulation: A Fable for Growthmen", *ibid.,* Vol.51(4), pp 638-643 (September 1961).

Phelps, E. S., "The New View of Investment: a Neoclassical Analysis", *Quarterly Journal of Economics,* Vol.76(4), pp 548-567 (November 1962).

Phelps, E. S., "Second Essay on the Golden Rule of Accumulation", *American Economic Review,* Vol.55(4), pp 793-814 (September 1965).

Phelps, E. S., *Golden Rules of Economic Growth, Studies of Efficient and Optimal Investment,* W. W. Norton & Company, New York (1966).

Phelps, E. S. and R. A. Pollak, "On Second-best National Saving and Game Equilibrium Growth", *Review of Economic Studies,* Vol.35(102), pp 185-199 (April 1968).

Pollak, R. A., "Consistant Planning", *ibid.*, Vol.35(102), pp 185-199 (April 1968).

Pollak, R. A. and E. S. Phelps, "On Second-best National Saving and Game Equilibrium Growth", *ibid.*, Vol.35(102), pp 185-199 (April 1968).

Pontryagin, L. S., V. G. Boltyanskii, R. V. Gamrelidze and E. F. Mischenko, "The Mathematical Theory of Optimal Processes", translated from the Russian, Interscience, New York and London (1962).

Porwit, K., "The Role of Optimization Methods in the Central Planning Procedure", Instytut ekonomiki i organizacgi przemysiu, Warsaw 279, 1966, Joint Meeting conference. Mimeographed paper.

Rader, T., "On Intertemporal Efficiency", *Metroeconomica*, Vol.17(3), pp 152-160 (September/December 1965).

Radner, R., "Optimal Growth in a Linear-logarithmic Economy", *International Economic Review*, Vol.7(1), pp 1-33 (January 1966).

Radner, R., "Efficiency Prices for Infinite Horizon Production Programs", *Review of Economic Studies*, Vol.34(97), pp 51-66 (January 1967).

Radner, R., "Dynamic Programming of Economic Growth", *Activity Analysis in the Theory of Growth and Planning*, Edited by E. Malinvaud and M. O. L. Bacharach, pp 111-141, Macmillan Company of Canada (1967).

Rahman, A., "The Elasticity of Marginal Utility in Optimum Growth Analysis", memorandum, Institute of Advanced Projects, East-West Center, University of Hawaii.

Rahman, A., "Optimal Savings with a Finite Planning Horizon", memorandum, Institute of Advanced Projects, East-West Center, University of Hawaii.

Ramsey, F. P., "A Mathematical Theory of Saving", *Economic Journal*, Vol.38(152), pp 543-559 (December 1928).

Rao, T. V. S. and G. Tintner, "Optimal Paths of Economic Development: A Stochastic Scheme", a memorandum, Department of Economics, University of Southern California, Los Angeles (February 1966).

Robinson, J., "A Neoclassical Theorem", *Review of Economic Studies*, Vol.29(3), pp 219-226 (June 1962).

Ryder, H. E., S. M. Goldman and H. Uzawa, "Optimum Patterns of Trade and Investment in a Two-sector Model of International Trade", Technical Report No.7, NSF: GS-420, Department of Economics, University of Chicago (January 1965).

Ryder, H. E., "Optimal Patterns of Foreign Trade and Investment in a Two-sector Model of Capital AccumulationII", Technical Report No.8, NSF: GS-420, Department of Economics, University of Chicago (January 1965).

Ryder, H. E., "Optimal Accumulation and Trade in an Open Economy of Moderate Size", *Essays on the Theory of Optimal Economic Growth*, edited by K. Shell, The MIT Press (1967).

Samuelson, P. A. and R. M. Solow, "A Complete Capital Model Involving Heterogeneous Capital Goods", *Quarterly Journal of Economics,* Vol. 70(4), pp 537-562 (November 1956).

Samuelson, P. A., "Efficient Paths of Capital Accumulation in Terms of Calculus of Variations", *Mathematical Methods in the Social Sciences,* edited by Arrow, Karlin and Suppes, Stamford University Press (1960).

Samuelson, P. A., "Comment on the Production Function Symposium", *Review of Economic Studies,* Vol.29(3), pp 251-254 (June 1962).

Samuelson, P. A., "A Caternary Turnpike Theorem Involving Consumption and the Golden Rule", *American Economic Review,* Vol.55(3), pp 486-496 (June 1965).

Samuelson, P. A., "A Turnpike Refutation of the Golden Rule in a Welfare-maximizing Many-year Plan", *Essays on the Theory of Optimal Economic Growth,* edited by K. Shell, The MIT Press (1967).

Samuelson, P. A., "Indeterminacy of Development in a Heterogeneous-capital Model with Constant Saving Propensity", *Essays on the Theory of Optimal Economic Growth,* edited by K. Shell, The MIT Press (1967).

Sandee, J. and C. J. van Eijk, "Quantitative Determination of an Optimum Economic Policy, *Econometrica,* Vol.27(1), pp 1-13 (January 1959).

Sen, A. K., "Some Notes on the Choice of Capital-intensity in Development Planning", *Quarterly Journal of Economics,* Vol.71(4), pp 561-584 (November 1967).

Sen, A. K., "On Optimizing the Rate of Saving", *Economic Journal,* Vol. 71(283), pp 479-496 (September 1961).

Sengupta, J. K., "On the Relative Stability and Optimality of Consumption in Aggregative Growth Models", *Economica, New Series,* Vol.31(121), pp 35-50 (February 1964).

Sengupta, J. K., "Truncated Decision Rules and Optimal Economic Growth with a Fixed Horizon", *International Economic Review,* Vol.7(1), pp 42-64 (January 1966).

Shell, K., "Patterns of Technical Change and Capital Accumulation", unpublished dissertation, Stanford University, Stanford, California (April 1965).

Shell, K., "Towards a Theory of Inventive Activity and Capital Accumulation", *American Economic Review,* Vol.56(2), pp 62-68 (May 1966).

Shell, K., "A Model of Inventive Activity and Capital Accumulation", *Essays on the Theory of Optimal Economic Growth,* edited by K. Shell, The MIT Press (1967).

Shell, K., (Editor), *Essays on the Theory of Optimal Economic Growth,* The MIT Press (1967).

Shell, K., "Optimal Programs of Capital Accumulation for an Economy in which there is Exogenous Technical Change", *Essays on the Theory of Optimal Economic Growth,* edited by K. Shell, The MIT Press (1967).

Sheshinski, E., "Optimal Accumulation with Learning by Doing", *Essays on the Theory of Optimal Economic Growth,* edited by K. Shell, The MIT Press (1967).

Skolka, J. and M. Cerny, "Outline of an Optimum Long-term Plan Model", English Summary, European, Meeting of the Econometric Society, Warsaw (1966).

Smith, V. L., "Problems in Production – Investment Planning over Time", *International Economic Review,* Vol.1(3), pp 198-216 (September 1960).

Solow, R. M. and P. A. Samuelson, "A Complete Capital Model Involving Heterogeneous Capital Goods", *Quarterly Journal of Economics,* Vol. 70(4), pp 537-562 (November 1956).

Solow, R. M., "Comment on the Production Function Symposium", *Review of Economic Studies,* Vol.29(3), pp 255-257 (June 1962).

Srinavasan, T. N., "Investment Criteria and the Choice of Techniques of Production", Yale Economic Essays, Vol.2(1), pp 59-115 (Spring 1962)

Srinavasan, T. N., "Optimal Savings in a Two-sector Model of Growth", *Econometrics,* Vol.32(3), pp 358-373 (July 1964).

Stoleru, L. G., "An Optimal Policy for Economic Growth", *ibid.,* Vol. 33(2), pp 321-348 (April 1965).

Stone, J. R. N., "Misery and Bliss", *Economia Internazionale,* Vol.8(1), pp 3-24 (January 1955).

Swan, T., "Economic Growth and Capital Accumulation", *Economic Record,* Vol.32(63), pp 334-361 (November 1956).

Strotz, R. H., "Myopia and Inconsistency in Dynamic Utility Maximization", *Review of Economic Studies,* Vol.23(3), pp 165-180 (June 1956).

Swan, T., "On Golden Ages and Production Functions", memorandum for the Round Table on Economic Development held in April 1960 in Gamagozi, Japan, under auspices of the International Economic Association. Mimeographed paper.

Swan, T., "Of Golden Ages and Production Functions", *Economic Development with Special Reference to East Asia: Proceedings of a Conference Held by the International Economic Association,* edited by K. Berrill, pp 3-16, St. Martins Press, New York (1964).

Szakolszai, G. Y., "The Pattern of Investments and the Rate of Growth", *Acta Oeconomica,* Vol.2(3), pp 190-211 (1967).

Teichroew, D. and M. Connors, *Optimal Control of Dynamic Operations Research Models,* International Textbook Company, Scranton, Pensylvannia (1967).

Tinbergen, J., "The Optimum Rate of Saving", *Economic Journal,* Vol. 66(264), pp 603-609 (December 1956).

Tinbergen, J., "The Optimum Choice of Technology", *Pakistan Economic Journal,* No.2, pp 1-7 (December 1957).

Tinbergen, J., "Optimum Savings and Utility Maximization Over Time", *Econometrica,* Vol.28(2), pp 481-489 (April 1960).

Tinbergen, J. and H. C. Boz, "The Optimum Rate of Development", *Mathematical Models of Economic Growth,* pp 24-31, McGraw-Hill (1962).

Tinbergen, J., "Optimalization – Of What?" *Co-Existence,* Vol.5(1), pp 1-5 (January 1968).

Tintner, G. and T. V. S. Rao, "Optimal Paths of Economic Development: A Stochastic Scheme", memorandum, Department of Economics, University of Southern California, Los Angeles (February 1966).

Tobin, J., "Economic Growth as an Objective of Government Policy", *American Economic Review,* Papers and Proceedings, Vol.54(2), pp 1-20 (May 1964).

Uzawa, H., "Optimal Growth in a Two-sector Model of Capital Accumulation", *Review of Economic Studies,* Vol.31(1), pp 1-24 (January 1964).

Uzawa, H., "Optimum Technical Change in an Aggregative Model of Economic Growth", *International Economic Review,* Vol.6(1), pp 18-31 (January 1965).

Uzawa, H., "An Optimum Fiscal Policy in an Aggregative Model of Capital Accumulation", Center for Mathematical Studies in Business and Economics, University of Chicago (1966).

Uzawa, H., S. M. Goldman and H. E. Ryder, "Optimum Patterns of Trade and Investment in a Two-sector Model of International Trade", Technical Report No.7, NSF: GS-420, Department of Economics, University of Chicago (January 1965).

van Eijk, C. J. and J. Sandee, "Quantitative Determination of an Optimum Economic Policy", *Econometrica,* Vol.27(1), pp 1-13 (January 1959).

von Weizsacker, C. C., "Wachstum, Zins und Optimale Investitoinsquote", University of Basel, Switzerland (1961).

von Weizsacker, C. C., "Das Investitionsoptimum in einer wachserden Wirtschaft", Appendix to "Optimales Wachstum und Gleichgewichtwachstum" *Schriften des Vereins für Socialpolitik,* Neue Folge, Band 27 (1962).

von Weizsacker, C. C., "Existence of Optimal Programs of Capital Accumulation for an Infinite Time Horizon", *Review of Economic Studies,* Vol.32(2), pp 85-104 (April 1965).

von Weizsacker, C. C., "Lemmas for a Theory of Approximate Optimal Growth", *ibid.,* Vol.34(97), pp 143-151 (January 1967).

Williamson, R. E., T. C. Koopmans and P. A. Diamond, "Stationary Utility and Time Perspective", *Econometrica,* Vol.32(1-2), pp 82-100 (January-April 1964).

Wan, H. Y., Jr., "A Note on the Ramsey Model", memorandum to the Econometric Society, First World Congress, Rome (September 1965).

Vosgerau, H. J., *Über optimales wirtschaftliches Wachstum,* Kyklos Verlag, Basel, Switzerland (1965).

Yaari, M. E., "On the Consumer's Lifetime Allocation Process", *International Economic Review,* Vol.5(3), pp 304-317 (September 1964).

Yaari, M. E., "On the Existence of an Optimal Plan in a Continuous-time Allocation Process", *Econometrica,* Vol.32(4), pp 576-590 (October 1964).

Yaari, M. E., "Uncertain Lifetime, Life Insurance and the Theory of the Consumer", *Review of Economic Studies,* Vol.32(2), pp 137-150 (April 1965).

Yaari, M. E. and D. Cass, "Individual Saving, Aggregate Capital Accumulation and Efficient Growth", *Essays on the Theory of Optimal Economic Growth,* edited by K. Shell, The MIT Press (1967).

Younes, Y., "Relation entre l'existence d'un programme regulier competitif et efficient et l'existence d'un programme optimal sur un horizon infini", Paper presented to the European meeting of the Econometric Society, Warsaw (September 1966).

SUBJECT INDEX

Admissible: 28; indefinitely, 85

Bliss: utility function, 52; condition of no Bliss, 70; level, definition, 122

Calculus of variations: terminal condition, 28; UMIT as a problem of, 36, 37
CC-O: 64
Conflict of interests: with respect to time, 24; with respect to income, 25

Efficiency: condition, 33, 37, 43; condition for Eulerian programs, 41; sufficient condition for, 161
Efficient: program, 32, 33, 40; strategy, 33; Eulerian, 37, 41, 42, 43; path, 60, 161; RUMIT, 163
EG: *see* Model, EG
Euler's equation (or condition): 30, 37, 38, 39, 108, 111, 116, 117, 122, 127, 143, 161
Exponential: MUEFT-solution, 56; UMIT-solution, 142. *See also* Golden Utility

Feasible: program, 18, 19, 20, 71; path, 18, 19, 102, 121, 140, 145, 155; strategy, 18, 21, 32, 34, 64; indefinitely, 19, 39, 40, 42, 44, 59, 80, 85; *a priori*, 156, 157
Flexibility, Frisch's: *see* Utility, elasticity of marginal

Golden Rule: 104, 105, 122, 142, 148, 149, 151, 161
Golden Utility: UMIT, 45, 46, 47, 52, 64, 65, 70, 126, 129; MUEFT, 57, 58, 61, 64, 65, 69, 70
Government: life span, 24; yearly, 24; instantaneous, 24, 25, 30, 68, 72

Growth: strategy, definition, 3, 18, 20, 21; efficient, *see* Efficient; optimal, *see* MUEFT and UMIT; path, definition, 18, actual US, 69; program, definition, 18; change of, 20, 22, efficient, *see* Efficient, optimal; *see* MUEFT and UMIT; superexponential, 80; model, *see* Model
Growth rate: value of, 132

Immortals, Society of: 23, 33, 50
Impatience: principle of minimum, 35, 52, 61, 72, 131, 158; principle of zero, *see* Patience, principle of infinite
Inefficient: MUEFT, 33; MUEIT, 33; Eulerian, 41; program, 41, 44; path, 60, 161
Instantaneous: consumption, 26; government, *see* Government

Labor equation: 5, 7, 8, 14
Law of diminishing returns: 6, 7, 10, 101
Lipschitz condition: 85

Minimum convergence: 37, 43, 44
Model: EG, definition, 4, 5; economic interpretation, 6, 7, 8; properties, 15, 16; Q-EG, definition, 8, 9; economic interpretation, 10, 11; properties, 16, 17; superexponential, 11; CC-O, 64
MUEFT: definition, 32; postulate, 33; solution, 33; under CC-O, 53, 59; properties, 53, 66, 67; properties of generalized, 55; optimal solution, existence of, 57; equation (or condition), under CC-O, 58; short-term properties, 61, 62; long-term properties, 61, 88; generalized, 67; applied to US, 70. *See also* Efficient, Inefficient, Exponential, Golden Utility and Time Horizon
MUEIT: 30, 31, 32, 54; inefficient, 33; generalized, 37, 54, 55; properties, 48

National: allegiance, 28, 30, 31, 72; preference pattern, 81, 102, 103, 118, 121, 141, 153, 159, 160

Optimal growth: classical theory of, 11, 12, 71, 138; problem of, 18, 23, 24, 25, 26, 71; program, 18; path, smoothness of, 18, 80; consistency of, 34; efficiency of, 60; voting rights in the determination of, 157, 158; classical definition of, 23, 30, 31, 33; definition of, 29; criterion, 71, 153, 156, 164
Overtaking principle: 34, 103